SPORTS CRISIS

COMMUNICATIONS

SPORTS CRISIS

COMMUNICATIONS

CASES AND CONTROVERSY

JIM ROCCO AND THOM WEIDLICH

Hart +
Harvest
PRESS

Cover design by Iman Swain

The materials contained herein represent the opinions of PRCG | *Sports*, and should not be construed to be the views or opinions of Hart + Harvest Press.

Printed in the United States of America

ISBN: 979-8-9873569-4-4

e-ISBN: 979-8-9873569-5-1

Library of Congress CIP is on file.

Discounts are available for books ordered in bulk.
Inquire at Hart + Harvest Press, 45 Broadway, Suite 3140, New York, NY 10006 or sales@hartandharvest.com.

www.hartandharvest.com

Hart + Harvest PRESS

To Gráinne and Simon: You're the reason why I am able to wake up in the morning feeling hopeful and go to bed at night feeling content.
— J. R.

To my mother and father (1931–2023), who never missed any of their kids' games
— T. W.

CONTENTS

FOREWORD

Welcome to *Sports Crisis Communications: Cases and Controversy*, a remarkable anthology of content and analysis more than a decade in the making.

I thought I'd tell you a bit about how this book came about. Nearly 15 years ago, my communications-consulting firm became involved in sports public relations. Up to that time, we had mainly handled crisis, legal, and litigation communications issues in other areas, along with a range of more general reputation-management and public relations services (my talented colleague Thom Weidlich — coauthor of this book — was often part of our team on crisis work). Sports-related assignments would come up rarely . . . but only rarely.

Over the years, this began to change, and we began to see more sports PR assignments, whether involving media, brand management, licensing, or other matters.

A few years later, an old friend and colleague — Jim Rocco, who had been at HBO Sports and Barclays Center in Brooklyn, New York — was looking for a new adventure. He joined us to head up a dedicated brand for sports communications: PRCG | *Sports*.

Our original intent was not necessarily to go into sports-related crisis work, but as we began to concentrate more heavily in the field, we realized that much of sports news these days *is* crisis news — dealing with sensitive matters that require high-level skills and advice from trusted advisors with what we call a "360-degree view" of reputation. Inevitably, therefore, we became more and more adept at advising clients on matters where the crisis happened to involve, or be in, the sports industry. A new practice within our firm began to grow.

This book springs from those seeds. *Sports Crisis Communications: Cases and Controversy* brings together some of the best thinking and ideas gleaned from our work, culled from some of the best content we've generated at our firm in recent years. For example: One of the great things we've been doing — for more than a decade now — is putting together weekly blog posts on crisis communications, under the supervision of the aforementioned Thom Weidlich, who had been a journalist at Bloomberg, *PRWeek*, and *The National Law Journal*.

Inevitably, as the sports world confronted more and more crises of various sorts, and our work began to follow, this content touched on sports issues with increasing frequency. Our blog posts covered the latest-breaking crises in sports from the perspective of what those involved did right and (more importantly) what they did wrong. With new introductions and "Postgame" updates, these blog entries form a good portion of the book. You may not even remember some of these crisis events, particularly from the pre-COVID days, but there are lessons in each.

Several years later, we also began a well-regarded podcast hosted by Jim Rocco called *Crisis Communications in Sports*, where we interviewed leaders in the sports world on issues related to sensitive reputational matters, media, special events, and other topics relevant to our work. The insights from our guests were often stunning. And while they are collected in podcast form on our website, we thought a broader audience should read and learn from these interviews as well. Included are fascinating discussions with some of the leaders of their respective fields including legendary commentator Bob Costas and Hall of Fame tennis broadcaster Mary Carillo.

Here's the overriding truth, particularly in crisis communications: Real learning comes not from memorizing strategic outlines and bullet points and PowerPoint slides, but from seeing what really happens, in the real world, in real time. This is what *Sports Crisis Communications: Cases and Controversy* is all about. This book highlights what teams, athletes, organizations, and others actually do when a crisis happens, and the lessons you can draw from their experiences to use in your day-to-day work. You'll find excellent commentary by Jim Rocco and Thom Weidlich, as well as from other members of the PRCG team, past and present.

We hope reading this book brings you to a greater appreciation of how difficult these issues are, and why proper planning is key. That's a takeaway as well. Management of a difficult communications situation is not about spin-doctoring, or hiding the truth, or chatbots and fake news — all those things you read about too often these days. Playing these sorts of reputation games in the public arena will give you something akin to a "sugar high": You may feel good in the short term, but don't be surprised when it all comes crashing down. It's my hope that my esteemed colleagues show that effective sports crisis communications is about preparation, responsiveness, and — most of all — truth.

Enjoy!

James F. Haggerty
President & CEO
PRCG | Haggerty and PRCG | *Sports*
March 2025

PART ONE:

THE FUNDAMENTALS

1

CRISIS COMMUNICATIONS IN THE SPORTS CONTEXT

This is a book about sports crises — specifically, crisis communications planning and response in the context of sports. The sports world experiences an astonishing number of negative situations that make headline news: players accused of domestic violence; accidents, incidents, and even violence at sporting events; leagues fingered for corruption or other wrongdoing. Disputes over political issues. Sexual assaults. Lawsuits.

The list goes on. We're crisis communicators who work in the sports arena as well as other areas. Just as every business sector has specific crisis scenarios they need to prepare for, sports organizations and individuals need to anticipate the adverse events unique to their universe (in addition to those common in any field). And there *are* many unique aspects to crisis communications in sports — many of which we'll discuss as this chapter moves along.

How This Book Is Structured

The bulk of this book is an anthology of blog entries we've posted over the past 10 years, along with excerpted transcripts of podcast interviews we've done with fascinating experts, including journalists and sports commentators. This content includes coverage of crises directly related to sports — athletes, teams, other organizations — and of what we call sports-adjacent crises, such as those involving retailer Dick's Sporting Goods and exercise-gear maker Peloton.

We look back at these crises to see what worked, what didn't, and what could have been done better. Our hope is that a deep dive into these concepts and stories will give the reader a solid foundation for confronting negative situations, whether they befall a player, team, league, sponsor, or other entity.

Who Should Read This Book?

We've aimed *Sports Crisis Communications* at any reader interested in sports and sports businesses; in the way reputation is maintained, and sometimes damaged, as a result of public actions; and in best practices for ensuring long-term protection of individual and organizational sports brands. Some of these audiences include:

- **PR pros, attorneys, agents, managers**, and **administrators** working in or for:
    - **Sports leagues**, whether the NFL or Major League Cricket
    - **Professional teams,** from Arsenal F.C. to the Carolina Chaos lacrosse squad
    - **Colleges** and their athletic departments, especially in light of new reputational challenges from NIL (name, image, and likeness) endorsements, conference realignment, and other matters
    - **High schools** and their athletic departments
    - **Youth sports** organizations
    - **Arenas**, stadiums, and other sports locales
    - **Marketing and public relations agencies** that represent athletes, teams, leagues, and schools
    - **Brands that sponsor** teams or leagues or have stadium or arena naming rights
    - **Brands endorsed by** professional athletes (who tend to find themselves in hot water)
- The book is also great for:
    - **Professional athletes** themselves

- o **Student-athletes**, especially with the rise of NIL
- o **Students studying** to work in sports, including sports communications
- o **Fans** simply fascinated by the drama of sports crises and controversies

Before we can look more closely at the particular types of crises facing the sports realm, we first have to understand crisis communications itself: what it's about, why it's important, why so many organizations don't prepare for it, and why so many are so bad at it. Then we can look at the unique aspects of crises in the sports universe and take a deeper dive into the basics — the fundamentals, to put it in sports lingo — of crisis communications, including what goes into a proper crisis communications plan. We'll do all of this in our first two chapters, then move on to substantive examples over the past decade that highlight these learnings . . . or not.

What Is Crisis Communications?

We begin with the most elemental question: What is crisis communications?

Imagine this: You've had a nice weekend and you're ready for the excitement of a new week working in the world of sports. This particular morning you're in the office with a set of meetings and Zoom calls on your calendar, and a list of things you need to accomplish.

You check your email and see the following from a colleague (maybe your boss):

RE: Important! Read ASAP!

The first line says:

We have a problem . . .

Welcome to the world of crisis communications!

Something has happened, something negative — an accident, an athlete's drunken episode, a cheating scandal — and it must be dealt with. Immediately. And by dealt with, we mean learning the facts of what's going on and communicating them (and your side of the story) to your "stakeholders" — your customers, vendors, employees, regulators, and (perhaps most importantly) *fans*. Often, this is done through the media, and a lot about crisis communications concerns media relations — dealing with both traditional and social media. But it can also involve direct communications to each of these stakeholder groups, through individual or group emails, messaging apps, or even the telephone (remember the telephone?).

To be sure, not all crises are the same. How can you know if your organization is actually in the throes of one?

All sorts of definitions exist, including the rule of thumb that holds if you can't say, "Let's forget about the whole thing," you're probably in the midst of a crisis.

But let's begin with a more clinical definition:

> Crisis communications can be defined as the process of ensuring an effective communications response to an unstable or critical state of affairs that threatens to have an undesirable or negative impact on an organization's or individual's reputation, business, or goals.

It's easier said than done. Sometimes, just accepting that no company or organization is immune to a crisis is half the battle. Unfortunately, most remain ill-prepared when a crisis hits, which raises the question: Why is that?

Why Don't Organizations Prepare for Crises?

Imagine sending your team out onto the field and only then making up the plays. Or deciding not to have plays at all since you can't prepare for every eventuality. You'd never do it. And, in fact, you'd be laughed out of the room for even suggesting it (or off the court or off the field . . . you get the idea). And yet this is what some very smart people do when it comes to developing a communications response to a crisis.

Based on our decades of experience in this field, we have some ideas about why this is. First, most people want to feel positive about their organizations. Optimism is good. But being *overly* confident — believing that nothing bad will ever happen to your company — is a recipe for disaster. Crises, both self-induced and otherwise, occur all the time. They'll happen to you: to your company or team, to your brand, to your players or other personnel. It simply isn't wise to pretend they won't and to be unprepared. This is particularly important in sports, given its prominence in the media, on social media, and in the day-to-day lives of most of the public.

Second, many executives will insist a budding crisis is merely a minor incident so as not to have their "regular job" disrupted. We call this the "yes in the presentation, forgotten at the desk" syndrome. Let us explain.

As you might imagine, we regularly speak before sports-related entities. Whenever we address these issues in a conference room or a hotel meeting room, we get the following response: "Yes ... Yes! Absolutely correct! We *do* need this sort of crisis communications planning to protect our team, our athletes, our brand."

And then the attendees go back to their desks. There are 147 unread emails in their inboxes and seven Zoom calls the rest of the afternoon. In the crush of pending assignments, they forget what they've just learned. Despite the risks, planning is pushed to the back burner.

Because, let's face it: It's not your "regular job." It's not part of your job description.

But it needs to be.

According to a 2022 survey by online software marketplace Capterra Inc., only 49 percent of U.S. companies have a formal crisis communications plan, 28 percent have an informal plan, and 23 percent have no plan (or don't know if they have one!)[1]

---

1. Zach Capers, "More Than Half of U.S. Businesses Should Be Worried About the Next Crisis — Here's Why," February 23, 2023, https://www.capterra.com/resources/crisis-communications-plan/.

Not having a plan is a mistake, particularly for sports brands and organizations so in the public eye. Potential incidents and issues need to be monitored because they may become blowout crises. That's not to suggest everything bad that happens should be treated as a five-alarm fire. Not everything is as dire as a natural disaster or an active shooter. But problems should be examined carefully since they may contain embers that can spark into a blaze before you know it.

With this in mind, one of the keys to effective crisis communications response is to know what to react to and what to simply keep an eye on. In certain instances, the need to respond will be obvious: a bomb threat at your stadium, for example. Other cases — for example, a rumor about an unhappy player looking to force a trade, or word of a pending lawsuit or government investigation — may require only monitoring and preparing in case a response is necessary.

What's the Damage if You Don't Plan for a Crisis?

We once had a sports team owner ask us: "Why should I prepare for something that may never happen?"

Our response: Think of crisis communications planning as an exercise in *risk management.* By planning effectively, you're insuring against the type of reputational damage that destroys revenues and reputation. The impact of mishandling a crisis can hang over a sports organization for years.

It's like insurance, a well-established concept in sports. You carry a second catcher on your baseball team in case your starter gets hurt. You sign a young arm out of college because your quarterback is getting up there in years. By paying that young quarterback, you're insuring against a negative event.

More directly, teams have for years bought actual insurance policies to protect against negative results. Consider this *Washington Post* headline from 2016, after the Washington Nationals signed pitcher Stephen Strasberg to a seven-year, $175 million deal: "Worried About Your Ace's $100 Million Arm? There Is Insurance for That."[2]

---

2. Barry Svrluga, "Worried About Your Ace's $100 Million Arm? There Is Insurance for That," *The Washington Post*, September 9, 2016, https://www.washingtonpost.com

Everyone in the sports field, from owners to players to brands, needs to understand that the risk of reputational damage from a crisis is at least as great — financially and culturally — as your $175 million pitcher going down. Proper crisis communications planning is the insurance against crisis reputational risk.

In so many crises that become front-page news and cause sustained reputational damage, the first few days are characterized by tone-deaf and often contradictory language, misinformation, legalese, banal clichés, or ultimately a profound lack of understanding and empathy. It's clear that organizations that respond this way don't have a plan in place for communicating publicly when a negative event happens. Put simply: They make it up as they go along. A fumbled initial response contributes to long-term reputational damage. Planning can help avoid that.

Smart response can even affect a stock price. For example, in 2019, two academics studied 128 events of negative publicity hitting a brand endorser (the majority of whom were athletes) affecting 230 publicly traded companies between 1988 and 2016. They found that fast announcements (within three days) of companies' reactions increased firm value by 2.1 percent over the next four trading weeks, while slow reactions decreased the value by 1.88 percent (see chapter 10).[3]

Even if you're not a publicly traded company, your value can suffer. This is becoming particularly important as private equity and other investment vehicles take on bigger roles in sports.

What Type of Crisis Am I Dealing With?

Let's dig a little deeper into defining types of crises. Just as in sports, simplicity is key. It's like your golf swing: If there's too much going on there, you're probably going to shank it. In the same way, if you have too many elements in how you define a crisis, you'll get tied up in knots rather than develop an effective response.

/news/sports/wp/2016/09/09/worried-about-your-aces-100-million-arm-there-is insurance-for-that/.

3. Stefan J. Hock and Sascha Raithel, "Managing Negative Celebrity Endorser Publicity: How Announcements of Firm (Non)Responses Affect Stock Returns," *Management Science* 66(3) (2019):1473–95.

With that in mind, we tend to divide crises into two broad categories:

1. **Exploding:** the sudden, event-related crisis that leaps onto the scene, such as an accident, fire, or violent incident
2. **Unfolding**: the long-term crisis that bubbles up over time, like a lawsuit or investigation

Let's distinguish a little more between the two.

Exploding: Exploding crises are the ones you can't miss: the undeniable, attention-grabbing, headline-making events or gaffes you have to deal with immediately — whether you like it or not, and whether you're prepared or not. *Your team's star player was caught up in an unsavory sex scandal following a drunken night at a club — and it's now front-page news!*

Unfolding: Unfolding crises are a little less obvious because they develop over time, but build in momentum. It's easy to ignore the warning signs at first with these crises, which can prove disastrous to your organization or client in part *because* they're less obvious. *Allegations about misappropriated taxpayer funds that were earmarked for a new stadium project have led to a government investigation of your team's owners and management.*

A blog post in chapter 11 directly addresses the issue of defining a crisis. Normally, we don't view a disappointing performance in an organization's everyday business as calling for crisis communications. For example, a publicly traded company having a bad quarter in terms of revenues or profits isn't necessarily a crisis. So, too, with a sports team or player having a bad year. That said, ongoing negative results could become an unfolding crisis. The blog post addresses such a scenario: the Brooklyn Nets' dismal 2023–2024 season.

I Can't Plan for *Everything!*

One of the most common misconceptions about crisis communications is that you can't prepare for a crisis if you don't yet know the exact details — that, since you can't anticipate everything, it's useless to plan for anything.

As you'll learn throughout this book, there's a great deal you can do ahead of an unflattering, public-facing crisis. Just as in sports, preparation is key. There are some basic elements for doing that right.

Before we get to that, let's discuss some issues that make crisis communications in the sports context unique.

Six Elements That Make a Sports Crisis Different

Yes, many aspects of crisis communications in sports are similar to those you find more generally — and you can certainly learn by looking at effective response across a range of industries. But there are aspects inherent to sports that make crises in this sphere unique. In this section, we'll enumerate six. It's important to understand these differences because this insight will at least partly dictate how you develop and implement your sports-crisis plan.

1.   'That's Passion, Baby!'

A rabid sports fan is one that boos a TV set.

— Jimmy Cannon

The main thing, perhaps, that sets sports apart is the passion people feel for it. For sports fans, there's sports, and there's everything else.

The dictionary defines passion as a "strong and barely controllable emotion." *Barely controllable.* How would you characterize the angst you feel when the team you rooted for your whole life is about to blow what appeared to be an insurmountable lead? How do you describe the euphoria you feel when your team wins a huge game against its biggest rival? Barely controllable.

As legendary basketball announcer Dick Vitale might say, *"That's passion, baby!"*

Fans' passion for sports, and for their favorite players and teams, makes any negative situation so much more intense. Thus, sports crises draw so much more attention, including media attention. This passion makes the sports crisis communicator's job more challenging. It also means that, for communications professionals, passion and emotion need to be front of mind when strategizing how to address a crisis.

Consider, as just one example, the situation Major League Baseball Commissioner Rob Manfred found himself in following his comment after the Houston Astros' sign-stealing scandal in 2017, when many people thought he should strip the team of its World Series title and trophy. "The idea of an asterisk or asking for a piece of metal back seems like a futile act," Manfred uttered, unwisely.[4]

That one sentence caused him to suffer the wrath of baseball fans everywhere. Manfred severely miscalculated the passion and awe that fans (*fanatics*) feel toward the World Series title and trophy. The commissioner of baseball had referred to the World Series trophy as *a piece of metal!*

Manfred's unwitting error resulted from his attempt to explain his reasoning solely with logic. Logic, however, is often the *antithesis* of passion — and it most certainly takes a backseat in sports. So while a crisis plan rooted strictly in logic might serve you well in other contexts, when it comes to high-stakes sports, it will fall flat. Fans' passion cannot be ignored or overestimated.

2. The Adoration of Sports Stars

If you were the greatest, you were the Michael Jordan of whatever business you were in.

— Ahmad Rashad

You've no doubt heard the cries of some higher-education professionals ruing that their schools' sports programs garner more attention and funding than their academic initiatives. The University of Michigan has produced a similar number of Nobel Prize winners to national football championship winners, but football gets the attention. The massive amounts of money generated by a top-notch college

---

4. Reuters, "Manfred Apologizes for 'Piece of Metal' Comment," February 18, 2020, https://www.reuters.com/article/idUSKBN20D06G/.

football or basketball program is, of course, at the root of such inequity. The glorification of star athletes, and in some instances coaches as well, further fuels this love affair between fans and athletes.

So another element that makes sports crises different is dealing with the gargantuan popularity of star players. That can work both against you and for you, especially in difficult communications situations. Because star athletes are put on a pedestal, any crisis they're embroiled in is magnified exponentially. But, conversely, an athlete's popularity can make it easier to garner a sympathetic public ear.

Let's put it this way: We're willing to bet that Patrick Mahomes has more adoring fans than Bob Iger, CEO of The Walt Disney Co., even given that the Magic Kingdom has a well-promoted reputation for making "dreams come true." As such, it would be a mistake to create the same crisis communications plan for Mahomes, and the teams and brands he touches, that you would for Iger and Disney. You need to take into account the reverence fans afford sports stars, which goes far beyond anything you might see in the business world.

More than this, such adoration often excuses bad behavior on the part of athletes. Consider Irish MMA superstar Conor McGregor — or, as he's called when he enters the octagon, "The Notorious" Conor McGregor. Despite his many public outbursts and confrontations (including alleged violent assaults), up until recently his bad-boy image had remained popular, particularly with young fans, and his earnings potential was unaffected. This was, in no small part, thanks to a well-thought-out public relations plan, focused largely on the United States, to ensure McGregor's side got spun properly when tales of his transgressions hit the news.[5] In fans' eyes, McGregor could do no wrong, and his bad behavior was not just excused but often leveraged to foster his brand.

All this said, however, a recent legal loss may be changing that. In November 2024, after an Irish jury found McGregor liable of sexual assault, Proximo Spirits said he would no longer be the face of Proper No. 12 Irish Whiskey, which he helped found and later sold to Proximo.

---

5. Kirik Jenness, "Meet Conor McGregor's PR Crisis Manager," MixedMartialArts.com, April 16, 2019, https://www.mixedmartialarts.com/editorial/meet-conor-mcgregors -pr-crisis-managerf16bcfef-4031-4d72-b760-e771b952eb50.

Video-game developer IO Interactive and other brands have also cut ties with him. (See our McGregor blog post in chapter 8.)

The general point is this: Along with athletes' prowess and success at play, the adoration of fans for sports stars plays a key role in fostering reputation — and may even overcome bad acts and events (see our "Postgame" update to the Deflategate post, for example, in chapter 3). But as McGregor appears to be learning, this popularity can also lull an athlete into a false sense of invulnerability. Winning on the field won't always aid in confronting a public backlash — and we'll see examples of this throughout this book.

3. Stars Bigger Than Their Teams

I'm going to take my talents to South Beach and join the Miami Heat.

— LeBron James

From the moment LeBron James uttered this now-infamous quote in 2010, on a roundly maligned ESPN special called *The Decision*, it became obvious that teams were beginning to take a backseat to individual athletes.

Sports purists like to say that no one player is bigger than the team, but that ideal has been put to the test in the 21st century. Thanks in large part to social media, athletes have become more cognizant of developing their own brands. Understandably, they're encouraged to do so by their agents, managers, teammates, and perhaps family and friends, because it translates into increased earnings potential. Top pro athletes earn more money off the field than on it.

Our point here is obviously related to our previous one about the hero worship of star athletes, but players overshadowing their squads is a special consideration for team (and sometimes league) public relations counselors.

The catch for these sports-communications pros is that an athlete's individual agenda and beliefs may not align with the team's. It would seem the two should peacefully coexist, but the bigger an athlete gets, the harder it is to reel him or her in. If then–Green Bay Packers quarterback Aaron Rodgers wants to be coy when asked by the media about his COVID-19 vaccination status — thereby causing a media crush and a distraction for the team — the club's crisis communicator will have to scramble to respond.

Finally, athlete sponsorships and co-branding opportunities, which began in earnest in 1984 when Nike hitched its wagon to Michael Jordan, present a whole other set of obstacles that crisis communicators need to navigate. A real challenge develops for PR pros when an athlete works with a company whose ideals, views, or politics contrast with those of the team or league. Gone are the days when Jordan, in explaining why he wouldn't endorse a Democratic candidate for the U.S. Senate in North Carolina, quipped, "Republicans buy sneakers, too." Things have gotten a whole lot more partisan since then.

(For more on the outsize personalities of professional athletes, see our interview in chapter 17 with former New York Mets PR head Jay Horwitz.)

4. Closed-Up Athletes

Their job was to get a headline, and I wasn't gonna give it to them.

— Derek Jeter

New York Yankees Hall of Famer Derek Jeter was known throughout his playing career for his guarded nature. He never trusted the media and consequently became a master at providing stock answers. He's not alone in this.

While professional athletes understand that reporters serve as a bridge to their fans, many of them don't like to reveal too much about themselves. To some extent, this is understandable. Repetition of the same questions can be draining. The sports stars may have security concerns about their families, or they may simply be introverted. Particularly for younger athletes at the start of their careers, this is a vulnerable time to be making statements to a reporter.

It's also become more common for athletes, such as Olympic swimming great Michael Phelps, basketball star Kevin Love, and tennis champion Naomi Osaka, to publicly admit their struggles with anxiety, while closely guarding where and how they discuss these issues. (See chapter 15 for Mary Carillo's discussion of Osaka.) So while leagues require professional athletes to make themselves available to the press, a lot of them don't like to be interviewed — and most don't say much. Bland clichés, stock answers, and blank stares are the norm. That's often not helpful in a crisis.

Some athletes, though, are getting the message — and it's to their benefit in a crisis situation. Baseball superstar Shohei Ohtani is known for his press shyness, but when a gambling scandal erupted in 2024 concerning his now-former interpreter, people were surprised that he convened a press conference to address the allegations. And he did quite well, though he didn't take any questions from reporters (see our blog post in chapter 5 and our interview with Bob Costas in chapter 20). Clearly he was convinced he had to go beyond his usual way of interacting with his public, given the severity of the issues he faced.

So, athletes' reticence about or outright hostility toward the press makes the job of the sports crisis communicators all the more difficult and requires them to be as nimble as the athletes they represent.

5. Sports Reporters vs. News Reporters

He who can, does. He who cannot, teaches.

— George Bernard Shaw

While the great playwright Shaw's statement may be snarky, it is true that some people are teachers because they didn't have the talent (or luck) to make it in the field. A similar statement can be made about sports reporters — or at least a lot of them.

While reporting on sports can be an exciting and rewarding career choice, we're sure most reporters would rather be the ones throwing the football or swinging the bat instead of holding a microphone or notepad. Chances are, most were good athletes in their youth. But not elite. Or maybe they sustained injuries that prevented them from going pro. Either way, their passion for sports outweighs their talent or ability to play them at the highest level, and so reporting on the games and the athletes is the next best thing.

This truth can lead to a unique dynamic that differs from other types of news reporting. "Hard news" journalism requires a serious tone and professionalism. Sports reporting is by its nature less stuffy and more snappy. The former athlete and the jock mentality are always lurking beneath the surface. As a sports crisis communicator, you have to adjust the typical media-relations approach to account for the heightened toughness, jealousy, and maybe silliness.

Another factor adding to the difficulty of dealing with sports journalists is that, in a world of sports radio and shoutfests on ESPN and other outlets, all sports news is, at some level, opinion. Even when reporting on a crisis, legal action, or other sensitive public issue, these reporters rarely play it straight. In fact, often they don't even call the subject of a negative news article to give an opportunity to respond — a standard journalistic practice if ever there was one. They figure if you disagree with a story, you'll call in . . . just like sports radio.

On top of this, we have a trend of current and former professional athletes hosting their own podcasts and other shows — circumventing the journalists altogether, which brings these issues only more to the fore. This trend was featured in a March 2024 *Columbia Journalism Review* article headlined "Can Sports Journalism Survive in the Era of the Athlete?" featuring some of these podcast jocks.[6]

To be sure, developments affecting journalism in general are also at play in sports journalism. For example, it used to be standard practice to fact-check and confirm media stories *before* publishing. Not so much anymore in the rush to be the first to post the news online and on social media.

Even major, "legitimate" sports media outlets — *Sports Illustrated*, ESPN, The Athletic, CBS, NBC, and the like — race to beat competitors on social media. They seem to take the position that they can

---

6. Josh Hersh, "Can Sports Journalism Survive in the Era of the Athlete?" *Columbia Journalism Review*, March 28, 2024, https://www.cjr.org/business_of_news/sports-journalism-survival-foul-territory-mcafee-braun-mlb.php.

publish fast and publish first, and if they learn that any information is wrong, they can revise the article later to reflect the truth. From a sports-media standpoint: no harm, no foul.

Here's the problem with that. In this internet and social-media age, that first version of a story is the one that's circulated across the globe, including through aggregators. It doesn't matter if the story is updated — the first version is the one that spreads worldwide, with any falsehoods intact. The revised stories may appear on the original media outlet's website or social media, but it's the older, false version that most of the world sees. Thus, from the standpoint of reputation, the damage is already done. So that's something that sports crisis communicators, like all crisis communicators, have to deal with.

6. Social Media

I'll promise to go easier on drinking and to get to bed earlier, but not for you, $50,000, or $250,000 will I give up women. They're too much fun.

— Babe Ruth

One thing's for certain, the Babe would have been a hell of an X (Twitter) follow!

There's no way of knowing if Ruth would have had a filter if he played now, but we do know that he played at a time when writers tended to keep hidden his exploits, such as his astronomical number of trysts with women and his once allegedly injecting himself with sheep-testicle extract as a performance-enhancing drug (it apparently didn't work). Cultural norms were different then, to say the least. It's a little more complicated for modern-day athletes.

Today, professional players' personal lives, like those of all celebrities, are viewed as fair game — people want to know everything about them. That's exacerbated by social media. Indeed, young pro athletes are only familiar with a world where social media plays a major role, and being an "influencer" can often be as compelling and profitable to a young athlete as setting records or winning championships. With this comes many obstacles that athletes, their reps, teams, and leagues have to maneuver around. Sure, social media is huge in other industries, such as Hollywood, but there's no question that it's transformed how athletes communicate and how they're communicated about.

Professional sports organizations should have social-media policies laying out their best practices. Yet the best plan imaginable can be effective only if it's carried out. And that can be a *real* challenge, because social media affords professional athletes, like the rest of us, the opportunity to provide their unfiltered, unchecked, and unabashed opinions with the tap of a thumb. The problem for communications professionals is that such opportunities give pro athletes the ability to . . . provide unfiltered, unchecked, and unabashed opinions with the tap of a thumb.

The amplifying nature of such unfiltered utterances — remember, as described above, the huge, devoted followings many of these athletes have — creates a phenomenon that prior generations of teams, leagues, advisors, and analysts never had to deal with. These impacts are especially visible when it comes to hot-button social-justice issues. This trend came to a head in 2016, when San Francisco 49ers quarterback Colin Kaepernick took a knee during a pregame playing of the national anthem to protest what he felt were injustices toward people of color. It certainly wasn't the first time an athlete used his platform to draw attention to a cause, but never had a similar instance blown up so quickly and with such ferocity. One reason for that is it went viral on social media. Strong viewpoints flared on both sides and the story became a major topic.

(See chapter 15 for Mary Carillo's discussion of athletes' use of social media at the expense of traditional media.)

So now we've defined what a crisis is, why it's so important to the long-term reputation of sports brands to communicate properly in response to one, why planning is so important, and why so few organizations and communications leaders engage in such planning. We also looked at some ways a sports-related crisis is different from those in other fields. In our next chapter, we'll discuss how to put all this into action . . . before delving into dozens of real-world examples.

2

CRISIS COMMUNICATIONS PLANNING AND RESPONSE: THE PLAYBOOK

The last chapter provided an overview of the importance of crisis communications, particularly in the field of sports, where events and incidents are watched so closely, by such devoted audiences, across a range of platforms and media outlets. Now let's look at best practices in preparing for a crisis, and ways to execute on those best practices in the heat of a negative reputational event.

These are really the basics of crisis communications planning, and not just in the area of sports. Companies and other organizations that have their acts together think long and hard about what negative situations could hit them and how they would respond to best protect their reputations. They create crisis communications teams and plans. The plans include what tough situations they're most likely to find themselves in (typically due to the type of business they're in) and the needs for responding to those particular scenarios. These organizations also constantly reevaluate their teams and plans.

We're going to move through this material pretty quickly, but it will give you a good overview of what's involved.

Preparing for a Crisis: The Crisis Leader and Team

Here are the four most important things an organization needs to do to prepare for a crisis:

1. Identify someone to head up crisis response
2. Choose a crisis team
3. Prepare a crisis plan
4. Train on that plan so everyone on the team knows what to do when a crisis erupts

It sounds simple, and it is simple if you do it right. Every organization, for example, needs a captain to steer the ship when a crisis arises. So if you haven't yet, you need to add a new C-suite title to your lexicon: Chief Crisis Officer.[1]

Who should be your Chief Crisis Officer — your crisis leader? Some obvious positions suggest themselves: CEO, COO, general counsel, head of public relations or communications. In the sports world, a general manager or assistant general manager can fill the role. Factors such as skillset, experience, and temperament should all be taken into consideration.

Your Chief Crisis Officer should be flexible and able to respond at a moment's notice. He or she must work across organizational lines and — importantly — have the authority and willingness to act. If your Chief Crisis Officer will be the crisis spokesperson, he or she should be an experienced communicator with the ability to speak with sensitivity and nuance before a variety of audiences.

What about the crisis communications team?

Organizations that haven't prepared properly for a crisis tend to throw together a haphazard committee to try to come up with a plan of action. When this approach is taken, a large group tends to gel around the crisis response — and gels can be messy, with too many

---

[1]. Some of the concepts and details in this chapter are from an excellent book by the founder and CEO of PRCG | *Sports*, our colleague James F. Haggerty. The book, coincidentally, is called *Chief Crisis Officer: Structure and Leadership for Effective Communications Response* (Hart + Harvest Press, 2023).

team members weighing in to justify their inclusion. A lot of time is wasted, and a clear, actionable course of action isn't achieved.

So when establishing your crisis team, less is more. The team should be small enough to make decisions rapidly and for its members to communicate with each other directly and decisively. It should be large enough to cover the tasks needed to be accomplished. Each member should also have an alternate in case the primary person is unavailable when the crisis comes. The team should have the buy-in of the higher-ups to make key decisions during the crisis.

Depending on whether you're the communications counsel for a team, league, or other organization, the members of this core crisis communications team could include the organization's leader, HR rep, comms people, lawyers, and others. You can designate different employees to be members depending on the type of crisis. For example, if it's a data breach, chances are you'll want your chief information officer at the table. The key is to assemble a manageable group of empowered and informed individuals ready to move quickly.

The Crisis Communications Plan

While many organizations don't even have a working crisis plan in place, the ones that do typically have created a grotesquely large and dusty binder filled with a lot of verbiage and not a lot of immediate help. Half the people listed in the plan may no longer be with the organization (this is particularly true in sports, where changeovers in personnel happen frequently). Or, if it's in electronic form, it's buried on a server somewhere and long forgotten and long ignored. It's plus-size, by the way, because whoever created it was probably getting paid by the page (or thought they were!). It's dusty because no one in the company ever looked at it.

We're not big fans of giant tomes. That's not what's needed. What's called for in a crisis communications plan is simple: It should be a guide for what to do before, during, and after a crisis. In fact, the plan should be divided into those three sections: one for actions before a crisis takes place, one for during a crisis, and one for the learnings after a crisis occurs.

Before the Crisis: This section should describe the organization's general goals for successful crisis response — such as limiting the number of negative articles or fan responses on social media, staunching a drop in overall reputation (using some of the common metrics out there), or preventing a loss of sales or decrease in attendance. It should include a list of the most likely crisis scenarios an organization might face. The plan should then be home to templates, checklists, and other useful material designed for those scenarios. Information for when training will be conducted, and how and how often the plan will be updated (at the very least annually), should also be included.

Most importantly, this section lays out what each team member will be responsible for doing during a crisis. Who will head up gathering facts? Who will retrieve and update the draft statements that have been prepared in advance? Who is responsible for signing off on those statements before they're released? Who will see that the statements are distributed through the appropriate channels?

Crisis team members should also be responsible for reaching out to various stakeholders. These include the media, team personnel, league officials, regulators, politicians, and others, depending on the crisis. All involved must communicate to all affected audiences what is going on and how it's being addressed.

During the Crisis: This section guides the team as it goes about its work. Here's the most important principle in creating this part of the plan: If you want it to be *used* in the crisis response, it has to be *usable.*

Therefore, this section of the crisis plan should be simple, with a lot of white space, bold headings, and simplified checklists. Color-coding the various sections will help since the eye makes connections to various colors. In computer parlance, it needs a clear *user interface.* Crisis team members should be able to glance at it and refresh their memories on what to do. It should be a "living" document that brings the crisis team together and aids it in developing messages quickly and effectively.

In addition to the simple plan, there's another great tool you can develop. You know those laminated cards football coaches have their plays on that double as low-tech anti-lip-reading devices? We recommend developing a tool similar to what football coaches carry to place an abridged version of your crisis procedures and contacts. In our work, we call it a "Crisis Flash Sheet," which can be stored where easily found. Created with laminated 8.5-inch by 14-inch (legal-size) paper, a Crisis Flash Sheet can be wedged conspicuously on a desk or shelf, sticking out above the books, for easy access.

Your crisis response plan should include plenty of lists, including contact information for team members and alternates, emergency responders (for physical crises), trauma counselors (for athletes or employees), lawyers, website personnel, and other important stakeholders.

It should also include information sheets for documenting calls going out for gathering information and media calls coming in with inquiries. Forms should be included for monitoring traditional and social media so you can track the coverage and gauge public interest and sentiment (and, importantly, how this sentiment is improving thanks to your stellar crisis response!).

The plan's crisis-response section should also describe initial procedures: where the team will meet (including virtually where appropriate) and an alternate location if the first choice isn't available, and shortened versions of who will do what function, such as getting the statement out to media, athletes, employees, and other key audiences.

We've learned over the years that the initial facts in any crisis are invariably wrong. The plan should remind those monitoring incoming information of this. Data points arriving must be vetted and confirmed — including by considering the source — before anything is used for public consumption. It's best to have multiple sources before releasing your first statement. This is especially true in sports, where rumor and speculation are all part of the game. The danger is that if you release what are purported to be facts that turn out not to be, you'll have to issue a new statement correcting that. Which isn't a good look (in fact, our experience has shown that if you have to issue a second statement to clarify what you put in the first, you may be fighting a lost cause).

Another important role during the crisis is monitoring both

traditional and social media. The information gathered should be analyzed to help understand if the crisis response is working. A certain amount of caution should be taken with regard to examining the results. While platforms can measure general consumer sentiment, they don't yet have the ability to accurately interpret specific perspectives while a crisis is playing out. Even with advances in artificial intelligence, or AI, trained human intervention is key to getting the most out of the data. In nearly every case, we have to drill down into social-media data to see the underlying sentiment — which often comes from articles written by sports journalists.

And again, always keep in mind a specific problem that typically occurs: When the crisis strikes, no one can find the plan. It's on a shelf gathering dust or deep in a drive on the server or (God forbid) buried deep inside the Microsoft Teams portal you have trouble accessing even for routine tasks. (It does make sense, by the way, to have analog and digital versions, as this increases the likelihood of finding at least one.)

Finally, consider how to effectively use technology to facilitate accessibility and ease of use. We've experimented with various software and apps, and if you tailor the right one, it can work well in aiding a rapid response.

After the Crisis: The third section of your crisis communications plan should lay out tasks for after the crisis. If you've promised to follow up with certain stakeholders, including media, make sure that's done. If the organization wants to pursue follow-up coverage, assign and handle that. But most importantly, you must evaluate how your organization responded to the crisis: what you did right, what you did wrong, and what needs to be changed in the plan. This might include an evaluation questionnaire to gather the data needed to assess performance, as well as plans for follow-up meetings.

Training Makes Perfect

> *The key is not the will to win. Everybody has that. It is the will to prepare to win that is important.*
> — Bobby Knight

A crisis communications plan isn't very useful if it isn't tested and understood by all the crisis team members. The moment you learn your goalie is found to have engaged in sexual assault or an employee is arrested for drunk driving is not the moment to start exploring the document that guides you through that crisis. The team needs to be trained in the plan.

There's much to learn from such training. You may see what in the plan doesn't work or needs to be fine-tuned. You may also see that certain team members aren't right for their roles and need to be replaced — because they don't seem interested in their assigned tasks, are too dominant, or don't believe in the mission of such preparation.

Having the training program also shows that the team or league is committed to getting crisis response right. Most importantly, training helps ensure that, when a crisis hits, the team is familiar with the procedures to follow and isn't just winging it.

There are basically three types of crisis training:

- Drills of discrete parts of the plan, where at least each member's responsibility is focused on
- Tabletop run-throughs of a simulated crisis, with team members playing their roles and developments worsening so that the response must alter
- Live run-throughs of a simulated crisis

We suggest that throughout the year one drill be done for each of the most important parts of the plan (such as formulating the initial and second messages) and tabletop run-throughs be done at least twice. We realize that that may sound like a lot. But training as much as possible should be the goal (just like for athletes!).

Live run-throughs can also be beneficial, though they're a lot to take on. Because of that, and because they can involve team members frantically running around the facility, we're not the biggest fans of live run-throughs. In this training type, trainers (usually outside consultants) portray, for example, reporters or regulators who phone in with demanding questions or employees providing new facts on the ground that change the scenario.

Just as with crisis communications planning in general, organizations too often let the training fall by the wayside. That's a mistake. Training in the plan is the only way to get it right. It shows you care about your organization's reputation.

A Roadmap for How to A.C.T. During a Crisis

To bring this all together: When creating a crisis communications plan, we often advise organizations to use the acronym **A.C.T.**, which stands for **Assess**, **Create**, and **Train**. If you want to create an effective crisis communications planning process, you should:

- Assess potential crises, what appropriate responses would look like, and the team(s) that will handle them
- Create a plan of action that includes the checklists, templates, and other resources you'll need in the event of a crisis
- Train the core team, as well as the broader team where applicable, in tabletop or other virtual scenarios to ensure the plan is executed properly in a variety of situations

It's best to think of A.C.T. not as a one-time project, but as a *cycle*. You should constantly be in ACTion. Crisis communications planning becomes a continual process through which you develop a living approach to crisis response. In other words, you're in a constant cycle of assessing the potential matters your organization may confront, you're creating the structure and resources needed to respond, and you're training to ensure the plan works in the heat of a crisis.

A Word About Language

Messaging is a central part of crisis communications, and language and tone are central parts of messaging. So, we need to say a few words about those subjects.

The statements you issue in response to a crisis really do matter. Depending on how high profile the episode, your words will ricochet far and wide. They may be repeated in dozens or more articles. They'll be picked up by aggregator sites that don't even do their own reporting. That's why it's so important to get it right.

Throughout this book you'll see discussions of what should substantively be included in a crisis statement (acknowledgement of the situation, what the organization is doing to address it, concern for those affected). In addition, the language used, and the tone, are crucial. People reading your words need to understand that actual human beings are behind them. You must use language that resonates so the audiences actually listen to what you have to say. After all, that's the goal. The tone must convey that you take the situation seriously. You also want to convince the reader or listener of your point of view.

Therefore, such crisis statements must be honest, sincere, and compelling. They should never rely on clichés or jargon. The world is already filled with too much of that (especially from companies!). Yes, it's a good idea to research how other organizations have commented in similar crises, but keep in mind that (alas) most statements are badly and stiffly written. That shouldn't be emulated.

A crisis communications statement should be forthright, not coy. Most people will forgive accidents. They'll forgive mistakes. They'll forgive uncertainty and less-than-perfect information. What they won't forgive is being *played*.

For example, in May 2024 when video was posted showing a Delta Air Lines baggage handler tossing the East Tennessee State University team's golf bags onto the tarmac without a care, the company wrote in response, "We apologize to the ETSU Golf team and ask for a mulligan on how their equipment was handled. We're in direct contact with the Bucs to ensure they have what they need to successfully compete in the NCAAs."[2]

No equivocating. No excuses. Just acknowledgement that the company was in the wrong (with an apology) and a nod to what it was doing to make it right. That's too rare. (A quick aside: Despite the successful "mulligan" joke, humor rarely works in crisis

---

2. Liz Keller, "Delta Apologizes After Video Shows Baggage Handlers Mistreating East Tennessee Golf Team's Clubs," *Knoxville News Sentinel*, May 23, 2024, https://www.knoxnews.com/story/sports/college/2024/05/23/east-tennessee-state -golf-team-video-mishandled-luggage-viral-gold-bags/73816330007/.

communications because people are too upset or angry about something — namely, the crisis!)

We are constantly astounded at how reluctant organizations are to inject humanity into, or to personalize, their press releases and statements issued in response to a crisis. These messages are too often so worked over, lawyered up, and sanitized that they seem designed to evoke boredom. They project that the organization employs only robots.

Personalizing crisis communications can help garner sympathy because it shows the organization is made up of human beings. The entity itself may not have human emotion, but the people who work in it, and run it, do. We suspect company leaders believe a too-informal or personal statement would seem unserious. But it's not wrong to share personal stories and experiences.

Here's our favorite example of this, though not one from sports. In 2023, the U.S. Department of Labor fined three McDonald's franchisees for illegally employing more than 300 children — two of them 10-year-olds — including working a deep fryer. Tiffanie Boyd, SVP and chief people officer of McDonald's USA, responded with some typical corporate verbiage such as, "We are committed to ensuring our franchisees have the resources they need to foster safe workplaces for all employees and maintain compliance with all labor laws."

But she added this: "As a mother whose teenage son proudly worked at our local McDonald's, I feel this on a very personal level." Boyd was saying, I'm not just a corporate suit. I'm a mother — of course I care about fighting child labor and promoting workplace safety.

It was a heartfelt response.[3]

Consistency in messaging is also important. Especially these days, even your initial message may appear in several places: a statement or press release, a tweet and other social-media posts, an employee email or memo, talking points for the spokesperson. A best practice is

---

3. Teddy Grant, "Over 300 Minors Found Working at 3 McDonald's Franchisees: Department of Labor," ABC News, May 3, 2023, https://abcnews.go.com/US/minors-found-working-mcdonalds-franchisees-labor-department/story?id=99053558.

to get a final version of the statement or press release (the "core" message) and write the others based on that. If you issue several statements over time they, too, must be consistent (which isn't to say you don't provide new information).

The basic rules and best practices of good writing also apply. These include avoiding the aforementioned clichés and jargon.

Clichés don't resonate for the simple reason that they're clichés. If you write "a picture is worth a thousand words," don't expect your reader to sit back in awe at your talent. Crisis communications itself has its own clichés, and these are what organizations too often rely on. This is tricky because messaging, especially the first statement, demands the substantive elements we mentioned above. Still, organizations often write, for example, "Safety is our top priority." It's become a cliché that doesn't make a positive impression with a skeptical public. If safety is the top priority, how did the accident happen? Better to lay out the safety measures in place and those to be adopted. And, of course, an explanation of what went wrong.

There are also common legal clichés. "This case is without merit and we will defend ourselves vigorously" is the knee-jerk response from companies when they're sued (we know a news editor who's so tired of seeing *vigorously* in these statements that he snips it off the end of the published versions). Again, don't write something like that and expect it to make any kind of a positive impression.

As for jargon, it's hard to avoid in sports because there's so much of it. There's some leeway here because the audience for your messages will most likely be fans familiar with the specialized language. If the audience *isn't* made up of sports fans (maybe regulators are an important stakeholder group for this particular crisis) you may have to define certain terms. Thought should always be given to whether the intended audience will understand what you write. If the crisis in question is over, say, a two-point conversion play, that may require a little explanation.

If it's a legal matter, avoid the jargon known as legalese (not *all* sports fans are lawyers). Not everyone knows, for example, what a summary-judgment motion is. And speaking of legalese, in most crises the language you use will be vetted and altered by attorneys. You may have to resist them "lawyering up" the language — in other words, making it bland or incomprehensible to the layperson.

Your crisis communications should be clear, concise, and understandable. For some reason, when people need to write a statement to be released to the public, they tense up and won't allow themselves to use everyday language. They write "at the present time" instead of "now." They insist on "in the event that" instead of "if." One way to avoid that is to, when discussing the crisis with the response team, jot down the plain language you're uttering and use those words in your press releases and the like.

Avoid wordiness, or "clutter," as famous writing teacher William Zinsser called it. The cardinal rule of writing is to not make your reader read a single unnecessary word. Avoid unneeded adjectives and adverbs (a particular problem with inexperienced writers). Avoid throat-clearing phrases such as "It should be pointed out..." As Zinsser says, "If it should be pointed out, point it out."

He writes: "Every word that serves no function, every long word that could be a short word, every adverb which carries the same meaning that is already in the verb, every passive construction that leaves the reader unsure of who is doing what — these are the thousand and one adulterants that weaken the strength of a sentence."

He also says — and we concur — "Writing is hard work. A clear sentence is no accident."[4]

The Windup

It's often said that admitting you have a problem is the first step to recovery. When it comes to crisis communications, *anticipating* that your company *can* have a problem at some point is truly the first step.

---

4. William Zinsser, *On Writing Well: The Classic Guide to Writing Non-Fiction*, 7th ed. (New York: Harper Perennial, 2006), 6–15.

In these first two chapters we covered:

- What constitutes a crisis
- Why organizations mistakenly don't take crises seriously
- What makes sports crises different
- The two main types of crises
- The importance of preparation
- Choosing a crisis leader and crisis team
- Creating a crisis communications plan
- The importance of training on that plan
- How to create messages that resonate, so that your response to a crisis is actually heard

Now it's time to move on to our deep dive into real-life crises that sports people and organizations have experienced and how they've handled them (the good, the bad, and the just-plain confusing). We do this through the use of more than a decade's worth of content we've created covering these subjects. Chapters 3 through 14 republish select blog posts arranged by categories, with an introduction for each topic and follow-ups for most entries (see "Postgames" where included). Chapters 15 through 20 are transcripts of some truly exciting podcast interviews we've done with in-the-know journalists and others who provide great insights into sports crises.

PART TWO:

PLAY-BY-PLAY

INTRODUCTION

The blog posts that follow cover a slew of sports drama going back to 2014, organized into chapters by crisis category. Simply looking at the chapter titles should give a sense of the crises that most befall, and are most dire for, athletes and sports organizations. They include domestic violence, sexual assault, discrimination, gambling, and questionable public behavior.

By delving into the details of these stories — the older ones will be a jaunt down memory lane — the reader will gain a solid grounding in the specific situations that arise and how they're best dealt with. A good way to learn the fundamentals of crisis communications is to develop an empirical knowledge base of the actual negative events.

Each chapter begins with an introduction that explores the crisis communications topics raised by the blog posts, such as apologies, fact-gathering, and working with lawyers. These subjects may appear to come up somewhat haphazardly, but there's a method to our madness: It's the incidents themselves that give rise to the points we lay out in the introductions. We believe that by familiarizing yourself with them, you'll be well on your way to becoming a crisis communications expert.

Within each chapter, the blog posts are presented chronologically. Most are followed by "Postgame" updates reporting what's happened with the personalities and organizations since the events in question and how their reputations have fared (in other words, how well the response worked).

3

WINNERS DON'T:
CHEATING

Introduction

One reason people are passionate about professional and college sports is the sheer joy of watching players in action who've worked incredibly hard to become among the best at what they do. Sports fans assume that also means playing by the rules, including practicing good sportsmanship.

That's why cheating scandals are such a jolt, a betrayal. Cheating hits at the heart of sports and harms the reputation of athletics in general. Sports are supposed to be about excellence, hard work, and achievement. Obviously, leagues and teams should strive to avoid such scandals by insisting that all involved hew to the highest standards.

Accusations of cheating are a major crisis that communicators must be prepared for. If a cheating crisis comes, it must be dealt with quickly and openly. (We'll address a particular type of cheating, the use of performance-enhancing drugs, in the next chapter.)

Cheating crises are an example of how important fact gathering is to crisis communications. If a player or organization is unfairly accused of cheating, you must bring together the facts to make that defense. That was especially highlighted in the University of Michigan's sign-stealing scandal and whether Coach Jim Harbaugh deserved any blame. We also have a post on the Team Penske race-car cheating scandal in which the leader, Roger Penske, took quick action but individual members tried to deflect complete responsibility.

Another issue, as with all crises, is that when the bad news arrives, your balance in what we call the "Credibility Bank" can either help or hurt you. As we've detailed in chapter 1, prominent sports figures are often perceived in a much different light than the rest of us, and often enjoy a unique reverence. The privilege afforded star athletes and coaches can come in handy for a sports-communications professional, but it can also breed a complacency that leaves a team or brand unprepared for responding when a crisis hits.

As you see from our original commentary in the "Deflategate" scandal, the New England Patriots had a negative Credibility Bank balance due to the earlier "Spygate" scandal. Things continued to go in a very bad direction for the team, Coach Belichick, and Tom Brady; a solid communications strategy wasn't in the playbook. Imagine if the crisis had been more serious than a few soft footballs.

Having a high balance in your Credibility Bank — by maintaining a strong reputation for integrity through positive actions and positive press coverage — can help blunt the negative reputational impact when the crisis comes. In other words, the crisis work begins long before the crisis alights.

Or (as you'll see below), win seven Super Bowls. That helps, too.

'Deflategate' Shows Importance of Having a Balance in Your Credibility Bank
First published January 26, 2015

The ongoing "Deflategate" situation — or, maybe, scandal — underscores the importance of companies and organizations maintaining a balance in their "Credibility Bank" to help ease damage, and maintain reputations, when a crisis hits.

The National Football League's New England Patriots continue to face suspicions that the team underinflated footballs to make them easier to catch during its January 18 victorious AFC Championship Game against the Indianapolis Colts.

And because of the way the team and Head Coach Bill Belichick have handled the accusation that they are cheaters, the issue simply isn't going away — just when they need to focus on defeating the Seattle Seahawks at Super Bowl XLIX on February 1.

The latest was January 24's press conference in which Belichick said the team followed all the rules for inflating footballs and that the air pressure in them could have been affected by the weather or rubbing them before the game. "I'm not a scientist," Belichick revealed.

The massaging allegation didn't impress Bill Nye "The Science Guy" — who admits he's rooting for the Seahawks. "What he said didn't make any sense," Nye said yesterday on *Good Morning America*. "Rubbing the football I don't think you can change the pressure. To really change the pressure you need one of these, the inflation needle."

During the press conference, Belichick admitted the team had been guilty of 2007's "Spygate" scandal in which it illegally taped the New York Jets' defensive signals — a liability on the Patriots' Credibility Bank balance sheet.

But the deficit is also there because Belichick has such a tense relationship with the press. He doesn't hide his contempt for reporters. It's not unusual for people to refer to Belichick as a "jerk" when it comes to the press — which encourages them to pile on, rather than giving the benefit of the doubt, when a crisis strikes.

Belichick and quarterback Tom Brady appeared at an earlier press conference on January 22. That performance garnered a *Saturday Night Live* spoof in which the coach blamed the quarterback and the quarterback turned responsibility over to an equipment manager, who invoked Jack Nicholson's tough-talking character from *A Few Good Men* ("You can't handle the truth!").

The point? The overall sense is that Belichick and the Patriots are not being straight with the public.

Also disappointing has been the NFL itself, which didn't put out a statement on the matter until January 23. The league said the investigation by outside experts, including Washington, D.C., lawyer Ted Wells, began the night of the AFC Championship Game and is ongoing. "We take seriously claims that those rules have been violated and will fully investigate this matter without compromise or delay," it said.

The investigators have conducted almost 40 interviews, the NFL said. Let's hope that effort to determine whether air was let out of a football finally pays off by putting this particular crisis to rest.

Postgame

Okay, this is a unique case, and it's interesting to look back now at the career of Tom Brady, who retired (finally) in February 2023. Back in 2015, Brady was still more than a few Super Bowl rings shy of his career total of seven, and he wasn't being called so much the "G.O.A.T." as "cheater." As we say, having a balance in the Credibility Bank can go a long way. If Super Bowl XLIX had been Brady's last, he might have been forever linked to the ball-inflation scandal rather than lauded as the greatest quarterback to play the game. Instead, four more Super Bowl victories later, it's barely remembered. There's a lesson here too, though: Don't count on being the G.O.A.T. to save you. They only come around once in each sport, after all.

Is Michigan's Standing by Its Man the Right Play?
First published November 16, 2023

The University of Michigan Wolverines football team is embroiled in a sign-stealing scandal that's brought about strong emotions and strong responses from the school. Michigan is boldly defending its coach, Jim Harbaugh. Is that the right move? Probably only time will tell.

The scandal broke last month when it was reported that college-sports governing body NCAA was investigating whether Michigan had sent scouts to its future opponents' games to learn their sign systems

— a no-no. On November 3, Connor Stalions, the team employee at the center of the scandal, was at first suspended with pay and then resigned. The probe is ongoing.

A major question is what, if anything, Coach Harbaugh knew about Stalions' alleged operation; he's denied being aware. On November 10, even with the probe pending, Tony Petitti, commissioner of the Big Ten conference Michigan belongs to, suspended Harbaugh for the final three games of the regular season. The first of those three games was played this past weekend.

Michigan has dug in and defended Harbaugh. It's almost a siege mentality. It seems the Wolverines feel they're accused of doing what other college gridiron squads do; they just got caught (allegedly). Part of the defensiveness stems from the team being undefeated and a possible contender for the national championship. The school doesn't want to jeopardize that.

Things came to a head this weekend. Michigan issued a forceful statement in response to Harbaugh's suspension. "We are dismayed at the commissioner's rush to judgment when there is an ongoing NCAA investigation — one in which we are fully cooperating," it wrote.

Even more boldly, it filed a lawsuit seeking a temporary restraining order to allow Harbaugh to coach. It was hoping for a decision before last Saturday's game, but that didn't happen. In fact, the first hearing in the case is scheduled for tomorrow.

A high-profile aspect of this came after last weekend's game against Penn State, which Michigan won 24–15 even without Harbaugh. In a postgame interview, Michigan's fill-in coach, offensive coordinator Sherrone Moore, broke down in tears. "I want to thank the Lord, and I want to thank Coach Harbaugh," he said. As we say, it's getting emotional. Harbaugh himself has been criticized for opining that the Wolverines should be considered "America's team."

On Sunday, University of Michigan President Santa Ono posted on X, "As our team showed so clearly yesterday, we will respond to any challenge head on with a conviction to do better and to emerge even stronger."

It's tough to say whether Michigan's tough stance is the right move. Too many facts are unknown. That's part of its argument: Harbaugh is being denied due process by being punished without having been found to have engaged in wrongdoing. But it's an interesting example of needing to decide what tone — strident or apologetic — to take in responding to a crisis.

Postgame

Later in the day after this post appeared, Michigan announced that Coach Jim Harbaugh would accept his three-game suspension, and the court case was dropped. The next day, the Wolverines fired its linebacker coach for allegedly instructing team members on how to respond to questions concerning the probe. In January 2024, Harbaugh accepted a job as head coach of the Los Angeles Chargers, leaving his college woes behind him, but not before leading the Wolverines to the National Championship title.

The Michigan situation described here is a little different from the typical cheating scandal in that it raised the question of how aware Harbaugh was of the sign-stealing efforts. Still, it shows how damaging allegations of cheating can be to reputation.

Team Penske Struggles to Steer Race-Car Scandal
First published May 9, 2024

Roger Penske, the 87-year-old owner of Team Penske, is struggling to stave off the damage from a cheating scandal rocking the car-racing world. On Tuesday this week, after an internal probe, Penske suspended two senior leaders and two engineers, and strove to communicate the team's position.

The scandal centers on Team Penske driver Josef Newgarden's use of so-called push-to-pass software in a March 10 race he won in St. Petersburg, Florida. Push-to-pass, which gives a horsepower boost, is not allowed to be used on starts and restarts. Sanctioning body IndyCar didn't discover it on the three Team Penske cars until April 21.

IndyCar then took away the March win from Newgarden and the third-place finish of teammate Scott McLaughlin. It penalized a third teammate, Will Power, 10 points and fined all three $25,000. The situation is unusual: It's the first IndyCar disqualification in 29 years.

Now this week, after the probe by his general counsel, Roger Penske suspended the president, the team managing director, and the two engineers for two races — including the Indianapolis 500. (Team Penske has won the Indy 500, called "The Greatest Spectacle in Racing," a record 19 times, and Penske Corp. owns the Indianapolis Motor Speedway where it's held.)

On Tuesday morning, Team Penske put out a statement about the suspensions, noting "significant failures in our processes and internal communications." It quoted Penske himself: "I recognize the magnitude of what occurred and the impact it continues to have on the sport to which I've dedicated so many decades. Everyone at Team Penske along with our fans and business partners should know that I apologize for the errors that were made and I deeply regret them."

Penske also did an interview Tuesday with the AP, which has been all over this story. He said the probe found "no malicious intent by anyone." The team had been testing the software on starts and restarts and inadvertently neglected to return it to legal form for the March race, he said. Newgarden has said he used it three times because he thought the rule had been changed. McLaughlin has said he used it once out of habit. Power didn't use it.

The coverage makes clear that a lot of people, including other team owners and drivers, aren't buying the explanations. "It's simply not believable that one of three cars owned by series leadership thought a major rule had been changed without any public announcement," the AP's Jenna Fryer wrote.

A major part of the story is that Penske, a former racer and a motorsports giant, has a sterling reputation. Now that reputation is under threat. It's a reminder that one misstep can imperil an otherwise golden name.

Fryer penned an analysis headlined "IndyCar Cheating Scandal Risks Sullying Roger Penske's Perfect Image." Just to show how damaging a reputational crisis can be, despite Penske's stature, Fryer managed to dig up a previous scandal he was involved in — in 1967!

"This is an unfortunate situation and when you're the leader, you have to take action," Penske said in his AP interview.

We couldn't have said it better.

Postgame

It turns out Roger Penske did one better than just saying the right thing and taking action. He doubled down by taking a page out of the Brady–Belichick handbook as his team went on a heater, racking up an impressive series of wins on both the IndyCar and NASCAR circuits in the immediate aftermath of the cheating scandal. Among the numerous accolades earned, statement wins by Penske drivers such as Joey Logano, Ryan Blaney, and especially Will Power — who had gotten caught up in the scandal — helped put Team Penske back into a positive light. The consensus among fans and the media was that the entire team seemed determined to re-establish Roger Penske as one of the greatest racing team owners in history.

4

JUST SAY NO:
PERFORMANCE-ENHANCING DRUGS

Introduction

A particular type of cheating scandal is the use of performance-enhancing drugs. Such accusations often involve investigations into the facts, but, as with nearly all crises, people want to hear something before the probe is completed. You must tell your stakeholders that you're aware of the situation, what you're doing about it, and when you'll be able to comment further.

Our 2016 post on tennis player Maria Sharapova and how she handled her crisis concerning a banned drug, for instance, offers a good template on how to respond when one is at fault: own up to it. In Sharapova's case, she was also able to get in front of the story. That goes to the heart of crisis communications: The goal is to respond quickly with the appropriate facts so a narrative that goes against you doesn't bury you — and your reputation.

The more-recent situation with sprinter Issamade "Issam" Asinga and Gatorade is unusual but shows the importance of gathering facts to make your case. We'll be interested to watch how that plays out. In any event, it underscores how devastating a scandal over performance-enhancing drugs can be.

We also include here a post on a crisis communications mainstay:

the apology. Apologies, whether in personal relationships, business, or sports, are usually poorly done. Former Yankees great Alex Rodriguez took a creative approach here — he produced a handwritten letter of apology. The problem was, it didn't come off as sincere.

Responding quickly is important in any crisis, and that includes apologies. One planning tool that might help in that regard is to have a collection of proven public apologies that can serve as a jumping off point for when it's your turn to do the mea culpa. Done right, you're not pulling template language off the shelf. Rather, you're starting with language you know will provide the right tone. Tailor accordingly.

Ultimately, apologies must be sincere. So take ownership of wrongdoing, outline what will be done to make amends, and make sure you're not engaging in self-indulgent exercises — i.e., discussing how the negative situation has upended your life ("It's been a nightmare for me since this happened"), rather than the lives of those you've affected.

A-Rod Handwrites an Apology but Forgets to Focus on the Content
First published February 19, 2015

This week has been abuzz with discussions of disgraced Yankee third baseman Alex Rodriguez's handwritten mea culpa. In addition to apologizing to the Yankees last week (most likely because spring training is about to begin), on February 17 A-Rod published a handwritten note to fans saying he was sorry for his actions. The note, including its personal touch, doesn't seem to be swaying negative opinions too much.

Rodriguez is returning to the Yankees after the longest suspension in baseball history, having missed 211 games, for steroid use. He's about to start what will most likely be an awkward season for him. Obviously, A-Rod wants to put his best foot forward.

The handwritten nature of the note was pretty unique and attracted a lot of attention — *The Wall Street Journal* devoted a whole article to analyzing his handwriting. Rodriguez mentions that his team offered him Yankee Stadium to conduct a press conference, which he decided against doing (often a wise move in a crisis situation).

In the note, published through Major League Baseball's website, Rodriguez directly apologizes to his fans, teammates, and the baseball community. "I take full responsibility for the mistakes that led to my suspension for the 2014 season," he wrote. "I regret that my actions made the situation worse than it needed to be. To Major League Baseball, the Yankees, the Steinbrenner family, the Players Association and you, the fans, I can only say I'm sorry."

The note has some nice elements but its vague nature doesn't give the impression the athlete is truly remorseful. Owning up to the behavior in question is one of the most important elements of an apology and A-Rod doesn't apologize for his steroid use. In fact, it's not clear what he's referring to.

He noticeably leaves out any mention of what he has done to reform himself — another important apology element because it shows you're taking steps to prevent the problem from happening again.

The note takes on a defensive tone. Rodriguez reminds everyone he has been harshly punished for his actions — seemingly forgetting he deserved the penalty.

"I served the longest suspension in the history of the League for PED use," he writes in the only mention of his infraction. "The Commissioner has said the matter is over. The Players Association has said the same. The Yankees have said the next step is to play baseball."

Clearly, he wants everyone to move on. But the responses to the note show people aren't moving on. Fans aren't buying it. The reactions have been sarcastic and skeptical.

One person tweeted, "It's going to be great when it turns out A-Rod did not hand-write his handwritten letter."

Another user wrote, "Few people take the time these days to craft a hand-written note. Especially when apologizing to Planet Earth. What a personal touch."

And yet another tweeted, "Give credit where credit is due. It is hard to write an apology letter on unlined printer paper. But I've seen more raw emotion on a prescription order sheet."

Even *The New York Times* wrote an article today with the headline "Lying, Lying, Gone? Fans Should Hope So."

Clearly, Rodriguez's apology isn't getting the reaction he wanted. It would have been more effective if he had fully admitted to his steroid use and hadn't pulled his punches (we realize there may be some legal implications there). Instead, Rodriguez half-assed it.

Maybe he focused too much energy on physically writing the note so that he forgot to focus on the content.

Postgame

The season following Alex Rodriguez's 2014 suspension for using performance-enhancing drugs ended up being his last, as he retired following the conclusion of the 2016 MLB campaign. A-Rod's ignominious record — professional baseball's longest suspension — has since been beaten by Trevor Bauer, who in 2022 was handed a 324-game suspension (eventually reduced to 194 games) due to allegations of sexual assault.

Since retiring from play, Rodriguez has shifted his focus from the diamond to redeeming his reputation by becoming a highly regarded analyst on both Fox Sports and ESPN and through the business realm, specifically investing. He's created a portfolio that includes many real-estate properties. Following his victory in a lengthy arbitration battle, and pending final NBA approval, it appears he may also be on his way, along with partner Marc Lore, to becoming a majority owner of both the Minnesota Timberwolves and Minnesota Lynx basketball franchises.

It remains to be seen if the controversial ex-Yankee will make it into the Baseball Hall of Fame, despite having a no-doubt-about-it baseball resume. The use of steroids continues to dog him, as suspicions of such use dog other players of his era, and may ultimately make it so he never reaches the Hall. It's safe to say his "sorry-not-sorry" apology didn't help his cause.

In Communications Over Failed Drug Test, Sharapova Stays in Front of the Ball
First published March 10, 2016

Russian tennis pro Maria Sharapova's handling of her positive drug test offers important lessons for those engaged in crisis messaging. Sharapova shrewdly got in front of the news, announcing it before anyone had an inkling. Also noteworthy: how quickly some of the companies Sharapova promotes suspended (and only suspended) their relationships with her.

Sharapova called a press conference in Los Angeles on Monday. The speculation was that she would announce her retirement. Instead, she admitted she had tested positive for the drug meldonium at the Australian Open in January. She was forthright in her subdued comments, unwavering in taking the blame. Some observers called it a "textbook apology."

"I did fail the test and I take full responsibility for it," Sharapova said. "I made a huge mistake."

She didn't rely on a press release or statement and didn't have her lawyer do the talking. Instead, she stood alone in front of a group of reporters.

Under its rules, the International Tennis Federation wouldn't have announced that Sharapova tested positive until the investigation was done. The tennis player apparently decided to be proactive and get her story out first. You might say: easy call — the news was coming out eventually.

But think of all the times a company is confronted with impending bad news and just can't get itself to take charge. Instead, the executives and lawyers and communicators huddle in a conference room hoping pixie dust will sprinkle upon them and make the whole horrible situation go away.

Under these circumstances, it doesn't.

And Sharapova did have a story to tell, though not one without its question marks. She said she'd been taking meldonium for 10 years for a variety of ailments. (The drug, which isn't approved in the United States, aids blood flow.) She said she monitored the banned-substances list to see whether it had been added.

In late December, she received the annual email to players from the World Anti-Doping Agency and the International Tennis Federation with a link to the updated list of substances that would be banned come January. But, she said, this time she didn't click on the link. So she didn't know that meldonium (which, to complicate things, she knew as "mildronate") had been newly banned.

Her explanation is being met with some skepticism. *The Times* of London reported that the tennis pros received four other warnings in December that meldonium would be banned. "Whether it was one notice of some kind or more than one, Maria has already acknowledged she should have known," her management team responded.

The stakes are not small. Sharapova will be suspended provisionally on Saturday until a final determination is made. She faces a four-year suspension for a knowing violation, two years if she's found not to have known.

She also faces losing a lot of money. Sharapova, 28, is reportedly the highest-paid female athlete in the world, taking in $23 million in endorsements last year alone.

Within hours of her admission, Nike, one of her sponsors with which she also has a clothing line, said it was suspending their relationship. Porsche and Tag Heuer made similar statements. Evian water owner Danone took a more wait-and-see attitude. Racket maker Head NV, on the other hand, said today it would seek to extend its contract with the tennis player.

The Nike deal alone was worth $12.5 million a year, according to Business Insider. Nigel Currie, a sports-marketing and sponsorship consultant in the U.K., told the business site that sponsors are distancing themselves more quickly from scandal-hit athletes, rather than waiting for the adjudication process. In this case, the sponsors are only suspending the relationship pending further events (Tag Heuer is suspending negotiations it had underway with Sharapova).

New York Times reporter Sydney Ember noted that Nike had defended Lance Armstrong for years when he was accused of doping. But more recently it terminated boxer Manny Pacquiao a day after he apologized for making anti-gay remarks.

Ember speculates that Nike's fleetness with Sharapova may have been due to fears of getting slammed on social media. That is a legitimate concern — certainly one for crisis communicators. The reporter also noted that other sponsors have been quick to drop spokespeople, such as Subway with Jared Fogle, now in prison for charges related to child pornography.

But perhaps Sharapova's adroit handling of her communications will bring her sponsors back before long. Minimizing impacts like that is the whole point of adept crisis communications — the type Sharapova just demonstrated.

Postgame

In June 2016, Maria Sharapova received a two-year suspension from the International Tennis Federation for testing positive for the banned substance meldonium. The ITF found that, although Sharapova's intention was not to cheat, she was the only one responsible for the positive test. She disagreed with the decision and appealed. That October she won a partial victory and had her suspension reduced to 15 months.

Her temporary banishment was considered to start in January 2016, when she failed the test, and she returned to the tennis court in April 2017. She played professional tennis for slightly less than two years before announcing her retirement in early 2020. Sharapova ended her career as one of 10 women to complete the career Grand Slam. Since retiring she has continued to work on her charity, the Maria Sharapova Foundation, as well as expand her Sugarpova line of candy. When she teamed with John McEnroe in a pickleball exhibition in 2023 (facing off against Andre Agassi and Steffi Graf), no mention was made of the prior suspension, and it would appear the incident has had no long-term impact on her reputation.

The lesson in all this for sports-communications professionals is clear: Although many people, including other tennis pros, were cynical about Sharapova's protestations of innocence, she managed to get through the drug-testing crisis with dignity because she owned up to what she did, quickly and directly, although she maintained she didn't know meldonium was banned. She was also wise to get out in front of the crisis and proactively announce she had failed the test. Sharapova may have lost a few sets, but it appears she won the match.

Gatorade, Sprinter Slug It Out in Reputation Ring
First published July 18, 2024

Issamade "Issam" Asinga, the teenager *The Washington Post* calls "the fastest high-school sprinter in history," and Gatorade, the drink brand synonymous with sports, are in a fierce reputational battle. It's heating up, as the runner just sued the company in federal court.

In May, following an investigation, anti-doping overseer Athletics Integrity Unit suspended Asinga, 19, from competing in track and field for four years after he tested positive for a banned substance, cardarine. The prohibition, which Asinga has appealed, includes the upcoming Paris Olympics and it may imperil his scholarship at Texas A&M University. It nixes his under-20 record for the 100-meter from last year (9.89 seconds).

Asinga contends the culprit is a bottle of Gatorade Recovery Gummies for Athletes the company gave him, along with other gifts, at a ceremony honoring him last year. The sprinter says the bottle tested positive for cardarine. He also contends the drinks brand is lying about its product to avoid reputational harm. He sued in Manhattan federal court July 10. Gatorade denies the gummies were tainted.

So, we have an athlete at the beginning of a promising career desperately trying to reverse his ban from his sport and save his reputation by pointing fingers at a big company, and the big company trying to aid its own reputation by arguing it's done nothing wrong.

And they're speaking out in the press, with both sides widely quoted, particularly in a lengthy *Washington Post* piece that comes off as a human-interest story, a PR win for Asinga. He gave *WaPo* an interview on Zoom with his lawyers (and apparently his father) joining in. "You're either guilty or you're not," Asinga said. "I know I'm not, so I've got to chase my dream."

For its part, Gatorade issued a more forceful corporate statement than is typical, a nice reminder that even big companies can give the public their side of the story during litigation. This crisis goes to the heart of what Gatorade does for a living, so it really can't play games (see what we did there?).

WaPo and Reuters quoted from Gatorade's statement:

"The product in question is completely safe and the claims made are false."

"Gatorade products are FDA compliant and safe for athlete consumption, which was validated by the findings of the Athletics Integrity Unit investigation."

"Gatorade fully complied with the Athletics Integrity Unit investigation, including producing evidence that was accepted by the AIU that the gummies were not contaminated with the banned substance in their original ruling."

That last paragraph gets to the heart of the matter: the twists and turns of the gummies testing. At first Gatorade told Asinga it couldn't find a sample from the same lot for him to test. It gave him a sample from a different batch, which came back negative. Then, six months later, it said it *did* find one from the same lot, but it too tested negative. Asinga contends that's because over time cardarine becomes undetectable.

His theory of the case is that Gatorade purposefully withheld a sample from the same lot until it would no longer test positive. The company originally refused to provide a sealed bottle from the same batch "because it feared harm to its own reputation — even though it knew this choice would devastate Issam's," according to his complaint.

Another major issue is that Asinga's gifted bottle was labeled "NSF Certified for Sport," an assurance it was free from banned substances. But it turns out NSF, which so certifies products, didn't test that lot, and this is a big part of Gatorade's embarrassment.

On June 4, NSF issued a public notice that the lot and one for a similar Gatorade product "have not been tested, evaluated, or certified by NSF and are not authorized to use the NSF certification mark or make any claims of NSF certification."

5

WHAT ARE THE ODDS?
GAMBLING

Introduction

Gambling is obviously one of the hottest topics in sports today. It's also a crisis minefield. That wagering on sports is legal in more places doesn't alter that it's controversial — especially online gambling and proposition betting, or prop betting, wagering on individual plays or a player's game stats. And while a big portion of the over-21 U.S. population can now place bets whenever and wherever they like with just a few taps, this doesn't include the athletes themselves.

Like cheating, a gambling crisis also shows the utility of gathering facts and comparing them to the reporting and the rumors. In one blog post republished here, on an NFL betting scandal, we show how, even when you're in a crisis because of your own actions, invoking facts can mitigate the episode's seriousness. You've got to tell your side of the story. That's also the lesson of a more recent gambling scandal that arose around baseball superstar Shohei Ohtani in March 2024 (see the post in this chapter; for a wider discussion of sports betting, see our interview with Bob Costas in chapter 20).

Truth is usually more complex than myth. Even if you're partially in the wrong, it's crucial to explain in a simple manner what the facts are and how they may (again, maybe partially) exonerate you. Too often, those mired in a crisis respond with a "no comment." That's usually a mistake.

NFL Gambling Scandal Shows How Facts Can Help in a Crisis
First published April 27, 2023

Late last week, the National Football League disclosed its biggest gambling scandal in decades. We were intrigued by the statement from one of the suspended players' agents because it shows how speaking out with facts can help alleviate a bad situation.

The NFL made its announcement on April 21 — a Friday, which is when you release news you don't want to get a lot of notice. Three players — two with the Detroit Lions and one with the Washington Commanders — were suspended indefinitely; the Lions immediately said they cut those players from the team. Two other Lions players, Jameson Williams and Stanley Berryhill III, were suspended for six games.

The NFL didn't provide much in the way of details, which was mentioned in the press coverage. The organization did say it didn't appear that the gambling affected any NFL games, clearly a point it wanted to make.

The three players with the harshest punishments had bet on NFL games during the 2022 season, a major no-no. Pro football players can bet on other sports, though not "in any club or league facility or venue," the NFL press release noted. But the release didn't connect that to any of the players punished.

It was up to Alliance Sports, the agency that represents Jameson Williams, to make the connection clear. The agency tweeted a statement. After noting its client took full responsibility and "is very apologetic," it wrote: "However, it is important to note that Jameson's violation was not for betting on football but rather due to a technical rule regarding the actual location in which the online bet was placed — and which would otherwise be allowed by the NFL outside of the club's facility."

So there you have it. It appears Williams made a bet at his

workplace, which is verboten. Too often people are reluctant to explain themselves in a crisis (we haven't seen any responses from the other players or their reps). But here, Williams' agents put out an explanation that probably had people thinking, "Okay, maybe the guy made a mistake, but it isn't *that* bad." And that statement was picked up in the media coverage we've seen.

The Lions' press release said that Williams and Berryhill were suspended "for other gambling policy violations, including betting from an NFL facility on non-NFL games." But that didn't precisely connect the dots. The move by Williams' agency was a good one.

Postgame

Three of the players involved in the gambling crisis, Quintez Cephus, C. J. Moore, and Stanley Berryhill III, have since been released by the Detroit Lions. Jameson Williams is still with the Lions, perhaps showing that getting in front of the crisis and telling your story if you have one to tell can work in your favor.

Now that the doors of the unsavory issue of player gambling have been kicked open, more NFL player-betting indiscretions are being uncovered. Just a couple of months after these initial findings, another rash of scandals was made public with at least four players suspended for betting on NFL games or on other sports in the workplace. Perhaps it's time for the league to take another look at its policies and think about what it can do to persuade its legions of fans that the integrity of the games isn't being compromised.

Oh, Ohtani! Gambling Scandal Has High Comms Stakes
First published March 28, 2024

One of the biggest crises currently rocking the sports world — the gambling scandal swirling around Los Angeles Dodgers superstar Shohei Ohtani — raises all sorts of tawdry communications issues with all sorts of important communications lessons. Not the least of those lessons arises from a presser Ohtani himself held.

On Tuesday, March 19, when the Dodgers were in South Korea to open their season (against the San Diego Padres), Ippei Mizuhara, longtime interpreter and friend of Japan native Ohtani, gave a 90-minute interview to ESPN. Ohtani apparently didn't know about it, but his spokesman did.

In the interview, Mizuhara claimed that Ohtani had covered $4.5 million in gambling debts the interpreter owed to a California-based bookmaker. Sports gambling remains illegal in California, and Mizuhara (who said he didn't bet on baseball) and the bookmaker are reportedly under federal investigation. Sports gambling, though accepted in many corners of the sports world, is controversial. It's not surprising this has blown up into such an issue.

The day after the interview, but before the ESPN article was published, Ohtani's spokesman (who reportedly was a recently hired crisis communications counselor whom we haven't seen named) recanted the story and said Ohtani's law firm would issue a statement. Which it did: "In the course of responding to recent media inquiries, we discovered that Shohei has been the victim of a massive theft, and we are turning the matter over to the authorities," said West Hollywood, California–based Berk Brettler LLP.

After that came out, Mizuhara changed his own story and said Ohtani didn't know about his gambling debts and hadn't transferred any money to the bookmaker. Mizuhara was on the Dodgers' payroll and, that same day, the team fired him. MLB has opened an investigation into the mess.

The first noticeable comms issue is that it appears Ohtani's spokesman didn't initially coordinate with the law firm. Even the accusation that Ohtani covered Mizuhara's debts was trouble. This is an unusual situation, but when it comes to high-stakes comms such as this, everyone has to be on the same page.

A second comms issue is that, probably because of that lack of coordination, we had conflicting narratives and unanswered questions, which kept intense focus on the story (that's why it's so important to get the facts straight from the get-go). Was Mizuhara covering for Ohtani's own gambling? Also, the law firm's statement didn't explain who did the thieving.

On Monday, the press-shy Ohtani held a news conference in which he appeared to clear up some (not all) of the questions. We're usually not fans of pressers because they can turn into zoos, but Ohtani's camp said in advance he wouldn't be taking questions, just making a statement.

In fact, Ohtani did a good job and, if he was truthful (which he seemed to be), he cleared up a number of things. He was more forthcoming than might have been expected.

He said he's never gambled or had any dealings with bookmakers. He said that, until the team was in South Korea, he was unaware of Mizuhara's "gambling addiction," his huge debt, or his alleged shenanigans with his money (though it's still unknown how Mizuhara accessed his accounts). He said he never agreed to pay off his friend's debt. After he learned of it, he informed his representatives and the Dodgers, and then went to authorities (his side is declining to say which ones).

"Ippei has been stealing money from my account and has told lies," he said.

In our view, Ohtani took the heat off himself and — again, if truthful — convincingly portrayed himself as the victim, not the bad guy. It shows the importance of invoking facts and telling your story.

Ohtani conducted his presser through an interpreter. Not Mizuhara, obviously.

Postgame

On April 11, 2024, Ippei Mizuhara was arrested, accused of stealing over $16 million — more than originally thought — from Shohei Ohtani. It became clear that the baseball player was indeed the victim of his former interpreter. Shortly after his arrest, Mizuhara apologized through his lawyer to Ohtani, the Dodgers, MLB, and his family.

He reached a deal with prosecutors, and in June 2024 pleaded guilty to one count of bank fraud and one count of tax fraud. His winning bets had totaled $142 million and his losing bets $183 million, a net loss of $41 million.

In February 2025, Mizuhara was sentenced to 57 months in prison.

Before the arrest, there was a lighter incident that occurred while Ohtani was in the spotlight. After he hit his first homer with the Dodgers, the woman who caught it complained about the team's treatment of her in its efforts to coax her into returning it. Instead of offering real money for the ball (one estimate put its worth at $100,000), the Dodgers bestowed her with signed gear: a ball, a bat, and two hats. Ohtani said he met with the woman, but she denied that. Given the focus at the time on the pitcher's reputation, it would have been a much smarter move to pay her something closer to the estimated value or even forgo the ball. Ohtani wasn't thinking long-term about that rep.

Still, he started the season with this scandal and ended it with helping his team win the World Series and being named league MVP. All in all, not a bad comeback from what could have been a disastrous year.

6

BAD BOYS:
ATHLETES' PUBLIC BEHAVIOR

Introduction

Many sports crises arise from athletes' behavior off the field, court, ice, pitch, track, what have you. It's similar for extracurricular activities of team personnel and league or athletic-department officials. The crisis communicator doesn't have the luxury of saying, "Sorry, this odious behavior occurred off the clock. Not our concern." In the sports galaxy, when an individual does something boneheaded, it doesn't reflect only that person's rep, but the organization's.

Athletes, and the communicators who advise them, must keep in mind that being in the public eye means having one's behavior particularly scrutinized. Yes, fame and respect for one's abilities can go some way in blunting criticism. But only so far. Eventually, boorish behavior catches up with you. It's part of the communicator's job to make sure players in the spotlight (and teams, leagues, and athletic programs) are aware of this.

A stark example came in 2023 at the University of Alabama, as laid out in the post republished below. One student-athlete, Brandon Miller, transported a gun used in a murder (though he wasn't criminally charged). Another, Tony Mitchell, was arrested for marijuana possession. Given the students' high-profile affiliation with the school and athletic program, both institutions were required to comment. Especially in the Miller incident, the response was harshly criticized, as we relate. Mostly this stemmed from the insensitive comments of basketball coach Nate Oats.

In his follow-up apology, Oats acknowledged that he "didn't have the details from the hearing" before his initial response because he "was coming straight from practice," which caused him to use "a poor choice of words, making it appear like I wasn't taking this tragic situation seriously."

One of the challenges of crisis communications is the dilemma of responding quickly versus taking time to gather facts. Both are vitally important to control the narrative and minimize damage. Oats erred on the side of speaking out too quickly, and then had to admit he hadn't done his due diligence, which came back to bite him in a big way.

There's a lesson in that. Yes, you have to respond fast, but you also must have the facts. If you don't have them right (and you won't at first), you should put out a statement saying you're aware of the situation, you're investigating, and you'll follow up when you know more.

The Alabama story shows that communicators can learn as much from bad examples of crisis communications as good ones. It's so important to get the messaging right from the start because having to follow up with clarifying statements is not a good look.

A less severe instance of bad behavior concerns tennis great Novak Djokovic's 2020 refusal to speak to the press after he was tossed from the 2020 U.S. Open for throwing a hissy fit on the court and hitting a line judge with a ball. It's an example of how the public is laser focused on athletes' behavior, especially on the court (and, in this case, just off it). Professional athletes are generally required to talk to the press as part of their jobs, so Djokovic's snub didn't go over well.

As we note in the post, deposits in the "Credibility Bank" — a good reputation — help fight a tough situation; unfortunately, Djokovic already had a negative balance in his account. On the other hand, he appears to have sincerely apologized for his behavior.

This chapter also provides another example of a badly done

apology, this time from Olympic swimmer Ryan Lochte. To expand on what we said in introducing chapter 4, a genuine apology is sincere and nonevasive. It names the wrongdoing and the perpetrator's understanding of why it was wrong. It must state how amends will be made. It doesn't mention how the situation impacts the wrongdoer — it focuses on the victims. It relays what will be done to make up for the mistake. While apologizers can mention that every effort will be made to avoid a repeat performance, they shouldn't make promises. If the perpetrator slips up again, he or she will just look foolish.

Here we also republish our post on NFL player Odell Beckham's odd incident on an airplane in 2022. The theme of that post, due to the agile communications of Beckham's lawyer, is the importance of invoking facts and downplaying emotion when responding to a crisis.

Our Man in Brazil: A Review of Ryan Lochte's 'Apology'
First published August 25, 2016

By now, barrels of ink and millions of pixels have given their lives in the effort to excoriate U.S. swimmer Ryan Lochte for his "apology" regarding his behavior at the Rio Olympics. Lochte contended he and his teammates were robbed at gunpoint when they, apparently, had engaged in some vandalism and were forced to pay for it. Earthlings don't agree on much, but they all seem to concur that Lochte's "apology" was The Worst Such Attempt in the History of the Universe.

Though the facts have been evolving, we generally agree that Lochte's non-apology apology was terrible. But we also think its amateur status offers lessons for crisis communicators who want to get it right. We have commented on approaches to apologies before, but the best practices in this area can't be repeated too often. When you confront a crisis, the guidelines need to be second nature — not newly learned.

So, here are the problems we see:

It took him five days. Lochte told NBC on Sunday, August 14, that he and three teammates had been robbed earlier that morning at gunpoint by men posing as police officers. It wasn't until Friday, August 19, that he fessed up and "apologized." His excuse for the delay? "I waited to share these thoughts until it was confirmed that the legal situation was addressed and it was clear that my teammates would be arriving home safely." He reportedly "apologized" to the public only after doing so to his sponsors (more on them below).

He did it on Instagram. Lochte lied to reporters about what happened, yet he presented his mea culpa on Instagram. Especially with social-media crises, but also more generally, the crisis should be addressed in the same medium in which it arose. The Instagram post seemed like not-so-artful dodging.

He never actually fessed up. To genuinely apologize means to genuinely own up to what you did wrong. In his Instagram post, Lochte only said he wanted to apologize for his "behavior last weekend — for not being more careful and candid in how I described the events of that early morning." That opened him up to endless ridicule that he wouldn't admit that he lied and that he falsely reported a crime. You might say he was reticent due to the legalities, but by his own admission "the legal situation was addressed."

His "apology" — though at the statement's opening — was an afterthought. The first words of the statement are "I want to apologize," but that's about as far as he goes in terms of contrition.

He never said what he would do to correct the situation. All he said was he had "learned some valuable lessons" from the ordeal, without elaborating on what they were. He didn't offer to change his behavior or make amends in some other way (see Speedo below).

He portrayed himself as the victim. From his post: "It's traumatic to be out late with your friends in a foreign country — with a language barrier — and have a stranger point a gun at you and demand money to let you leave." What actually happened, according to reports, is that the athletes got drunk, went to a gas station very early in the morning, urinated outside when they couldn't access the bathroom, and damaged a sign or poster. The Americans were confronted by the gas station's owner (or his guards), who demanded payment for the sign or poster. They paid (probably overpaid) for the damage. (Earlier accounts had the teammates trashing the bathroom or at least its door, which appears not to have been the case. And Lochte originally said a gun was pointed at his head, but he later admitted that that wasn't true.)

He continued to not fess up. The day after his Instagram post, Lochte appeared on NBC. He didn't admit to lying. He said he "over-exaggerated that story," which gave rise to more ridicule. *Today* show host Al Roker to his on-air colleagues: "He lied. He lied to you, he lied to Matt Lauer, lied to his mom. He left his teammates hanging while he skedaddled. . . . There was no robbery, there was no pull-over, no-body cocked a gun to his head, he lied!" (On Tuesday, August 23, fellow swimmer Jimmy Feigen, through his law firm, issued a much more effective and detailed [and 867-word!] statement about the incident.)

Well, Lochte is paying the price. At least four sponsors have decided to end their relationships with the swimmer or to at least not renew their contract — sponsorships reportedly worth $1 million a year. The four are Speedo, Ralph Lauren, skin-treatment company Syneron Candela, and mattress maker Airweave.

In a classy move, Speedo said it would donate $50,000 of Lochte's sponsorship fee to a charity for poor children in Brazil.

Now, that's smart crisis communications.

Postgame

U.S. Swimming and the United States Olympic Committee suspended Ryan Lochte from all competitions affiliated with the U.S. team for 10 months, along with imposing a list of smaller punishments. Lochte's three teammates were suspended for four months in addition to the other penalties. Lochte originally faced charges in Brazil of filing a false police report, but they were dropped due to the statute of limitations expiring, as well as the judge ruling that Brazilian prosecutors would be unable to prove their case against him.

In 2018 the U.S. swimmer received another suspension, this time for receiving a prohibited intravenous infusion, during which time he went into rehab for alcohol abuse. Lochte attempted to compete in the 2020 Summer Olympics in Tokyo but failed to qualify. The 2016 episode in Brazil is a reminder of an important aspect of crisis communications: the effective apology. In-the-spotlight athletes should train for them just as they train in their sport. Lochte showed how *not* to do it.

Crisis Comms Lessons From a Tennis Tantrum
First published September 10, 2020

Novak Djokovic, the No. 1 ranked men's singles tennis player, threw a hissy at the U.S. Open on Sunday and bashed a ball that hit a line judge in the throat. Djokovic was ejected from the tournament, was fined, and suffered a blow to his reputation. The incident provides crisis communications lessons even for those of us outside the world of tennis.

Lesson #1: Have some money in the Credibility Bank.

Djokovic's reputation precedes him. He's been involved in some iffy situations. Yet a positive public profile is essential to protect against damage when you inflict yourself with a crisis.

Just last month, Djokovic formed a breakaway players association criticized for promoting division. He organized a tour that was lambasted for a lack of social distancing; several players and others tested positive for COVID-19. He also publicly opposed vaccination.

Then there's the lack of control displayed by the September 6 incident at the New York tournament, which he was strongly favored to win; Djokovic whacked the ball in anger after losing an important point and did not aim at the female judge. Still, one report was headlined "Novak Djokovic's Latest Misguided Moment Does Irreparable Damage to His Public Image." Which is not to ignore that he gives generously to charity and has his own foundation to help disadvantaged children.

Lesson #2: Talk to the press.

As many news reports mentioned, Djokovic left the stadium without talking to the press. It's a rare crisis that recommends not communicating with journalists. In this case, Djokovic may have felt he needed to cool down first (not a bad instinct). But the Grand Slam (he's won 17) demands that the players give interviews. For ignoring reporters, he was fined $7,500 — his total lost prize money and fines from the stunt came to $267,500, according to the Associated Press.

Lesson #3: A genuine apology is a beautiful thing.

Crises in which you are at fault (tennis pun intended) require you to actually apologize. The night of the incident Djokovic issued a statement on social media. For all the deserved criticism rained down on him over his temper, the statement was pretty good. In it, he apologized several times: "I'm extremely sorry to have caused her such stress." "I apologize to the @usopen tournament and everyone associated for my behavior." "Thank you and I'm so sorry."

He even addressed the anger issue: "As for the disqualification, I need to go back within and work on my disappointment and turn this all into a lesson for my growth and evolution as a player and human being."

Two short, sharp sentences in his statement were catnip for the press: "So unintended. So wrong."

So true.

Postgame

Novak Djokovic's self-inflicted woes after being kicked out of the U.S. Open in 2020 continued. Mostly these centered around his opposition to COVID-19 vaccines. During the height of the pandemic, he refused to be vaccinated, and so was unable to travel to or play in tournaments. The Australian government looked to make an example of him before the Australian Open in 2022 — despite being given an exemption and despite being the No. 1 seed. It denied Djokovic access to travel into the country and took his visa away for his vaccine refusal. He was also unable to play at the 2022 U.S. Open.

One fact can't be denied: Djokovic is masterful at not letting bad publicity stand in the way of his success on the court. In 2023, he became the men's player with the most Grand Slam championships, and he's still going strong. Still, his ability to elude controversy has proven to be a more difficult task to master. At the 2025 Australian Open, he refused to do an interview after he felt a presenter insulted him and his fans. He ended up retiring from the tournament due to an injury.

For most "ordinary" athletes, it's still advisable to work on controlling their emotions and, maybe more importantly, their crisis-response skills.

(*See chapter 15 for Mary Carillo's discussion of the Djokovic incident.*)

Odell Beckham's Lawyer Responds to Plane Flap
First published December 1, 2022

The bizarre incident in which NFL free agent Odell Beckham Jr. was hauled off an American Airlines plane in Miami prompted a response from his lawyer. It's tough to vouch for the truthfulness of the statement, as we weren't there. But it's an example of invoking facts rather than emotion — though there was some of that — in publicly making one's case.

During the Sunday episode, the flight crew reportedly called on the Miami-Dade Police Department because of a medical emergency; Beckham was "in and out of consciousness" as the crew tried to wake him before takeoff, according to a police statement. Fearing his illness would worsen during the flight to Los Angeles, the crew asked him to deplane, but he refused. So everyone was forced off and then the officers got Beckham to vamoose.

American Airlines issued a statement saying "a customer" refused to follow the crew's orders and fasten his seatbelt, according to ESPN.

Later on Sunday, Beckham's New Orleans–based lawyer, Daniel E. Davillier, put out a statement taking issue with these characterizations of events.

Davillier said his client "fell asleep with his blanket over his head, which is his normal practice for long flights." Wakened, he was told he needed to exit the plane because he refused to buckle up, the lawyer said, adding that Beckham told the attendant he had been snoozing and would don his seatbelt. But he was informed it was too late.

That was a very factual defense that at least made his client sound less unreasonable than the "official" statements. In crisis messaging, facts are your friends — or should be.

Davillier did then go in for some emotion, referring to the "over-zealous flight attendant" who "wanted to prove that he had the authority to have Mr. Beckham removed from the flight." Davillier concluded: "This incident was unnecessary. Sleeping on a plane should not be a cause for removal from a flight."

So what's the upshot of this? We hear about people being booted from planes all the time, just not people this famous. Beckham wasn't arrested, and the event seems not to have hurt him too much. The timing is strange in that the wide receiver, who hasn't played since being injured in February's Super Bowl, is meeting this week with new teams to sign with.

The consensus seems to be that the Dallas Cowboys are the front-runners to nab him. The Miami incident isn't of concern, Cowboys owner Jerry Jones said. "His overall team compatibility, his judgment, his behavior is not an issue with him."

Postgame

Odell Beckham Jr.'s plane fiasco has mostly faded behind the horizon. "It just was crazy, it was something that, it is what it is," he said in an interview two weeks after the incident. "I learned my lesson — put my seatbelt on before you fall asleep." In January 2023, police released the video footage from the plane, but it didn't provide many answers as to what led to the strange event.

Despite all the speculation, Beckham didn't sign with a team during the 2022–2023 NFL season, a time during which he was recovering from a serious knee injury. While he seemed to indicate he had been offered only $4 million a year, he denied he was holding out for $20 million. Beckham ended up latching on to the Baltimore Ravens for the 2023–2024 season, signing a one-year incentivized contract that included a guaranteed $15 million. He was released after that season and signed with the Miami Dolphins, which also waived him at the end of 2024.

March Sadness: A Tale of Two Student-Athletes
First published March 23, 2023

Well, this is a bit messy. Two University of Alabama student-athletes have gotten themselves into varying degrees of hot water in separate incidents. The circumstances and consequences are different, but both bring agitation. This is especially so because one of the jocks is a basketball star currently shining in a wee tournament.

The Crimson Tide is the No. 1 seed in the NCAA March Madness basketball extravaganza. That would all be fine and dandy except back in January its star player, Brandon Miller, transported — he says un-wittingly — the gun that was used in a killing. Two people have been charged with capital murder, but authorities said they had nothing to charge Miller with, and he wasn't. Charged, that is.

Some people feel the team should have at least suspended Miller. They're also upset at basketball coach Nate Oats' comments at the time, which seemed to belittle the event. "Can't control everything everybody does outside of practice," Oats said. "Nobody knew that was going to happen."

When those utterances didn't go over well, Oats issued a more considered statement — giving us yet another example of what happens when you don't get the crisis messaging right the first time. "In no way did I intend to downplay the seriousness of this situation or the tragedy of that night," the statement said in part.

Fast forward two months. On Monday this week — the first day of football practice — Nick Saban, the Crimson Tide's longtime coach, said freshman defensive back Tony Mitchell was suspended until further notice due to his arrest in Florida last week. Mitchell was charged with possession of marijuana with intent to sell and/or deliver (he also reportedly drove 141 mph fleeing police).

"Everybody's got an opportunity to make choices and decisions," Saban said. "There's no such thing as being in the wrong place at the wrong time." He added: "There is cause and effect when you make choices and decisions that put you in bad situations."

In what might be a reach, Fox News' Scott Thompson wrote that Saban's comments "could've been a subtle jab at a fellow Crimson

Tide head coach." Meaning, Oats and his allegedly lackadaisical management of the Miller matter.

The circumstances were handled differently, but the facts were also different. Brandon Miller denies he knew the gun was in the car. He hasn't been criminally charged. Tony Mitchell has. It's an example of how facts shape crisis response.

Another (more cynical) difference is that we're at the climax of the college basketball season where the stakes are highest, and football hasn't yet kicked off. Yes, coaches seek to protect their players. But might Oats have acted more forcefully against Miller (as in, suspended him) if it were the off-season and he weren't a star? On Tuesday, the U.S. Basketball Writers Association named Miller its National Freshman Player of the Year.

The way the play is going, Alabama will probably make it into the Final Four. It is likely, therefore, with the spotlight burning brighter on the team, concerns about its handling of the Miller episode will intensify. The team must be prepared to deal with that.

In the meantime, the Tide rolls on.

Postgame

The University of Alabama shielded Brandon Miller from the media after this story erupted. In his first game back after being publicly linked to the deadly shooting, he scored 41 points, including the winning basket. The team was a No. 1 seed in the March Madness tournament, but fell short of winning a national championship, ultimately being eliminated in the Sweet 16 by the upstart San Diego State Aztecs.

There's no way to definitively conclude that the troubling incident had a substantial impact in the team's earlier-than-expected elimination, but it didn't hurt Miller's draft stock, as he was taken by the Charlotte Hornets with the second overall pick in the 2023 NBA Draft.

Tony Mitchell eventually apologized for the behavior that led to his arrest, via video of a speech he gave at a banquet, which he posted on Twitter, according to news reports. "I was doing things knowing I shouldn't, to try to fit in," he reportedly said. Mitchell pleaded no contest and, in May 2023, the court sentenced him to three years of probation and 100 hours of community service. Alabama lifted his suspension the next month.

1

ACTS OF CRUELTY I:
DOMESTIC VIOLENCE

Introduction

As we noted in the last chapter, athletes' bad behavior away from the field of play will always be something communicators have to deal with. That's only heightened when the accusation is criminal, which domestic violence is (as is sexual assault, discussed in the next chapter).

Domestic violence is a perennial problem in professional sports. For communicators — particularly those working with players at all levels — family-violence incidents should be on your list of crisis scenarios. Obviously, conducting counseling sessions with players to teach them the horrors of domestic violence and to prevent incidents is key to minimizing the abuse itself, in addition to the reputational toll it can have on players, organizations, and brands.

But while this can help minimize incidents, experience shows that, sadly, they'll still occur. Your team and leadership should be ready to respond with messages that are empathetic and refrain from victim blaming or other excuses and deflection. Communicators should be aware of the historic problem of blaming victims in domestic-violence cases; thankfully, that's becoming less common.

In our second post here, the original incident involving former

Yankee Domingo Germán was a rare example of various organizations coming together to speak in one voice. It's difficult to do, but it should be part of all crisis preparation. If a player is accused of family abuse, many groups — the team, the league, sponsors, companies that use the athlete as a spokesperson — will be called on to comment.

The crisis communications team, including the wider team — those across organizations — need to be brought together just as a coach brings a team together. When the accusation rises to the level of criminality, communicators must work closely with lawyers to ensure nothing is said publicly that shouldn't be.

The demise of Germán's career with the Yankees (the team let him go after the 2023 season) shows that, while winning cures a lot of ills, not winning allows teams to shed players with reputational baggage without any regret or fear of backlash from fans.

A much more high-profile and haunting incident of domestic violence concerned the NFL's Ray Rice, going back to 2014. Intimate-partner abuse has particularly plagued the professional football league. The league has been criticized for imposing what are perceived as lenient punishments, most notably in more recent cases involving Kareem Hunt, Tyreek Hill, and Xavien Howard.

The specter of the league's handling of the Ray Rice situation continues to haunt it as each new incident crops up. Simply put, thanks to fumbles like the Rice incident, nobody gives the NFL the benefit of the doubt when it comes to effectively addressing domestic violence.

A final irony: As mentioned above, in the years since the Rice scandal, we've seen countless high-profile cases of NFL players violating the league's personal-conduct policy, especially concerning domestic violence, but also sexual assault and illegal drug use. None of this has derailed the NFL's success. This may be another example of the way (as discussed in chapter 1) sports are different from other products or services. Will the NFL remain impervious? Maybe. But our experience with reputation and crisis communications tells us that if you play with fire long enough, you'll eventually get burned.

Lessons From the NFL Fumbling of the Ray Rice Story
First published September 9, 2014

The communications surrounding yesterday's news that the Baltimore Ravens fired running back Ray Rice have been frustrating in their paucity and finger-pointing and show that even wealthy organizations like the National Football League can make enough fouls that the penalty flags should be flying.

Rice was fired by the team and suspended indefinitely from the league after celebrity news outlet TMZ yesterday posted the video of him punching his now-wife in the face in an elevator in Atlantic City's now-shuttered Revel casino.

In February, the month of the incident, TMZ had released initial video showing Rice dragging his then-fiancée, Janay Palmer, out of the elevator. The NFL announced in July it was suspending Rice for this season's first two games. Following the wide outcry that this punishment was much too lenient, NFL Commissioner Roger Goodell in August admitted the league had fallen "short of our goals" to "create model workplaces filled with people of character" and upped the penalties for domestic violence.

Which brings us to the latest video disclosure. Everyone involved seems to be saying they hadn't seen the first part of the video, from inside the elevator, until TMZ posted it yesterday. Those protestations, especially Goodell's — the league insists the police never gave the video to the NFL — are meeting with some skepticism.

"[W]hat we all need now is total transparency, from Roger Goodell and the National Football League, from the people who run the Baltimore Ravens and, perhaps most of all, from the Atlantic County (N.J.) Prosecutor's Office," which had let Rice enter an intervention program, the New York *Daily News'* Mike Lupica wrote in his column today. (According to Lupica, the prosecutor's office put out a statement last night saying it made that decision "after careful consideration of the information contained in Mr. Rice's application in light of all the facts gathered during the investigation." Both Rice and his wife had been arrested after the incident.)

The Ravens' reaction yesterday was straightforward, if brief: "The

Baltimore Ravens terminated the contract of RB Ray Rice this afternoon," it said. Then came the NFL's tweet: "Roger Goodell has announced that based on new video evidence that became available today he has indefinitely suspended Ray Rice."

The league further defended itself last night in a statement: "We requested from law enforcement any and all information about the incident, including the video from inside the elevator. That video was not made available to us and no one in our office has seen it until today." (Apparently the players union thought it needed to defend itself, too. "I was one of the last people to see the video," DeMaurice Smith, executive director of the National Football League Players Association, told *Sports Illustrated*.)

Many commentators have said Rice should have been fired after the initial video clip was posted — that part is disturbing enough (a Fox Sports headline: "It Shouldn't Have Taken a Second Rice Video for Ravens, NFL to Get It Right").

All in all, it seems a situation being handled badly all around. No doubt, just as with the domestic-violence penalty tightening after the original slap on Rice's wrist, the NFL will have more explaining to do.

Postgame

Ray Rice's reputation has never recovered from the 2014 scandal. Even after he was reinstated into the NFL, no organization jumped at the opportunity to sign him, due to the criticism they might receive. The running back's professional-football career came to an abrupt end shortly afterward. In an attempt to rejuvenate his reputation, Rice began working with football teams across the country — both NFL and college — to spread awareness of domestic violence. Yet, a decade later, it seems his name will always be linked to the ugly and illegal behavior.

Rice and Janay Palmer are still married and have two children together.

Yankees, MLB Karaoke 'Kumbaya' Amid Domestic Violence Crisis
First published January 9, 2020

We may never know exactly what happened during the alleged domestic-violence incident between New York Yankees pitcher Domingo Germán and his girlfriend, but there's little doubt the details are well-known to both the team and Major League Baseball. Maybe because of that, all sides responded to the crisis with similar reserve.

Following a charity gala on the evening of September 16, 2019, the 27-year-old Germán was reported to have slapped his girlfriend during an altercation. It was believed at the time that a member of Major League Baseball's commissioner's office may have witnessed the incident. No charges were ever brought against Germán, nor was there even a police report filed, leaving fans and all other interested parties to speculate what may have transpired.

Despite the lack of public clarity, on September 19, Germán was placed on administrative leave, presumably until more information could be gathered. Then, less than a week later, MLB and the Players Association agreed to extend his leave through the end of the season, which accounted for nine games, as well as the postseason, which ultimately amounted to nine more games.

Anyone who follows the all-too-common trials and tribulations of professional athletes would have deduced that, despite a lack of hard evidence presented publicly, the powers that be must have known pretty quickly the situation did not bode well for Germán. This theory was bolstered by the fact that Germán himself, MLB, the players union, and the Yankees all seemed to be on the same page (for a change), as the administrative leave was never challenged.

The only open question was how much longer into the 2020 season Germán would be suspended. On January 2, MLB announced the full suspension would consist of 63 more games. Coupled with the 18 games already served, that came to 81, exactly half of a full season. It's the longest domestic-violence suspension ever given without criminal charges being brought against the player. It's believed that neither the players union nor Germán himself will challenge the ruling.

The public messages underscored the unanimity. The statement issued by the Yankees was both straightforward and well written, as were the comments by the commissioner's office. (Neither the pitcher nor his union appears to have released statements.)

MLB simply laid out what the discipline was and noted that Germán agreed not to appeal.

"We remain steadfast in our support of Major League Baseball's investigative process and the disciplinary action taken regarding Domingo Germán," the Yankees wrote. "Domestic violence — in any form — is a gravely serious matter that affects every segment of our society." It noted Germán's "acceptance of his discipline."

One should give the benefit of the doubt that these statements were genuine. However, when you dig deeper, it's pretty easy to find other, less-sincere reasons this played out the way it did.

First, despite having no public information that speaks to what happened that night, it's probably safe to assume the incident may have been recorded or, as mentioned earlier, someone reputable may have witnessed it. Perhaps Germán simply owned up to it. Whatever the case, keeping the details of the incident out of the public eye saved everyone a tremendous amount of embarrassment.

While what is truly known may never be revealed to the public, what seems certain is this: When the player, his union, the team, and the league are all in lockstep on an issue like this, it's because it's in ALL of their best interests to keep it under wraps.

It seems now that the excessive amount of time it took for the commissioner's office to issue this ruling had nothing to do with the gathering of additional facts, and everything to do with the negotiation of the maximum amount of games Germán could be suspended without pushback from Germán himself, the Players Association, and the Yankees. If this weren't the case, then history tells us that, at the very least, the Players Association would have challenged the fourth-longest domestic-violence suspension in MLB history.

So, kudos to the baseball community for working together and presenting a unified front, but in reality it was probably just in everyone's best interest to stick together on this particular issue.

Postgame

Domingo Germán finished serving his 81-game suspension, which led to him missing all of the 2020 shortened COVID-19 season. But that didn't end his domestic-violence profile, as new, unflattering details from the incident continued to be revealed, including that his girl-friend allegedly hid in a locked room to protect herself.

He again made headlines in 2022, when Yankees relief pitcher Zack Britton commented to the media about Germán: "Sometimes, you don't get to control who your teammates are. I don't agree with what he did. I don't think it has any place in the game or off the field at all." Germán chose not to respond.

It appeared that Germán's career had come full circle when, in June 2023, against the A's, he threw the fourth perfect game in Yankees history and the 24th in MLB history. The celebration was short-lived, as he remained inconsistent throughout the rest of the season and was ultimately released by the team in the off-season with little fanfare. In 2024, he played for minor-league teams affiliated with the Pittsburgh Pirates, and in October filed for free agency.

8

ACTS OF CRUELTY II: SEXUAL ASSAULT

Introduction

Unfortunately, like domestic violence, sexual assault by powerful people in sports is all too frequent. It's a particularly sensitive topic for crisis communicators. It's a high-level scenario in which communicators must work closely with the legal team, as obviously there are legal implications: The rights of the accused must be respected while simultaneously showing empathy for victims.

Yet it's an area where communicators may experience pushback, in terms of speaking out publicly, from lawyers involved. And as we discuss elsewhere in this book (see chapter 12), the best legal strategy is often not the best communications strategy. Also note that sexual assault is raised in civil lawsuits, not only criminal matters. We have examples of that here with NFL quarterback Deshaun Watson and MMA fighter Conor McGregor.

All teams and leagues should have crisis plans for accusations of sexual abuse and assault. They should have statements drafted for initial comments on allegations, whether they're against players or employees. Organizations should train on the plan for how to respond to such a crisis. And spokespeople should undergo media training so they're prepared to talk to reporters and answer tough questions.

Usually, when allegations come, an investigation will be conducted, including a criminal investigation. Teams and leagues don't determine guilt or innocence, but they can inform fans and other stakeholders that they're aware of the situation and are keeping on top of it.

Our post on the Canadian hockey scandal shows that, especially in sexual-assault cases, many organizations and individuals will be expected to comment. The public will closely monitor these statements. Will you take the accusations seriously and investigate them (if your organization is accused of wrongdoing)? Will you speak out against sexual assault while respecting the right to due process? Will you apologize and make amends if your organization (or a member of your organization) is found to be at fault?

One of the most notorious sexual-assault cases in sports concerned Jerry Sandusky, the former assistant football coach at Penn State who in 2012 was convicted of molesting young boys. The ugly episode had profound reputational implications for Joe Paterno, the legendary Penn State coach Sandusky worked under. One post here highlights a movie made about the episode. The film gives a behind-the-scenes look at how the school and others dealt with the crisis.

A takeaway from that movie is that a major crisis can be extremely chaotic, with too many people providing conflicting counsel. That's why it's best to determine the chain of command and decision-making as part of the crisis planning and training. Obviously, many crises are fast-moving and confusing, and flexibility should be built into the plan. But when the crisis strikes, everyone should know what his or her role is. Everyone should be prepared to perform that function. It's just like a quarterback having one job to do and a defensive tackle another.

The Paterno film also shows that the proactive action required to respond to a crisis can be drastic: in this case, the decision for Paterno to announce he would retire at the end of the season (though he was fired before he could leave voluntarily). It's a good tack in a crisis to take substantive action whose main, or significant, purpose is to communicate that something is being done about the problem. The public may demand action. This could mean a front-office reshuffling of management or the firing of a key player. Such action should be properly communicated to demonstrate that the matter is being taken seriously and handled.

A second post concerning Penn State noted the implications of the sexual-assault scandal arising from the criminal behavior of Larry Nassar, the doctor for the U.S. national women's gymnastics team and assistant professor at Michigan State University.

This post raises the question of how to determine public sentiment during a crisis. These days, this is typically done by "listening" to social media. But the Penn State fundraising team, concerned about the negative impact of the Sandusky crisis on donations to the school, crunched data based on the emails and phone calls coming in. Gauging the sentiment of stakeholders in a crisis is essential, and helps determine whether the response is changing negative views or whether the approach needs to be rethought.

The post is also a good reminder that monitoring how other organizations, even competitors (maybe especially competitors!), respond to crises can help inform your own approach. You can prepare by maintaining a portfolio of examples of how similar situations were handled by others. Ask yourself what you think they did right and what they did wrong. What would you have done differently? Should you copy their approach? Don't make the mistake of believing that, just because it's a different league or team, there's nothing there you can learn.

You may view the other guys as the enemy on the field, but it doesn't mean you have to view them as the enemy when it comes to learning crisis communications.

Nassar Scandal Gives Rise to Statements From USA Gymnastics, Michigan State
First published February 1, 2018

The wrenching victim-impact statements last week by gymnasts who had been sexually assaulted by physician Larry Nassar when they were girls intensified the focus on two institutions: USA Gymnastics, for which Nassar was the national team doctor, and Michigan State University, where he also worked. Both institutions released several media statements — some more impressive than others.

More than 150 girls and women spoke in a Michigan courtroom during Nassar's weeklong sentencing hearing (his total number of victims is as many as 265). On January 24, he was given a term of 40 to 175 years in prison, in addition to 60 years he previously got for child pornography. Other victims began speaking against him yesterday in another Michigan court, where he will be sentenced on further charges. (Gold medalist Simone Biles has said Nassar abused her, but she didn't speak at either sentencing.)

Both USA Gymnastics, the governing body for the sport, and Michigan State University have been criticized for their handling of the matter. Questions are swirling about why they hadn't detected and stopped the abuse sooner. Instead, it went on for more than two decades. Several investigations are underway.

USA Gymnastics, which said it didn't know of the abuse until 2015, when it fired Nassar, has lost several corporate sponsors. Its president, Steve Penny, resigned in March 2017 over the scandal. The day Nassar was sentenced, USA Gymnastics released a statement in the name of President and CEO Kerry Perry, in which she praised the long prison term and said the organization was focused on changing its culture.

The United States Olympic Committee has been more impressive in its communications, but then again it is not as accused of wrongdoing. On January 22, USA Gymnastics had said three board members had quit. In response, the USOC wrote, "New board leadership is necessary because the current leaders have been focused on establishing that they did nothing wrong. USA Gymnastics needs to focus on supporting the brave survivors. The Olympic family failed these athletes and we must continue to take every step necessary to ensure this never happens again."

On January 24, the USOC put out a long statement demanding change at USA Gymnastics, announcing an internal probe into the

Nassar matter, and calling for the rest of the USA Gymnastics board to resign.

USA Gymnastics responded (ignoring the resignation demand), "USA Gymnastics supports an independent investigation that may shine light on how abuse of the proportion described so courageously by the survivors of Larry Nassar could have gone undetected for so long and embraces any necessary and appropriate changes." (President Perry also issued a statement lauding the victims' courage.)

Yesterday USA Gymnastics announced that its entire board had resigned.

As for Michigan State, it fired Nassar in 2016 after an exposé in *The Indianapolis Star*. In February 2017, its gymnastics coach resigned for allegedly rejecting the sex-assault claims. The day of Nassar's sentencing, the state legislature had passed a resolution calling for Michigan State President Lou Anna Simon to step down or be fired. She announced her retirement later that same day. Her letter doing so has been criticized for its self-reference and defensiveness.

In it, Simon mentions that she had planned to retire in December 2016, but the crisis put that off. She humblebragged about being pilloried: "As tragedies are politicized, blame is inevitable. As president, it is only natural that I am the focus of this anger. I understand, and that is why I have limited my personal statements."

The board was officious in its acceptance of her resignation ("We agree with Dr. Simon that it is now time for change").

Two days later Michigan State Athletic Director Mark Hollis resigned. He wrote, poetically, "I am not running away from anything, I am running toward something. Comfort, compassion, and understanding for the survivors and our community; togetherness, time, and love for my family."

Both the Michigan attorney general and the National Collegiate Athletic Association have launched investigations into the school's handling of the scandal.

Postgame

Larry Nassar appealed his sentence, arguing that remarks made by

Judge Rosemarie Aquilina were unfair and vindictive. He lost that appeal.

In 2021, USA Gymnastics and the U.S. Olympic and Paralympic Committee agreed to pay $380 million to settle lawsuits filed by survivors of Nassar's abuse. It was reported that the settlement amount would compensate hundreds of gymnasts Nassar abused, including Olympic gold medalists Simone Biles, McKayla Maroney, and Aly Raisman.

In 2022, over 100 women, including Biles, Maroney, and Raisman, filed claims against the FBI, alleging it mishandled the investigation into the former team doctor and allowed him to continue his actions after they reported him to the agency back in 2015. In April 2024, the U.S. Justice Department announced it would settle 139 claims against the FBI for a total of $138.7 million. That agreement brought total payments related to Nassar's crimes to $1 billion, according to *The New York Times*.

A Lesson for Michigan State in Penn State's Sex-Assault Scandal
First published February 8, 2018

It is typically a good idea in a crisis to examine how other organizations dealt with similar situations, whether looking at simply what they said or at their larger strategic approach. A recent article reexamined the 2011 sex-assault scandal at Pennsylvania State University to see what lessons it might have for Michigan State University and its Larry Nassar sex-assault scandal — specifically with regard to fundraising.

The recent *Crain's Detroit Business* article invoked a 2014 story in *The Chronicle of Philanthropy*. In that earlier piece, writer Holly Hall depicts how devastating to the school community was the arrest of Penn State former assistant football coach Jerry Sandusky for sexually abusing boys. That was in November 2011. The school was more than two years from completing a drive to raise $2 billion.

Clearly, the ability to bring in donations was connected to Penn

State's overall reputation, which was in tatters due to the scandal. The university was widely criticized (as Michigan State and USA Gymnastics are now) for its inadequate, ostrich-like original response to the crisis, which eventually did entail the firings of school president Graham Spanier and longtime (and legendary) football coach Joe Paterno.

(Yesterday, the *Los Angeles Times* reported that donations are down at the University of Southern California amid scandals at its medical school, though the university rejected the crisis was the cause.)

Most fascinating in the *Chronicle of Philanthropy* story (as noted by *Crain's*) was the explanation of how the Penn State fundraising team, led by Senior Vice President for Development Rodney Kirsch, dealt with the situation. Kirsch mined the emails and phone messages that had been pouring into the school from alumni, donors, and others, to decide how to proceed.

Hall writes:

> Mr. Kirsch did an analysis of 4,000 emails, assessing whether the content was supportive or negative and whether and how much each individual had given to Penn State before. He noticed a pattern.

> Donors who had given $5,000 or more were much more likely to be supportive of Penn State through the crisis (79 percent of those people who donated $25,000 or more) than those who had given less. People who had never contributed to the university were the most negative, with 66 percent making disparaging comments.

That led Kirsch and his team to decide to meet with donors, or at least communicate with them, especially focusing on those who maintained a loyalty toward the school.

In the end, the sex-assault crisis did not have much effect on fundraising. Only nine pledges were withdrawn because of the scandal. In April 2014, Penn State announced it had raised $2.1 billion — more than its goal and before the deadline. It's an interesting example of using technology (and data mining) to learn what an audience is thinking and how to respond.

HBO's 'Paterno' Offers Insight Into the Importance of Crisis Discipline
First published April 12, 2018

This week, HBO debuted *Paterno*, starring Al Pacino as Joe Paterno, the eponymous football-coaching legend at Penn State who in 2011 found himself navigating a dire scandal. His former assistant coach, Jerry Sandusky, was arrested for sexually abusing children. In the movie, crisis communications gets a rare Hollywood depiction — especially the effort to convince a respected leader that he *is* in crisis.

While the dramatization invokes a healthy dose of artistic license, director Barry Levinson poignantly captures raw moments familiar to many who suddenly face an exploding crisis. In the scenes set in the Paternos' living room, the aging coach and his family struggle to comprehend and then contain a crisis rapidly unfolding in the media.

Paterno, as portrayed by Pacino, spends much of the week following Sandusky's arrest in various stages of denial, refusing to appreciate the gravity of accusations levied against him. His advisors draft statements and develop strategies that veer from Paterno denying he knew anything about Sandusky's crimes to throwing the university's administration under the bus. Sitting around with his family, the octogenarian equivocates on what he knew and what he did, preoccupied with scouting his next opponent.

The fraught deliberations inside the Paterno home show the importance of discipline in crisis communications. With the patriarch proclaiming his lack of guilt, his attempts to craft a response quickly fail. "It's a press conference, guys, not a deposition!" he says at one point. It's clear his resistance hindered his response.

The family finally brings in a crisis expert, who bluntly tells them that crisis communications isn't the same as regaling the press with tales of that day's football-field exploits: "He can't go out there. He's used to being the emperor, holding forth in front of a press corps after they watched you win. You're not disciplined enough to go in front of the press."

He also tells them what Paterno refuses to see for himself: "You need to resign before somebody does it for you."

As depicted in the film, four days after Sandusky's indictment Paterno announced he would retire at the end of the season, only to be fired by the school's Board of Trustees hours later.

Also this week, we saw an example of the flip side of Paterno's lack of discipline in crisis communications. Facebook CEO Mark Zuckerberg appeared before Congress to apologize for and explain the company's data-handling issues. An enterprising AP photographer snapped a picture of Zuckerberg's extensive talking points. For example, if he were asked if he should quit the company (which he wasn't), the response was to be, "Founded Facebook. My decisions. I made mistakes. Big challenge, but we've faced problems before, going to solve this one. Already taking action."

Zuckerberg was generally lauded for his staying-on-message performance.

So, even for Paterno, a legendary coach with tremendous goodwill and a half century of media experience, failing to immediately respond to allegations negated any future strategic efforts. In 2011, and significantly more so today, not responding immediately to adversity counts as a fumble.

Postgame

Joe Paterno died in 2012 from complications from lung cancer, just 74 days after the school fired him. Many people disagreed about whether the longtime head coach was an innocent bystander to the sex-assault scandal or if he played a role in covering it up.

A probe commissioned by Penn State and conducted by former FBI Director Louis Freeh uncovered emails from 2001 that showed the school's president, vice president, and athletic director and Paterno himself knew of an account by a witness who said assistant coach Jerry Sandusky raped a child in one of the school's athletic buildings. The school leaders decided against reporting the incident and instead confronted Sandusky themselves to protect the football program. The Paterno family disagreed with the Freeh report and commissioned one of its own that argued he was not part of a conspiracy of silence.

While Paterno the man will always be remembered as a legendary football coach, it's now impossible to tell his story without mentioning the Sandusky scandal.

The Penn State football program has had its ups and downs in the intervening years — including an NCAA-sanctioned, multiyear postseason ban in the wake of the Freeh report, followed by a Big Ten Championship in 2016. While present-day successes and the passage of time can help blur past indiscretions, the Penn State football story will forever be a difficult and complicated one to tell — especially outside of Happy Valley.

Watson Settlement Leaves Cleveland Browns Fumbling
First published September 1, 2022

Following the settlement between the NFL and the NFL Players Association over Browns quarterback Deshaun Watson's punishment for violating the league's personal-conduct policy, the Cleveland team has been left to clean up the mess Watson created. Its performance hasn't been impressive.

Since March 2021, 24 female massage therapists have sued Watson alleging they were sexually harassed and assaulted during their sessions. Amid the accusations and earlier this year, he was traded from the Houston Texans to the Browns. Watson has now received an 11-game suspension along with a fine of $5 million and mandatory mental-health training. This was an increase after the uproar over an initial penalty of six games and no fine.

This has left fans, media, and other players frustrated over his seemingly still-too-light penalty. Despite Watson's and the Browns' hopes that the allegations would be buried under the piles of sports news we see every day, they have remained in the public eye and are unlikely to go anywhere anytime soon. And Watson continues to maintain his innocence.

Some on both sides have taken to social media to express their outrage over the settlement. Among those asserting dismay is former Heisman Trophy winner from Baylor University Robert Griffin III, who tweeted:

"The NFL had an opportunity to show it had learned from its ugly history on standing up for Women with this Deshaun Watson case and IT FAILED. 11 games and a 5 million dollar fine doesn't fit what he was accused of doing and found to have done by [arbitrator] Judge Sue L. Robinson. Sickening."

Watson and the league are not the only ones receiving backlash. The Browns, known for being (let's face it) a dysfunctional team, once again find themselves in a hole they can't dig themselves out of. The Cleveland organization hasn't done much to help its image in the face of the negative attention that followed Watson from Houston to the Browns — they keep dropping the ball in their attempts to move forward in the wake of the scandal. Or think of a quarterback scrambling farther into his own endzone.

During an August 18 press conference following the settlement announcement, for example, co-owner Jimmy Haslam, asked about Watson's behavior, replied, "It's important to remember that Deshaun Watson is 26 years old, and he's a hell of an NFL quarterback."

You won't be surprised to learn that Haslam's comments were received in a negative way. His remarks suggest that Watson's age and talent are excuses for him to not take accountability for his actions. The comments also showed that Haslam values sticking by Watson and defending him to the media more than fixing the team's image and getting on the public's good side. That's bad crisis communications.

During the same press conference, co-owner Dee Haslam (Jimmy's wife) spoke of Watson growing as a person. "It's not going to happen overnight," she said. "He's 26 years old, and he's just getting into counseling." The Haslams seemed to want to change the subject to the wider issue of sexual assault rather than this specific story.

From a perception standpoint, rather than worrying about repairing the franchise's image and easing the tension between Watson and the public, the Haslams' comments make it seem as though they just want to forget this ever happened and move on with a controversial quarterback at the helm.

Although the wish to move forward is logical for the Haslams, this situation isn't leaving the news cycle anytime soon. It will likely follow Watson for the rest of his career. It will certainly follow the Browns for as long as he's their quarterback. The sooner Watson, the team, and the league acknowledge the depth of Watson's alleged infractions, the quicker they can move past this situation.

Postgame

The Cleveland Browns' response to the Deshaun Watson incident is yet another example of an NFL team not taking sexual abuse seriously — seriously enough to learn how to respond to such allegations.

It didn't go well for Watson when he returned to play after his 11-game suspension. In his first game back, the Browns played his former team, the Houston Texans. In fact, it was his first regular-season game since demanding in 2020 to be traded from Houston. Though the Browns beat the Texas 27-14, Watson threw an interception and many of his passes missed their targets. Texans fans booed him throughout most of the game.

Not much changed for Watson or the Browns for the remainder of the season as they finished with an unflattering 7−10 record. Given Watson's extended period of inactivity, that outcome wasn't terribly surprising. In 2023, he underwent season-ending surgery and was cleared to begin play for the 2024−2025 season. With most of the lawsuits against him having since been settled, Watson would now be judged by the results he got on the field. Those results were not good as the Browns finished last in the AFC North. Watson was at the helm for the first seven games of that season before he sustained a debilitating Achilles injury.

And then, finally, in March 2025, Browns co-owner Jimmy Haslam admitted that signing Watson was "a big swing-and-miss" due to his suspension and injuries.

Hockey Scandal Engenders Police Apology, Blah Statements
First published February 8, 2024

This past week saw a major development in the long-running, nasty scandal in Canada concerning its national religion, ice hockey. Five professional players were charged with a 2018 sexual assault, and the police apologized to the victim for the case taking so long. The scandal has governing body Hockey Canada bruised and battered.

At a press conference Monday, the police chief in London, Ontario, apologized to the unnamed victim. "I want to extend, on behalf of the London Police Service, my sincerest apology to the victim, to her family, for the amount of time that it has taken to reach this point," he said. The players were charged on January 31.

In 2018, they were on Canada's world junior hockey team, which that year won the world championship against Sweden. To celebrate that feat, they attended a Hockey Canada gala in London. They are accused of sexually assaulting the woman in a hotel room after that event. Lawyers for the accused, who all went on to play for professional teams from which they are now on leave, have denied the allegations.

The case has caused an uproar in Canada. The police probe that was opened in June 2018 was closed in February 2019 without charges being brought. The case was revived after TSN, the Canadian sports channel, reported in May 2022 that Hockey Canada had paid an undisclosed amount to the woman to settle a suit she'd brought.

Further reporting by other outlets uncovered that Hockey Canada had a slush fund from children's membership fees that it used to settle $7.6 million in sex-assault claims, including this one, according to the AP. This caused a huge outcry and eventually the resignation of the entire Hockey Canada board and CEO.

Hockey Canada's reputation is basically in tatters. It still needs to do a lot of work to restore its name. Back in 2022, the group reportedly adopted certain measures such as mandatory sexual-violence training for its players, coaches, employees, and volunteers.

In a column Monday, the *Toronto Star*'s Rosie DiManno lambasted how the case has been handled (including by the police) and wondered if — as often arises when celebrated athletes are involved — the players' status had something to do with the delay. Sports organizations need to learn that celebrity is no excuse for not doing the right thing. We have a feeling the nondisclosure agreement as part of the settlement had something to do with this.

The scandal hasn't given rise to inspired public statements. On Monday, Hockey Canada posted, lamely, on X, "#HockeyCanada has cooperated fully with the London Police Service and we are committed to continuing to support the legal process."

Katherine Henderson, the current CEO, commented on the recent developments. "Hockey Canada recognizes that in the past we have been too slow to act and that in order to deliver the meaningful change that Canadians expect of us, we must work diligently and urgently to ensure that we are putting in place the necessary measures to regain their trust, and provide all participants with a safe, welcoming, and inclusive environment on and off the ice," she said, according to *USA Today*.

We'll see.

Postgame

The sex-assault scandal engulfing Canadian ice hockey is particularly notable for how long it dragged on and the intensity of the public's upset. Some of the anger was focused on police and prosecutors. But Hockey Canada, the governing body for the sport, came under brutal fire, as this post relates.

Noteworthy communications aspects include that the organizations involved had rather uninspiring statements about the case, which didn't convince people it was being taken seriously. And Hockey Canada and the National Hockey League conducted investigations shrouded in secrecy.

The NHL teams that the players went on to play for didn't have much to say. Those teams were: the New Jersey Devils (Michael McLeod and Cal Foote), Philadelphia Flyers (Carter Hart), Calgary Flames (Dillon Dubé), and Ottawa Senators (Alex Formenton). A trial is scheduled for April 2025.

What Should Conor McGregor Do Now?
First published December 5, 2024

On November 22, a civil jury in Dublin found Conor McGregor liable for sexually assaulting a woman in a hotel room and awarded her about $260,000. Since then, brands associated with the mixed martial arts star have kicked him to the ground. In other words, his reputation is in tatters. What should he do?

It's not like the Irish fighter had a pristine rep to begin with. Accusations of assault, sexual and otherwise, have been hurled against him for many years. In fact, his bad-boy cred was part of his appeal, especially with young fans. McGregor "built his brand on his patriotism and brash persona," a recent BBC piece put it. He also had a PR campaign in place to manage the ripples.

But the general agreement now seems to be that he's crossed a line. Accusations are one thing, a jury verdict quite another. A jury verdict against you is a third-party endorsement that you're in the wrong. This has led to headlines such as "There's No Defending McGregor This Time, Lads" (Gript Media) and the BBC's "'People Want Nothing to Do With Him': How Ireland Turned Away From Conor McGregor."

It's also hitting him in the pocketbook. Proximo Spirits said McGregor would no longer be the face of Proper No. 12 Irish Whiskey, which he helped found and later sold to Proximo. IO Interactive, creator of the *Hitman* video game, cut ties with him. Retailers are pulling McGregor-related products from their shelves.

The Irish Sun even reported that elbow benders have been avoiding the fighter's Black Forge pub in Dublin to the advantage of nearby drinkeries.

McGregor is 36 years old, has a life ahead of him, and needs to restore his reputation, such as it is. First of all, he should step back and think about what he's doing. People need to see him make major changes. He should lie low for a while and work on cleaning up his act. He needs to party less and apologize more. There comes a time to put away childish things.

While known for his prowess in the octagon, McGregor hasn't fought since 2021. He says he wants to get back to that. He should. As former UFC fighter Matt Brown put it in an MMA Fighting podcast, "Get the f*ck out of the clubs. Put down the straws and get back in the gym."

Another big potential move: McGregor has said he will appeal the verdict, which is certainly his right. That makes it hard to apologize. But he should consider giving up that fight and admitting culpability. That would be a start down the road to reputation redemption.

9

WHEN TRAGEDY STRIKES: ACCIDENTS AND INCIDENTS

Introduction

As Elvis Costello sang, accidents will happen. Injuries and other incidents such as game violence, too. Whether they occur to players or fans, accidents give rise to fairly major and, alas, frequent crises. Whether the problem comes to pass on the field or in the stands (or indeed, as with the Kobe Bryant tragedy, in private life), communicators will be called on to provide responses.

One consideration in communicating an accident or injury is how responsible the individual or organization is for it. But even if it results from an act of God, responses will be expected, if only to hear expressions of sympathy.

Fan safety is a major concern for leagues and teams. Accidents and game violence should always be crisis scenarios planned for and trained in. Communicators need to be briefed on operational issues so they can properly inform the public if something goes wrong. The messaging will have to walk a fine line between showing empathy for victims and not admitting liability before the facts are known. Obviously, communicators have to work closely with lawyers on these types of issues. The incident at the UEFA Champions League soccer final in France, explored below, is a case in point. It then morphed into the French government blaming the alleged victims. All around, not good.

Damar Hamlin's dramatic injury underscores the importance and difficulty of gathering information and responding quickly to an accident or injury. You don't necessarily have to respond with all the facts — you probably don't have them yet — but something must be said.

A standard practice in crisis communications is to predict what negative scenarios your organization might face, especially given the business or other endeavor you're in, and then determine how you would respond to such situations. In sports, serious injury to a player is an obvious scenario. Others, as we've seen, include accusations of cheating, drug use, sexual harassment, and domestic violence. They also include crises that any company could face: severe weather, service disruptions, lawsuits, and, indeed, public safety.

Also, communicators should be aware that, while crises can be short-term, there are those, such as fan safety, that feed into longer-term so-called issues management. Crisis communications and issues communications are separate disciplines, but they share certain features and concerns. They're becoming blurred. Fortunately, issues tend to allow more time to strategize. As one post below demonstrates, the longer-term issue of fan safety — specifically netting at baseball stadiums — became an immediate crisis when a spectator died after being hit by a foul ball.

Kobe Bryant's tragic accident underscores a cardinal rule of crisis communications: At the start of a crisis, most if not all the information received will be incorrect. It's the role of the crisis communicator to keep a cool head when others are panicking, and calmly and methodically gather the facts, vet the facts, and convey the facts.

While facts can be damning, they can also exonerate you if you aren't in the wrong. Trust and reputation are gained only by showing that you're a stickler for truth. This is an absolutely crucial component of crisis communications.

An accident resulting from equipment failure is a rare sports crisis, but it does happen. We have a stellar example of one here, when

Zion Williamson's "equipment" — his sneaker — broke. That was an acute crisis for Nike, the footwear's maker. The company did a good job responding. Equipment failure can also lead to injury, which could be a crisis for any team or league.

Nike's response was impressive because it took the situation, which had its humorous aspects, very seriously; product makers should always view questions about quality as potential crises. Crisis communicators in sports can learn from this example. The crisis team must evaluate the growing negative situation and determine how severe it is. That will influence how strong the response should be. And, yes, it may entail having the organization's leader fly to the scene of the crisis. This shows the company taking the crisis to heart and responding appropriately, as Nike did, as you'll see, when it sent senior executives to Duke.

One post here provides an excellent example of crisis response. The Edinburg school district in Texas did a great job of responding when one of its football players purposefully knocked down a referee. It apologized and removed the team from the playoffs, even though it had won the game in question. That shows taking ownership of a crisis.

Granted, high-school sports have a lot to do with teaching kids about sportsmanship, so drastic measures were called for. Even if this were a professional team, the district's actions are a lesson: Often in a crisis you need to be shown doing something substantive to address the incident. In sports, you sometimes must recognize that maintaining or repairing a reputation is more important than winning on the field.

Two Sporting Stories Underscore Communications Subtleties
First published February 14, 2019

Two recent stories from the sports world show opposite handling of crises. In neither case did the party confronted with the crisis say much. But in the first the reticence came off as discreet, while in the second it appeared evasive. This shows how subtle crisis communications can be.

On February 5, ESPN published a story that revealed that back in August a 79-year-old woman named Linda Goldbloom died days after being beaned by a foul ball as she sat watching a Dodgers game in the team's Los Angeles stadium. The ball had flown up behind home plate and just beyond the reach of the protective netting.

The incident wasn't shown on the TV coverage of the game or mentioned in any news reports, according to ESPN. When Goldbloom died, the team made no mention of it, though it gave the sports-news site a statement for its story this month.

"Mr. and Mrs. Goldbloom were great Dodgers fans who regularly attended games," it said. "We were deeply saddened by this tragic accident and the passing of Mrs. Goldbloom. The matter has been resolved between the Dodgers and the Goldbloom family. We cannot comment further on this matter."

The team did, however, give a further statement to *The New York Times*, saying it hadn't publicly disclosed Goldbloom's injury because "the Dodgers generally do not make public reports of accidents that take place at Dodger Stadium." It added: "We avoid doing so out of respect for the privacy of the persons involved in the accidents and their families."

One could argue the Dodgers don't want bad publicity, but it's somewhat odd that the team didn't proactively reveal such an accident to get in front of the story. Goldbloom's death was only the third in all of baseball history to result from a fan in the stands being hit by a ball, according to ESPN. Perhaps the team does have a policy against such disclosure.

The example of a crisis not so well handled comes from a recent article on Golf.com. In November, professional golfer Matt Kuchar won the Mayakoba Golf Classic in Playa del Carmen, Mexico — his first victory in more than four years.

But then it leaked out that Kuchar had paid his caddie, David Giral Ortiz, who was from the area and not his regular man, only $5,000. Based on Kuchar's haul, Ortiz's payday should have been closer to $130,000.

Ortiz said Kuchar at one point offered him another $15,000, but he turned down the insult. When he won, Kuchar had called Ortiz his "lucky charm." The caddie said he believes he deserves $50,000.

The story became known after an ex–PGA Tour player had tweeted, "Who's gonna b the one to identify the player the [sic] paid his caddy 3k after winning a PGA tour event last fall???"

Naturally that caused some talk on social media. Ortiz disclosed emails between him and Kuchar's agent, Mark Steinberg ("I am out of the country. What Matt has offered is fair," Steinberg wrote, unwisely).

Neither golf pro nor agent commented much publicly. That's a mistake. The flap could have a negative effect on their reputations, though Kuchar's is maybe strong enough to withstand it. In fact, just today Golf.com published another story in which he said he was "disappointed" and "sad" over the disagreement.

Postgame

The Los Angeles Dodgers eventually offered Erwin Goldbloom, widower of Linda Goldbloom, an opportunity to honor his late wife at a game during the 2019 season. Erwin declined. "We don't need their sympathy," he said. "We want action." He told ESPN's *Outside the Lines* that he would "go down there" only if changes were made to improve fan safety. The two sides did settle, for an undisclosed amount, the wrongful-death suit Goldbloom filed.

While teams have taken steps toward adding protection for fans in their stadiums, petitions to improve netting for fan security continue to circulate. Fan safety presents potential crises for all professional teams — the issue should not be ignored.

Matt Kuchar eventually paid his local caddy, David Giral Ortiz, $50,000 from his winnings at the PGA Tour event in Mexico. This came after much pressure was put on him by golf fans, especially on social media. The amount eventually paid was still less than what most regular caddies would have received considering how much prize money Kuchar won ($1.3 million).

But Ortiz expressed gratitude and said the money would help him expand his business and renovate his home. Kuchar said he regretted the situation and his initial comments on it. He still actively golfs on the PGA Tour.

The Kuchar incident shows the challenges of deciding whether and when it's appropriate to speak out on a crisis — and what to say. Communicators advising players must always be sensitive to the spotlight constantly on them. It's hard to make everyone happy, and there will always be critics, but athletes' acts that show them to be inconsiderate or out-of-touch can ruin reputations. If such a mistake is made, be prepared to repair it quickly.

Nike Reacts Fleet-Footedly to Zion Williamson Incident
First published February 28, 2019

Nike Inc. did a fairly good job dealing with a crisis last week. It responded seriously and quickly, which is appropriate for a company named after the goddess of speed. Now it will have to follow through even if, as happens, memory of the incident eventually fades.

As is now well known, just 33 seconds after the start of a game on the night of Wednesday, February 20, Duke University basketball star Zion Williamson was downed when one of his Nike sneakers split apart. Williamson's spill was particularly high profile because Durham, North Carolina–based Duke was playing archrival University of North Carolina, located 10 miles down the road in Chapel Hill.

Nike had a statement out that night. "We are obviously concerned and want to wish Zion a speedy recovery," it said. "The quality and performance of our products are of utmost importance. While this is an isolated occurrence, we are working to identify the issue."

That was an appropriate response. The company acknowledged the issue and its seriousness, but didn't speak beyond the facts it knew at the time. It emphasized that it was investigating.

The next day, Nike officials met with Duke personnel — again, highlighting the seriousness with which it was taking the situation. It was a smart move reminiscent of Starbucks CEO Kevin Johnson traveling to Philadelphia after a racial incident in a store there last year.

"There was no way Nike was going to let one of their top clients chew on just a statement," wrote Jeff Gravley, sports anchor for WRAL-TV, the NBC affiliate in Raleigh, North Carolina. "Phone calls and their trip to Durham followed."

The story became huge. The day of that meeting, Thursday, Nike's stock dropped 1.1 percent, though it recovered on Friday.

Paul George, the player for the Oklahoma City Thunder and name-sake of the sneakers Williamson wore, felt the need to speak out. "I talked to Nike to see what went wrong, what happened with the shoe and I take pride in that," he said. "My shoes have been a successful shoe not only in college but in the NBA."

The episode brought up, once again, the contentious issue of whether college basketball players should be paid. If Williamson's injury had been serious (it wasn't), it could have ended his chances at a multimillion-dollar professional career. He is a favorite to be the NBA's No. 1 draft pick this year, and some say he should sit out the rest of the college season so as not to blow his chances with an injury.

Nike, of course, is implicated in the connection between money and college sports; for one thing, it pays Duke millions for the school to mandate that its players wear the brand.

The incident raises another basic idea about crisis communications: Equipment makers should be prepared for crises that involve equipment failure. Nike itself had warning that such a mishap could occur. According to *The Wall Street Journal*, this wasn't the first time a Nike shoe fell apart during a game: "In 2016, the Orlando Magic's Aaron Gordon's Nike shoe tore open. NBA players Manu Ginóbili and Andrew Bogut have also experienced similar malfunctions."

Even though Williamson's injury wasn't dire, the shoe failure could raise questions about Nike's quality. When its probe is complete, the company should release the results to show it's transparent and to assuage fears customers may have about that.

Postgame

After Nike officials traveled to Duke's campus in Durham, North Carolina, to deal with the Zion Williamson episode, the company sent the malfunctioning sneaker to China with custom measurements so a shoe could be built to withstand the power Williamson applies during games. We can't find any information that the sneaker company released details of its findings on the incident, which is a shame.

Williamson returned to play from his injury that March wearing a pair of shoes from Kyrie Irving's line as opposed to the PGs he had on when originally injured (interestingly, Nike dropped Irving in 2022 due to alleged antisemitism — another crisis). Williamson scored 29 points that first game back, shooting a perfect 13-13 along with 14 rebounds and zero issues involving his footwear. That, at least temporarily, silenced doubts about Nike's shoe quality.

Williamson did end up being the No. 1 pick in the 2019 NBA Draft and is now a power forward for the New Orleans Pelicans. *And* he has his own signature shoe line with none other than Nike — a seven-year deal worth a reported $75 million. But the faulty-quality issues resurfaced in a 2021 preseason game when Lakers rookie Chaundee Brown blew out a Nike-released Zion Williamson shoe in a fashion almost identical to Zion's own shoe explosion. Oh, the irony.

Kobe Bryant Accident Shows Challenges of Misinformation
First published January 30, 2020

The confusion over the facts of the terrible helicopter accident in which basketball phenom Kobe Bryant, his daughter, and seven other people tragically died reminds us that, when a crisis occurs, initial information typically is wrong.

This caused some soul-searching among journalists; it's also an important lesson for communicators.

Anyone riveted to the news on Sunday understands this. The facts about the accident near Los Angeles were in constant flux. *The New*

York Times did an instructional summary of the early reporting.

Celebrity site TMZ was first to report the news. More mainstream media outlets, which typically don't report victim names until families are notified, held back. Some posted on their Twitter accounts that they were trying to confirm the story.

Once, for example, the *Los Angeles Times* reported the story, it incorrectly said five people in total were killed. ABC's chief national correspondent wrongly reported that all four of Bryant's children were on board. It came out that one of his daughters was with him, then that she wasn't. At one point it was reported that Rick Fox, a former L.A. Lakers teammate of Bryant, was on the helicopter (the *Times* says that rumor arose from social-media chatter).

In fact, a total of nine people, all on the helicopter, including the pilot, died. Bryant's 13-year-old daughter was the only family member on board. Rick Fox was not. It's a cautionary lesson showing that, in the beginning of a crisis, communicators shouldn't assume the information they're getting is correct — it is most likely wrong.

In addition to the outpouring of bereaved commentary from global friends and fans of Bryant, official statements were required from certain companies.

Sikorsky, owned by Lockheed Martin, made the helicopter. "Safety is our top priority; if there are any actionable findings from the investigation, we will inform our S-76 customers," Lockheed Martin said in a statement.

Island Express Helicopters, which owned the helicopter, put out a terse statement that gave too little recognition to its pilot. "We are deeply saddened by this tragedy," the company wrote. "Our top priority is providing assistance to the families of the passengers and the pilot."

Some brands also adjusted their marketing messages in response to the tragic accident. For example, Kraft Heinz has a major campaign going concerning the (metaphorical) death of Mr. Peanut: Its Planters brand is retiring its mascot going back to 1916. The company pulled spots from Twitter and YouTube that showed him falling to his death after his car goes off a cliff.

That was a smart, crisis-preventing move.

Postgame

After Kobe Bryant's death, media outlets were shamed for their spread of misinformation, which was viewed as inconsiderate toward the grieving family. None more than TMZ. The celebrity-news outlet was first to report the tragic incident, just under two hours after it took place — and before Vanessa Bryant learned of her husband's untimely passing. TMZ was called out by both Los Angeles County Sheriff Alex Villanueva and Kobe Inc. President Molly Carter.

"It would be extremely disrespectful to understand that your loved one has perished and you learn about it from TMZ," Villanueva said. Carter discussed the false reports and said that "no one has been authorized to speak on behalf of the family regarding any personal details surrounding Sunday's tragedy."

TMZ founder Harvey Levin defended the media outlet's reporting by saying that it contacted Kobe Bryant's people an hour before it published the story and that it was told Vanessa Bryant had been notified prior to the release. In February 2023, Los Angeles County agreed to pay Vanessa Bryant and three of her daughters nearly $29 million to settle claims that public employees shared graphic photos of the helicopter crash.

Texas School District Scores Crisis-Response Touchdown
First published December 10, 2020

A school district in Texas gave us an early holiday gift: an example of expert crisis response and communications. The unfortunate incident arose from a student-athlete who — shall we say? — fumbled when it came to sportsperson-like behavior.

During a football game the night of Thursday, December 3, an Edinburg High School defensive end, Emmanuel Duron, charged onto the field and knocked down a referee who had just announced he was being ejected from the game. Duron had shoved an opposing player to the ground and tried to tackle the opposing quarterback after the whistle, according to *The Monitor* of McAllen, Texas.

After the attack on the ref, police escorted Duron from the stadium; he was charged with Class A assault, according to ESPN. (The Texas Association of Sports Officials decried the "vicious and deliberate assault.") The game continued and the Edinburg Bobcats won 35–21, which meant it advanced to the playoffs.

Not so fast. The next morning, the Edinburg Consolidated Independent School District — Edinburg is in the Rio Grande Valley — announced it was removing the team from the playoffs. It apologized to the referee and his family and also "to the athletes, staff, and our school community."

"We will take the appropriate disciplinary action once we understand the facts and circumstances underlining this incident," it said.

The short statement was astute crisis communications. The district acted swiftly. It apologized. It took action in yanking the team from the competition. And it said it would act further once it better understood the facts.

Later that day, the district updated its statement to note that it came to its decision after consulting with its lawyers and the University Interscholastic League, which, despite its name, administers rules for primary- and secondary-school athletics.

The district admitted the UIL "would have removed the football team from the playoffs if the district did not withdraw the team. Under Texas law and district policy, the interim superintendent was authorized to move forward with the decision."

So, okay, the district did the right thing even though it really had no choice. But the statement emendation was smart in that it probably staved off public criticism of its action.

The district included the UIL's own statement on the matter. "We applaud the Edinburg CISD administration for addressing this situation swiftly and taking appropriate action in removing themselves from the playoffs and for dealing with the student involved in the incident," it said.

We too applaud.

Postgame

Following the 2020 event, Emmanuel Duron went on to apologize to referee Fred Garcia and publicly acknowledged he had anger issues he needed to work on. The Edinburg school district was a real winner in showing how to be proactive when a crisis comes. Unfortunately, attacks on referees at high-school basketball and football games have persisted since the Duron incident. School districts around the country should take heed and be prepared if they find themselves in a similar situation. Fortunately for them, Edinburg provided a good blueprint.

France Under Fire for Its Soccer Play
First published June 2, 2022

France will have to engage in some fancy-footwork communications ahead of Paris hosting the 2024 Summer Olympics after a disastrous crisis Saturday night at the UEFA Champions League soccer final. The chaos outside the stadium has people questioning whether the country can handle a major sports event. It must convince the world that it can.

Liverpool and Real Madrid faced off at the Stade de France, the national stadium in Saint-Denis, just north of Paris (spoiler: Real Madrid won 1–0 in the biggest annual match for European soccer). According to French officials, between 30,000 and 40,000 Liverpool fans showed up with either fake or no tickets, numbers others say are wildly inflated.

The crush of fans outside the stadium meant an estimated 2,700 never got inside to see the game, whose start was delayed 36 minutes. Authorities locked down the stadium and wouldn't let people leave at halftime, saying it wasn't safe. Both teams' fans said they were harassed and mugged outside after the match. Police used tear gas and pepper spray.

"For France, the optics were not good," *The New York Times* put it.

The situation has the French and the British, not exactly a mutual-admiration society, sniping at each other.

The French sports ministry held a crisis meeting Monday that included local, UEFA, and police officials. French interior minister Gérald Darmanin, at a press conference that day, blamed "massive, industrial, and organized fraud of fake tickets" for the chaos and violence. He had unkind things to say about British soccer fans in general.

Liverpool Chairman Tom Werner, in a letter to French sports minister Amélie Oudéa-Castéra on Monday, demanded an apology for the treatment of his team's fans and for French officials blaming them. Werner criticized Darmanin for making "a series of unproven pronouncements on a matter of such significance before a proper, formal, independent investigation process has even taken place," according to the letter leaked to the *Liverpool Echo*. (The two ministers appeared at a Senate hearing yesterday.)

Werner has a point. One reason France, which will also host the 2023 Rugby World Cup, is coming under so much fire is that it has been quick to blame fans of the Liverpool club (owned by Boston-based Fenway Sports Group). Information at the start of a crisis is almost always wrong. Darmanin would have been wise to wait until tensions cooled.

U.K. officials have also gotten involved. Liverpool Mayor Joanne Anderson tweeted that she is writing French authorities, including President Emmanuel Macron, demanding some answers ("Shameful to pin blame on fans"). Police officers from Merseyside (which includes Liverpool) who had gone to France as observers reported that "the vast majority of fans behaved in an exemplary manner, arriving at turnstiles early and queuing as directed," according to a police statement.

UEFA, European soccer's governing body, has tapped Portugal's former education minister to conduct an independent investigation into the causes of the incident.

Postgame

The day after this post appeared, UEFA apologized to Liverpool and

Real Madrid fans. A week later, Didier Lallement, chief of the Paris Police Prefecture, apologized for the use of tear gas. It was also revealed that surveillance footage from the stadium had been destroyed.

In February 2023, Tiago Brandão Rodrigues, Portugal's former education minister tapped to conduct the independent investigation into the incident's causes, released his report. The probe put "primary responsibility" on UEFA, including for marginalizing its own safety and security unit. The French police came under fire for not working jointly with the other organizations to prepare for the event and for failing to prevent congestion.

The report rejected claims that thousands of Liverpool fans without valid tickets were to blame for the problems. That was an attempt by authorities to evade responsibility, the report said, which is a major mistake in crisis communications.

We haven't come across any operational issues with the 2023 Rugby World Cup. Host France lost in the quarterfinals; South Africa won the final. And in 2024, Paris was generally credited with hosting a first-rate Olympics, with a couple of hiccups as we discuss in a post in chapter 11.

Hamlin Injury Calls Into Question NFL Response
First published January 5, 2023

The injury that put Buffalo Bills safety Damar Hamlin in critical condition is a horrible tragedy. The main communications issue raised was the NFL taking more than an hour to announce the game would not go on. The league will have sensitive comms decisions to make related to this incident going forward.

Hamlin, 24, collapsed and suffered cardiac arrest after making a tackle during the game against the Cincinnati Bengals. Hamlin remains in critical condition at University of Cincinnati Medical Center. The players on the field, some in tears, had surrounded Hamlin as medical professionals restored his heartbeat.

The players were traumatized and at least some had no intention of continuing play. This was unique: Apparently, no injury has led to the cessation, rather than simply a delay, of an NFL game.

The league's lag in officially announcing the postponement gave those on Twitter and other social-media platforms time to speculate that it would force the players to carry on. This was not greeted with kind words: Commenters argued, correctly, that the focus should be on Hamlin's health.

ESPN announcer Joe Buck contributed to the confusion when he said the players would be given five minutes and then play would resume. "That's the word we get from the league and the word we get from down on the field, but nobody's moving," Buck said, according to *The New York Times*. Buck's statement seemed to fuel the anti-league ire.

But in a press conference hours later, an NFL official denied this was the case. "How do you resume play after you've seen such a traumatic event occur in front of you real time?" said Troy Vincent, the league's executive vice president for football operations. "And that's the way we were thinking about it."

Either Buck or Vincent had it wrong, and someone should provide clarity. It's an important question: Does the organization care so little about player safety or is it getting a raw deal from fans ready to pounce? Of course, resuming play would have been even worse.

Obviously, it took some time for the NFL to get its statement together. It could have announced that play would be halted and that further comment was forthcoming.

The public's insistence that the focus should be on Hamlin's recovery means that the league must be sensitive in communicating going forward, including about how and when the game will be resumed. In a Tuesday memo, NFL Commissioner Roger Goodell said he notified both teams that that won't be happening this week.

Postgame

Damar Hamlin remained hospitalized in Cincinnati. Four days after the incident he was finally able to breathe on his own and, with the tube removed, to speak. On January 9, he was flown to a hospital in

Buffalo, where he continued to recover and was released. He made an on-field appearance with medical staff at the Super Bowl the next month.

Much to the delight of NFL fans everywhere, on August 12, Hamlin played his first game since suffering cardiac arrest on the field seven months earlier. It was a preseason game that otherwise wouldn't have been notable. But for Hamlin, the league, and fans, it was another highlight in a memorable feel-good story.

The NFL had announced three days after the game between the Bills and the Bengals that it was officially canceling it.

The story had at least one more twist. Strictly from a football standpoint, Hamlin was anything but a lock to secure a spot on the Buffalo Bills' 2023–2024 roster. Rumors that the team would have to consider cutting him were being written and spoken about publicly. Cutting Hamlin would potentially be a major PR nightmare if not handled properly. Fortunately for the Bills, Hamlin bailed them out by playing well enough in the preseason to earn his way onto the team.

Insights From Police Response to Super Bowl Parade Shooting
First published April 4, 2024

On February 14, one woman was killed and 22 people were injured from gunshots fired just after the conclusion of the parade celebrating the Kansas City Chiefs' Super Bowl win. A recent and fascinating interview with the police officer who oversees the department's communications provides insight and sage advice.

In the interview with Police1, a news and information site, Captain Jake Becchina of the Kansas City Missouri Police Department offers some counsel particular to public-information officers in police departments. This includes having instructions at the ready for perimeter officers dealing with massive news trucks barreling in to cover such a major event. But a lot of what Becchina said is helpful to crisis communicators in general.

Here are four points he makes:

Create a good reputation before the crisis comes.

We're big believers that one way to prevent a crisis from spiraling out of control is to have deposits in the "Credibility Bank" — to do the work to have good relations with, and high regard from, your stakeholders.

Interestingly, Becchina said he was well aware of the opportunity the Super Bowl parade presented for the police department to do just that. He encouraged officers working the parade to use it to promote goodwill with the public.

"Our message that morning as we made roll calls is this is something to soak up," he said. "Everybody's here for a positive reason. Everybody's here to celebrate. And we don't often get those interactions or those opportunities to have those interactions in a universally positive environment. So our message to the officers as they headed out there was soak this up, use this to charge your batteries, use this to gain energy as a community interaction."

When a crisis hits abruptly, confusion reigns and sorting out information is hard.

We often say that the information that comes at the start of a crisis is usually wrong. That's especially true during an abrupt crisis. In this case, add in the contrast of the elation of the parade with the sudden tragedy of the shooting.

Or as Becchina put it, "That convergence of those two things — coming to the end of a celebration and then hearing 'multiple shots fired,' and knowing in your head that it's literally at the same location, your brain's got a lot of things to process all at once there."

Sorting out information in this case was especially hard because it was coming from so many sources: officers at the scene, 911 calls, broadcasts airing the horror live. "That all goes into that sensory input about what's taking place," Becchina said.

Social media can be extremely helpful.

Becchina said that within about seven minutes of hearing "shots fired," his team got out an email to its local media list and a tweet. After that, the focus was mostly on social media because he could barely keep up with the press inquiries flooding his email inbox. His solution was to point people to the social-media posts.

"The quicker you can drive everybody to that Twitter page ... that's your best and most efficient way of communicating in a time-line-type format information that is easily digestible and easily able to be gathered from anywhere in the world," he said.

Have buy-in from the boss.

Finally, it's crucial for the boss and others at the top to understand the importance of media relations in a crisis, Becchina said. He's fortunate in that his boss, Kansas City Police Chief Stacey Graves, used to have his job.

"If your chief is not somebody who speaks that [media] language, it's on you to educate them," he said. "Let them know what a situation like this is going to look like. Take half a day and do a tabletop exercise. Bring in a media professional if you don't have one on your staff."

He added that the buy-in is needed because the time when the crisis hits isn't the time to start deciding how you'll respond. For one thing, if you wait until you experience a crisis, too many voices will be in the room offering too many conflicting opinions about how to proceed. It will hamper acting decisively.

Postgame

The prosecution of people allegedly involved in the shooting had been slow going, but three men are expected to face separate trials arising from the incident. The trial for the man accused of firing the fatal shot is scheduled for January 2026. Prosecutors say a verbal argument quickly escalated to weapons being fired.

A Missouri man brought litigation against several politicians for, early on, wrongly identifying him in social-media posts as an illegal immigrant and the shooter. It's another example of the need to be cautious with information at the onset of a crisis. This post also shows that crisis communicators in sports can learn a lot from those working in areas outside of athletics.

On the Caitlin Clark Drama
First published June 6, 2024

Caitlin Clark, the WNBA rookie super-duper star, had quite the drama-filled few days. She was body checked during a game. Then a competing player complained she was getting too much credit for the popularity of women's basketball. Then Pat McAfee defended her — with a vulgar insult. Yet Clark appears to be mostly (and wisely) staying above the fray.

Clark's team, the Indiana Fever, played the Chicago Sky on Saturday. In the third quarter, while the ball wasn't in play, opposing guard Chennedy Carter hip checked her, knocking her to the floor. The refs later deemed it a "flagrant foul" (one involving excessive or violent contact). Debate rages about how serious a matter it was. Carter said she has "no regrets."

"I think at this point, I know I'm gonna take a couple hard shots a game," Clark said at a presser. "It is what it is, I guess. I don't know."

On Monday, Carter's teammate Angel Reese complained that Clark, the No. 1 pick drafted out of the University of Iowa in April, was too much the focus concerning the recent upsurge in the WNBA's popularity. "I'll look back in 20 years and be like, 'Yeah, the reason why we're watching women's basketball is not just because of one person. It's because of me, too.' And I want y'all to realize that," she said.

Also on Monday, Pat McAfee, the former NFL kicker and current controversial sports commentator, praised Clark on his ESPN talk show. McAfee said she was being badly treated. Part of his defense was to say that Clark transcends the new slew of players.

"I would like the media people that continue to say, 'This rookie class, this rookie class, this rookie class,'" McAfee said. "Nah, just call it for what it is: There's one white b— [rhymes with *witch*] for the Indiana team who is a superstar."

Later that day on X he apologized for using the vulgarism. "My intentions when saying it were complimentary just like the entire segment, but a lot of folks are saying that it certainly wasn't at all," he said. He sent an apology to Clark through the Fever's PR operation, and she accepted it, he said.

All this adds up to a crisis scenario for the rookie. All eyes are upon her. She's not saying much. This may be one of those rare instances where, for one's reputation, it's best to be restrained. Clark has been playing professional basketball for a month.

The Wall Street Journal's Jason Gay opined that what she's undergoing is typical. "Almost every celebrated newbie goes through harsh trials early in a professional career, often because they're situated on a lousy team," he wrote.

The Fever's current record is 2–9.

Postgame

As the 2024 WNBA season wore on, Clark continued with her stoic approach and it eventually began to pay dividends. The Fever surged, finishing at 20–20, good for third place in the Eastern Conference and a playoff berth, their first since 2016.

Clark averaged 19.2 points and 5.7 rebounds per game and led the WNBA with 8.4 assists per game. She was a near-unanimous selection for Rookie of the Year and set the league's single-season record with 337 assists. It's not difficult to imagine, however, how things could have gone awry had Clark's unflappable demeanor not prevailed.

10

YOU GOTTA PROMOTE: ADVERTISING, MARKETING, AND SPONSORSHIPS

Introduction

Advertising, marketing, and sponsorships lead to all sorts of crises in sports. Communicators need to be attuned to whether their organization's advertising or marketing campaign will upset people and cause an uproar. Having professional athletes as product spokespeople becomes a crisis when that celebrity does something untoward (or illegal). Another important consideration is whether to pull your advertising temporarily if it suddenly and unexpectedly looks bad due to something happening in the news, such as a mass shooting (it might be a bad time to advertise your charity basketball shootout).

Marketers must think through their campaigns and focus on how outsiders would view them, lest they backfire. Crisis communications means planning for what could go wrong. What if your sports team is launching a new ticket promotion? Is there anything about it that people could have a negative reaction to? Be prepared for that, including having a plan in place and statements ready.

We have two good examples here of a team's effort to promote itself and instead bringing fierce criticism: the Sioux Falls Stampede junior hockey team's "Dash for Cash" campaign and Boston's new women's soccer team unveiling its promotional campaign. As the post on the Peloton ad shows, organizations not attuned to public sentiment will err in reacting to a negative situation — they'll downplay it or, worse, ignore it. Listening to what the public is saying about your actions, including on social media, is a crucial part of crisis communications. Read the room!

It may be that the organization feels it didn't do anything wrong; the public is wrong to react the way it is. But crisis communications doesn't always mean being strictly logical; public reaction is often deeply emotional and, even if an organization doesn't agree, it has to swallow its pride. On the other hand, there are many examples of organizations being in the wrong and not being able to admit it.

When a mistake is made, the default should be to apologize. Yes, the apology itself may invite further criticism — you can't please everyone — but the effort is important. Nationwide's insistence in 2015 to not apologize for its Super Bowl ad that upset so many people, as recounted below, was tone-deaf.

Broadly speaking, the issue of corporate sports sponsorships has only become more sensitive in recent years, and companies that are marketing themselves through sponsorships must remain attuned to the reputational dangers as well as the rewards. Sports sponsors should be prepared to comment when scandal befalls a player, a team, or — indeed — a league (see the case of soccer governing body FIFA). Conversely, the sports world must be ready for when a reputational issue whacks a sponsor. In either case, pressure is often exerted to end the relationship.

The severity of the crisis must be weighed, and decisions as to whether to demand changes or to take other remedial action, or to disengage as a sponsor entirely, become key issues for the crisis communications team. This highlights once again the importance of having a team at the ready — one that is well-trained, well-versed in all elements of the crisis communications plan, and comfortable working together to ensure a cogent and speedy response.

Marketers of all types must be prepared for scandals involving their celebrity brand ambassadors. Often, those endorsers are profes-sional athletes, who aren't immune to publicity problems. As our post on a study about sports brand ambassadors shows, many questions go into how the marketing company should respond, including the level of the athlete's responsibility for the problem. The higher the blame, the higher the potential crisis. In gauging the potential severity of a crisis, one's responsibility for it should always be a factor considered. If your brand ambassador gets into hot water, will you suspend or end the relationship, or will you come to the famous athlete's defense?

Say, for example a high-profile athlete is involved in a barroom scuffle. The initial reaction will be to punt and for organizations to say they're waiting for the investigation or legal procedure to be com-pleted before commenting. That's not a wrong first impulse. Crisis planning includes having so-called holding statements — messaging that says you're aware of the situation and are trying to ascertain the facts. But eventually the public will want to hear more than that. If it's obvious the athlete was wronged, say that. If it's obvious the athlete was *in* the wrong (for example, maybe he sucker-punched someone), say that.

Usually a scandal involving a professional athlete raises reputa-tional issues for all involved: the player, the team, the league, and, yes, the brands the athlete endorses. So, they can involve coordination across (friendly) parties to ensure consistent messaging. Yes, the var-ious organizations will have different needs and maybe even different takes on the situation, but the public wants to hear a coherent story.

One negative example here concerns star quarterback Aaron Rodgers, spokesperson for insurance giant State Farm. The then–Green Bay Packer tested positive for COVID-19 after he seemed to imply he had been vaccinated when he hadn't. Instead of acknowledg-ing the harm that Rodgers' misleading response and careless actions caused, State Farm bet that its reputation and Rodgers' star power would be enough to weather the storm.

A major development in sports marketing has been the rise of NIL in college sports. After the Supreme Court's unanimous ruling in *NCAA v. Alston* in June 2021, college athletes across America scurried to find and sign deals that would allow them to, for the first time, profit from the use of their "name, image, and likeness," or NIL.

As recounted here, Louisiana State University gymnast Livvy Dunne was one such athlete who was positioned perfectly to leverage her popularity. While LSU likely didn't mind the attention Dunne's fame brought to the school, a conflict of interest arose that it was forced to address publicly.

Athletes are ambitious people not known for their moderate egos. Sports organizations have guidelines for behavior, but even then incidents will crop up. Communicators must be prepared to confront those incidents when they happen. A lot is at stake in getting it right. For college athletes, the rise of NIL only makes that concern more acute.

(See chapter 16 for Kery Davis' discussion of NIL.)

Flap Over Nationwide Super Bowl Ad Shows Sometimes an Apology Is in Order
First published February 2, 2015

Nationwide Mutual Insurance Co. is under attack for its Super Bowl ad that depicts a young boy reciting the things he won't be able to do, such as "ride a bike or get cooties," because he died in a preventable accident (drowning, apparently). Viewers called the spot "dark," "depressing," and — worse. Twitter was afire with those who thought Nationwide crossed the line in trying to sell insurance. In response, the company quickly put out a defensive press release that offered no apology. That may have been a mistake.

Press reports are quoting viewers' tweeted reactions about the ad such as " 'Hope you guys are having a great day. Did you know your kid is probably gonna die soon? Enjoy your nachos & funeral planning.' — Nationwide."

Amobee Brand Intelligence found that 64 percent of the 238,000 social-media mentions about Nationwide yesterday were negative, according to *The Wall Street Journal*'s report on the furor ("Nationwide Insurance Stands By Controversial Super Bowl Ad"). Nationwide was "playing with fire" with the ad's content, a marketing professor told the U.K.'s *Daily Mail.*

(To be fair, other companies ran Super Bowl ads this year that were considered downers and Nationwide did run a second, humorous spot with *Mindy Project* star Mindy Kaling.)

The Columbus, Ohio–based company's statement said it recognizes the commercial "started a fierce conversation" about preventable injuries around the home. "The sole purpose of this message was to start a conversation, not sell insurance," it said. The ad was about "an issue that is near and dear to all of us — the safety and well being of our children. We knew the ad would spur a variety of reactions."

It added: "While some did not care for the ad, we hope it served to begin a dialogue to make safe happen for children everywhere." It launched a website on household safety, MakeSafeHappen.com, to accompany the ad.

So Nationwide spent more than $5 million to air a 45-second commercial because it wanted to start a dialogue about safety — not because it wanted to sell insurance? We're not sure a lot of people will buy that. The ad had a tagline that sounded like a pitch for insurance: "At Nationwide, we believe in protecting what matters most — your kids."

What's clear is many were offended by the ad. An apology to those viewers may have been in order. Instead, we got a defensive tone. Not exactly endearing.

The statement reads like it was written ahead of time. Maybe it's true that Nationwide knew the ad would get a strong reaction. We think it hasn't heard the last.

Postgame

The Make Safe Happen ad — the infamous Nationwide Super Bowl XLIX commercial — was taken off the air hours after it premiered and it never returned. The spot continued to receive negative reviews after Nationwide defended its promotion.

A few months after the ad's broadcast, the chief marketing officer responsible for it unceremoniously left Nationwide. The next year, many wondered what direction the company — one of the NFL's biggest advertisers — would go with its Super Bowl commercial. In fact, it decided to skip out on Super Bowl 50. "Nationwide has historically been selective in our marketing approach around the Super Bowl," it explained. Not many people bought it.

While many consider Nationwide's Make Safe Happen spot to be one of the all-time worst Super Bowl ads, the company's relationship with the NFL is flourishing. In December 2023, Nationwide and the league announced a multiyear renewal of their partnership, the centerpiece being the insurance company's continued role as presenting sponsor of the Walter Payton NFL Man of the Year Award.

FIFA Scandal Points Up Need for Sponsors to Hone Their Crisis Skills
First published May 28, 2015

Yesterday's arrest of a slew of World Cup soccer officials and others in a $150 million corruption prosecution is a reminder that event sponsors have to concern themselves with crisis communications even in situations where they are not responsible.

In the wake of the arrests of officials at FIFA (the Fédération Internationale de Football Association, which organizes the World Cup), major brands including Visa, Coca-Cola, and McDonald's issued statements, with Visa hinting it might pull out of its sponsorship. The BBC's headline addressed the situation most pithily: "FIFA Scandal a 'Disaster' for Sponsors."

In these sponsorship situations (where the sponsor is not culpable), a statement should include at least these three elements:

- Outrage over the behavior
- An affirmation that the behavior goes against the sponsor's own ethics
- Notice that the sponsor has been in contact with the body governing the event

Of all the FIFA sponsors, Visa put out the most complete and effective (if ungrammatical) statement. It began, "Our disappointment and concern with FIFA in light of today's developments is profound." The payment-card company said that it supported the World Cup because it brings communities together and that FIFA needed to rebuild an ethical culture. And Visa said in no uncertain terms that it had spoken to FIFA: Should FIFA not make changes, "we have informed them that we will reassess our sponsorship," it said.

The statement by McDonald's could be judged as adequate: "McDonald's takes matters of ethics and corruption very seriously, and the news from the U.S. Department of Justice is extremely concerning. We are in contact with FIFA on this matter. We will continue to monitor the situation very closely."

Adidas' statement was comparatively anemic: "The Adidas Group is fully committed to creating a culture that promotes the highest standards of ethics and compliance, and we expect the same from our partners. Following today's news, we can therefore only encourage FIFA to continue to establish and follow transparent compliance standards in everything they do."

But Anheuser-Busch's was even more feeble: "We expect all of our partners to maintain strong ethical standards and operate with transparency."

The beer maker's effort was especially disappointing because last November it released a sponsorship statement that hit all the right elements. The company found itself in the unenviable position of having to address a raft of domestic- and child-abuse allegations against National Football League players. It said: "We are disappointed and increasingly concerned by the recent incidents that have overshadowed this NFL season. We are not yet satisfied with the league's handling of behaviors that so clearly go against our own company culture and moral code. We have shared our concerns and expectations with the league."

Yesterday's arrests are only the latest nightmare for the FIFA sponsors (which also include Hyundai and Gazprom). Last week, Visa, Coca-Cola, and Adidas addressed concerns over the use of migrant workers to build the stadium in Qatar for the 2022 World Cup.

According to today's BBC story, one bookmaker is already offering odds on which sponsor will be the first to pull out of the World Cup.

Visa is currently the favorite.

Postgame

FIFA's corruption scandal did affect its relationships with sponsors, mainly Visa, McDonald's, and Coca-Cola. Visa would go on to threaten to drop its sponsorship multiple times if it wasn't satisfied with reforms being put in place. The other two companies made it known they backed Visa's stance. Yet all three remained sponsors, even as FIFA attempted to make changes in the scandal's wake.

FIFA went on to suspend its president, Sepp Blatter, and UEFA President Michel Platini from any football-related activities for eight years. In 2021, the U.S. Department of Justice determined that, because of the actions of leaders such as Blatter and Platini, FIFA itself was a victim of the corruption scandal and would receive a $200 million payout to be shared with two affiliates. In 2015 alone, at least eight people pleaded guilty in the scandal.

Unfortunately, despite having a new leader and the benefit of lessons learned from past indiscretions, FIFA once again found itself embroiled in a sponsorship controversy in 2023. It was revealed that it was courting Visit Saudi, Saudi Arabia's state tourism authority, as a major sponsor for the Women's World Cup.

Vehement objections arose from organizers and players given Saudi Arabia's appalling human-rights record, especially regarding women. FIFA President Gianni Infantino called the backlash hypocritical because some countries that were complaining also trade with Saudi Arabia. But ultimately football's governing body reversed course and declined to add Visit Saudi as a sponsor for the Women's World Cup.

Study Explores the Effect on Brands of Celebrity Endorsers' Scandals
First published June 20, 2019

We have had occasion to address the sad situations in which a company is harmed by a scandal rocking its celebrity brand ambassador. New research reveals the impact these occurrences can have on the brand's stock price. It also shows factors to consider when deciding how to respond to such a crisis.

The research by Stefan J. Hock, a marketing professor at the University of Connecticut in Storrs, and Sascha Raithel, a marketing professor at Freie Universität Berlin, explored a wide field: 128 events of negative publicity for a brand endorser affecting 230 publicly traded companies between 1988 and 2016. Of the celebrity endorsers, 59 percent were athletes while the rest were TV and radio personalities or musicians.

Hock and Raithel found that, in terms of effect on stock price, the crucial questions were whether or not the brand reacted to the scandal, how fast it reacted, and whether it maintained or suspended the relationship.

The researchers also found that the most important factors in terms of how to respond were the level of blame to the celebrity, how close the scandal related to the celebrity's profession, how close the celebrity's profession was tied to the product, and whether the celebrity apologized. (To determine some of these they surveyed marketing professionals. They also analyzed stock movements.)

The research finds the worst thing you can do is to make no statement about the situation and take no action. Yet that's the path most companies follow. Overall, 59 percent of the companies in the study did nothing, while 20 percent announced they'd keep the relationship and 21 percent suspended it or ended it, according to an article in the May-June 2019 issue of *Harvard Business Review.*

It's a shame most companies react as they do. One of the study's conclusions is that handling such a crisis well can help the stock price. "The most surprising finding is that firms can gain value depending on their response," according to the study's abstract. "Announcements of firms' reactions positively affect [abnormal stock returns], especially if they occur quickly after negative publicity surfaces."

The researchers found that fast announcements (within three days) of firms' reactions increase firm value by 2.1 percent over the next four trading weeks (while slow ones decrease it by 1.88 percent). Most importantly, the study shows it's best to act: Issuing statements suspending or maintaining the endorser yielded more positive stock-price results than not reacting at all.

This provides a matrix for how to respond to these sad events. According to the abstract, "Firms have more positive [abnormal stock returns] when they (1) suspend higher-blame endorsers, (2) suspend endorsers whose negative publicity is related to their occupation, (3) maintain endorsers with a high product fit, and (4) do not suspend apologetic endorsers."

Back in March 2016, we praised the handling by Russian tennis pro Maria Sharapova of her positive test for a banned drug. In terms of how the brands she endorsed might respond, she was clearly to blame (though she said she didn't realize the drug was banned) and the scandal was related to her occupation. On the other hand, she strongly apologized.

As we noted, the two brands least related to tennis, Porsche and Tag Heuer, dropped Sharapova (Tag Heuer dropped negotiations with her), and another, Danone (Evian water), took a wait-and-see attitude. But one with a close fit to the tennis player — Nike — also suspended the relationship, while another, racket maker Head NV, stood by her.

The *HBR* article highlights a similar situation: Tiger Woods' December 2009 altercation with his then-wife. Woods, whose sponsors included Accenture, AT&T, Gatorade, General Motors, Gillette, and Nike, was given low marks for his attempt at an apology. Yet the *HBR* notes that, while nonsports brands were more likely to drop him, Nike and others related to golf stood by him.

We suspect celebrity scandals aren't going away. It's good for marketers to know how they will affect them — and how to respond.

Postgame

Sharapova retired from professional tennis in 2020 and most recently resurfaced in a celebrity pickleball tournament — no word to this point on whether she'll pursue a professional pickleball career that would entail new sponsorships.

Woods, slowed by extensive injuries, rarely plays pro tournaments anymore. Given his status as one of golf's all-time greats, however, he maintains a number of sponsorship relationships. One of his most lucrative and well-known deals, a nearly three-decades-long relationship with Nike, recently came to an amicable but still-surprising end. There were no scandals this time around, though, as in recent years Woods' public image has softened and he is mostly regarded as a loving father and a revered aging star.

Peloton Risks Nonresponse Response to Ad Flap
First published December 12, 2019

From a crisis communications point of view, the decision by Peloton, the fancy exercise-bike maker, to basically ignore the brouhaha over its controversial ad is the episode's most interesting aspect. We rarely see a nonresponse response — maybe for good reason. The company continues to be stalked by the issue.

The advertisement heard around the world features a woman whose husband gives her a Peloton bike as a Christmas gift (they sell for more than $2,200). The wife, who is by no means out of shape, is then shown filming herself using the equipment over a year, usually in some existential panic. She says she "didn't realize how much this would change me."

The spot, entitled "The Gift That Gives Back," has been viewed more than 8 million times on YouTube. It has been described as sexist or, at the very least, insensitive, even fat shaming (*The Washington Post* called it "dystopian"). Some said the message should have been about building strength rather than losing weight. In response,

Peloton's stock dropped 9 percent in one day (some say its bad Black Friday performance contributed).

New York–based Peloton issued a statement that did not apologize, let alone announce the promotion would be nixed. "While we're disappointed in how some have misinterpreted this commercial, we are encouraged by — and grateful for — the outpouring of support we've received from those who understand what we were trying to communicate," it said, without explaining what it was trying to communicate.

Company CEO John Foley spoke at a conference on Monday, December 9, and didn't mention the flap, not even to make fun of it, according to *The New York Times*.

But is ignoring the protest the right thing to do? Richard Carufel, editor of marketing publication *Bulldog Reporter*, called it "a pretty radical move" and asked whether it marks "a new era of crisis response."

We hope not. We think the move was risky. Yes, it might seem cocky to say "to hell with it," but many people, especially women, were offended by the ad (some weren't). Even when a company is in the right (and we're not saying Peloton is), it's important to acknowledge people's emotions.

Peloton has moved on to other worries. Famed short-seller Andrew Left released a report Tuesday, December 10, arguing Peloton, which did its IPO in September at $29, would drop to $5 a share next year (unrelated to the ad). The price went down 6 percent on that news, and Peloton hasn't fully dealt with it. It closed yesterday at $32.03.

The backlash over the ad got so bad that Monica Ruiz, the actress who played the wife, issued her own statement. "To say I was shocked and overwhelmed by the attention this week (especially the negative) is an understatement," she wrote.

Perhaps some exercise would help.

Postgame

Peloton's stock dropped so much after the incident portrayed here that at one point the company lost $1.5 billion in value. This would not last long, however. The COVID-19 pandemic began a few months later, forcing gyms to close — which presented an opportunity for Peloton. With everyone forced to quarantine at home and nowhere for them to work out, the company was able to offer high-end machines for home routines. By September 2020, Peloton's sales were up 172 percent.

That didn't prevent the company from experiencing further scandal (and since the end of the COVID-19 pandemic, its sales and stock price have been dismal). In addition to major problems with its treadmill, it had another kerfuffle in December 2021. In an HBO Max reboot of *Sex and the City*, Mr. Big, played by Chris Noth, has a heart attack and dies while exercising on his Peloton. Peloton, of course, knew about the product placement, but didn't know the role it would play.

The scene surprised those who watched, especially Peloton investors. The company's stock dropped 11 percent. In response to the Mr. Big episode, Peloton shot and quickly released an ad with actor Ryan Reynolds that garnered much positive feedback.

Alas, Peloton removed the ad when Noth was accused of sexual impropriety. Several weeks after it debuted, another show, *Billions*, featured a character having a heart attack after using Peloton equipment. And so it goes. . . .

The company was roundly criticized for ducking its head in its nonresponse response to the 2019 ad flap. It shows that it's usually an unforced error to ignore even minor threats to one's reputation.

How Do You Solve a Problem Like Aaron Rodgers?
First published November 11, 2021

Like a bad neighbor, State Farm is not there. Aaron Rodgers, Green Bay Packers star quarterback and pitchman for the insurance giant, wasn't quite truthful about his COVID-19 vaccination status. Yet State Farm is standing by its man. Its messaging on that might have been better had it not missed the point.

Last week, Rodgers tested positive for COVID-19 and then revealed he hadn't been vaccinated. The problem is that at an August presser he said, when asked, "Yeah, I've been immunized." Turns out he didn't mean he'd gotten a shot. Did he mean he gained protection by someone reading his tarot cards? Rodgers is now on a 10-day quarantine.

With Rodgers appearing in its commercials, State Farm had to say something. What it said was that it wouldn't drop him, which disappointed a lot of people. "Aaron Rodgers has been a great ambassador for our company for much of the past decade," it said in a statement quoted in *USA Today* Monday morning.

It continued: "We don't support some of the statements that he has made, but we respect his right to have his own personal point of view. We recognize our customers, employees, agents, and brand ambassadors come from all walks of life, with differing viewpoints on many issues." And: "We encourage vaccinations, but respect everyone's right to make a choice based on their personal circumstances."

The problem is that this doesn't address the problem. The issue isn't one of personal freedom. It isn't even about not getting vaccinated. The issue is that Rodgers lied, or was at least sneaky, about his vaccination status — to fans, reporters, the NFL, and teammates. He also, in violation of the rules, appeared at press conferences without a mask and attended a Halloween party with the other players.

State Farm didn't address any of that. We suspect at some point it may have to. The blowback against Rodgers has been harsh. The NFL has now fined him nearly $15,000 and the Packers $300,000 for violating COVID-19 protocols.

One thing that fed the fury was Rodgers' Friday appearance on the SiriusXM sports program *The Pat McAfee Show*, during which he spewed a lot of nonsense about vaccines and, sheesh, quoted Martin Luther King Jr. He returned to the show Tuesday and was more apologetic. "I misled some people about my status, which I take full responsibility for those comments," he said.

His original comments appear to have convinced another marketer, Wisconsin-based medical-clinic group Prevea Health, to end its relationship with Rodgers on Saturday.

"Prevea Health remains deeply committed to protecting its patients, staff, providers, and communities amidst the COVID-19 pandemic," it said in its statement. "This includes encouraging and helping all eligible populations to become vaccinated against COVID-19."

The difference in response from the two companies is interesting. When a company spokesperson, including from the sports world, gets in hot water, how much the scandal relates to the firm's business can affect the response. Rodgers is attacking medical science, and Prevea is a medical company. State Farm, based in Bloomington, Illinois, is the U.S.'s largest property and casualty and auto insurer.

But State Farm may have conducted a stealth operation of its own. It aired nearly 400 television ads on Sunday and only 1.5 percent of them featured Rodgers, according to Apex Marketing Group. Two Sundays before, 20 percent did. There were similar figures for the comparable Saturdays.

Maybe State Farm is as sneaky as Aaron Rodgers. Still, we wouldn't be surprised if it has a rethink of its relationship with him. That would be neighborly.

Postgame

The negative attention State Farm and Rodgers received was certainly unwelcomed, but State Farm remained the largest insurer of its kind and Rodgers signed a lucrative deal with the New York Jets less than a year and a half later. State Farm *did*, very quietly, end its 12-year partnership with Rodgers at the conclusion of the 2022–2023 NFL season. That's a long time for an athlete and company to be aligned, so it's likely the relationship ran its course. It remains unclear if Rodgers' missteps played into the decision, but they couldn't have helped.

'Dash for Cash' Made a Splash but Was Rash
First published December 16, 2021

Have you ever had what you felt was a brilliant idea and then, when you make it a reality, get hit with an epiphany: *What was I thinking?* That seems to be what went down with the Sioux Falls Stampede junior hockey team, CU Mortgage Direct, and their "Dash for Cash" event. At least they realized their mistake fairly quickly.

The South Dakota squad and the lending company, which supplied the cash, dreamed up a contest that took place on Saturday, December 11, during the first intermission of the match at the Stampede's arena, the Denny Sanford Premier Center in Sioux Falls. (Alas, the Stampede lost to the Tri-City Storm in a 3–2 shootout.)

The competition had 10 schoolteachers, wearing hockey helmets, battle for as much of $5,000 as they could grab by crawling on a rug at center ice and scooping up the one-dollar bills. The money was for their classroom activities. Each teacher collected between $378 and $616.

The event went viral on social media (where else?) and it didn't take long for the criticisms to rain down, mostly that the spectacle was humiliating to educators. Comparisons were made to *The Hunger Games*. The word *dystopia* was invoked. Commenters noted that teachers in South Dakota are rather badly paid. "Dash for Cash" now has its own Wikipedia page.

Randi Weingarten, president of the American Federation of Teachers, tweeted: "This just feels demeaning . . . teachers shouldn't have to dash for dollars for classroom supplies . . . No doubt people probably intended it to be fun, but from the outside it feels terrible."

By Monday afternoon, the team and the mortgage lender had a statement on the team's website. "Although our intent was to provide a positive and fun experience for teachers, we can see how it appears to be degrading and insulting towards the participating teachers and the teaching profession as a whole," they wrote. "We deeply regret and apologize to all teachers for any embarrassment this may have caused."

Most importantly, in terms of crisis response, the team and

sponsor were making amends. They said they would give an additional $500 to each teacher (including 21 who vied unsuccessfully for a spot in the competition), plus another $15,500 to area educators. The team and mortgage company said they would continue to support North Dakota pedagogues, though, one would hope, in a more respectful fashion.

One negative: They ended their statement by saying "CU Mortgage Direct and the Stampede will have no further comment at this time." We doubt that deterred media inquiries. One thing about crises: They're hard to just bat away. They're not hockey pucks.

Postgame

In February 2023, the Stampede held a Mental Health Awareness Night with players wearing warmup jerseys specially made for the event that were then sold to fans via an online auction. All proceeds from the jersey sales and a portion of ticket sales went to a local organization that works to address the importance of mental health. Always something to be said for learning from past mistakes.

LSU Confronts NIL and AI
First published March 9, 2023

It's always fun when two raging phenomena come together. We have that in the recent flap over a TikTok video by LSU gymnastics star and uber-influencer Olivia "Livvy" Dunne. The LSU (Louisiana State University) incident brings together controversies over NIL (name, image, and likeness) and AI (artificial intelligence). How's that for alphabet soup?

Dunne posted a 10-second clip, for which she was paid, promoting AI outfit Caktus, which aims to help students write their papers based on verbal prompts. The 20-year-old Dunne has 7.2 million TikTok followers.

The spot shows the caption "Need to get my creativity flowing for my essay due at midnight" and Dunne using the service. The phrase "gymnastics is the hardest sport" appears on her laptop screen and then is magically transformed by Caktus into a full composition. Dunne gives the thumb up (only one thumb).

AI has become all the rage the past few months especially with the rise of AI platform ChatGPT, which will apparently replace everyone's job, including plumbers. NIL has been all the rage since 2021, when the NCAA, the body that oversees sports at 1,000-plus U.S. schools, allowed student-athletes to profit from their — well — name, image, and likeness.

The On3 NIL 100 database of student-athletes' projected annual values lists Dunne third, at more than $3 million. She's the highest-paid NCAA female athlete, making seven figures.

NIL raises many reputational issues, such as what happens to sponsors when their athlete representatives do something stupid like get arrested for drunk driving. Then there's young people signing contracts they don't understand. While the universities aren't technically involved, they still have to worry about the reputational implications.

So here we have LSU faced with a student-athlete doing something sort of untoward in an NIL deal: encouraging students to possibly violate their school's code of conduct.

But LSU handled it pretty well. It didn't freak out. It didn't "cancel" Dunne, who probably didn't violate any rules. It simply issued a statement, picked up in the press, relaying its concerns — especially about how using AI could get students put on double secret probation.

"At LSU, our professors and students are empowered to use technology for learning and pursuing the highest standards of academic integrity," it wrote, according to press reports. "However, using AI to produce work that a student then represents as one's own could result in a charge of academic misconduct, as outlined in the Code of Student Conduct."

LSU's conduct code reportedly does not mention AI (we bet it will soon), but it does of course condemn plagiarism, a major academic no-no. AI's rise is new enough that the rules aren't clear on how it intersects with literary cribbing. And not just in academe.

Postgame

Livvy Dunne continues to be a marketing and social-media sensation. She remains atop the On3 Women's NIL 100 list. Later in 2023, she said she received more than $500,000 for a single social-media post (she didn't name the marketer). Also in 2023, she launched the Livvy Fund at LSU to help female athletes connect with brands for NIL deals. She graduated from LSU in May 2024, but announced she would stay on to compete with the school's gymnastics team for another year.

Fans Call Foul on Boston's New Soccer Team
First published October 24, 2024

It's remarkable how often a marketing campaign meant to promote an organization instead blows up in the organization's face and devolves into a crisis. Such was the recent experience of the National Women's Soccer League's newest expansion team.

On October 15, the Boston-based squad held a major event at a Dick's House of Sport to officially unveil its name, BOS Nation F.C., and its marketing campaign, including a one-minute promotional video. Unfortunately, the ad, whose theme has been expressed in news reports variously as "Balls, Balls, Balls" and "Too Many Balls," didn't go over well.

After showing several Boston-based male professional athletes throughout history with a "balls" voice-over commentary ("old balls, new balls, steel balls"), the video declares, "Yeah, Boston loves its balls. But maybe there are too many balls in this town. So let's add a new chapter to our city's legacy."

Oy vey.

As you can imagine, fans had a few things to say about this, and they weren't positive things. Even during the ceremony, one person held up a sign that read "No Room for Transphobia," which the protester said was in response to the ad, according to The Athletic.

"Why would a women's soccer team, noted for its diverse fan base and especially its passionate LGBTQIA+ fans, choose 'too many balls' as a concept?" asked Yahoo! Sports Staff Writer Liz Roscher.

Good question. The requisite follow-up statement, which came the next day, didn't provide much of an answer. "While we had hoped to create a bold and buzzworthy brand-launch campaign, we missed the mark," the team admitted. "We fully acknowledge that the content of the campaign did not reflect the safe and welcoming environment we strive to create for all, and we apologize to the LGBTQ+ community and to the trans community in particular for the hurt we caused."

In our view, that statement also missed the mark in not explaining how this happened and what the team would do about it. Footie fans, and the Boston public, deserve better. More broadly, it's a little astonishing that, in this day and age, organizations don't have processes for vetting how a bold marketing campaign might be heard differently from what's intended. Put it on the to-do list.

This is especially so because BOS Nation had a longish run-up to this highly anticipated moment. The NWSL announced the Boston expansion, the league's 15th team, in September 2023. Official play is slated to start in 2026.

All the statement had to say about making amends was "Thank you to all who have held us accountable by calling for us to do better. We hear and we will, together."

We'll see. But the story didn't end there. People were also upset with the name. The team explained that BOS Nation, pronounced "Boss Nation," is an anagram of Bostonian (which it is). The criticism's crux is unclear, but the general feeling seems to be that it's a horrible name. We know this from comments on X, such as "Horrible name" and "That's horrible."

Plainly, BOS Nation has more explaining to do. It can drop the marketing effort (it apparently shuttered the toomanyballs.com website). But more convincing will be needed on the name front.

Postgame

Since its disastrous announcement, BOS Nation has apparently been doing some soul-searching. It said in an "Update to the Community" on its website it was reconsidering its moniker. "Your voices have made it clear that revisiting our team name is essential, and we're fully committed to building a club identity that reflects the ambition of a women's professional soccer team in Boston."

In addition to reaching out to the other professional women's teams in Boston for guidance, the ownership group said it would seek fan input for direction moving forward. It did just that in the form of a fan survey that got over 1,000 responses; a summary of those responses was made public. This is the type of community engagement the Cleveland Indians successfully used from the outset when undergoing its own name change to the Guardians (see the next chapter), proving that getting a project like this right from the get-go means never having to say you're sorry.

In March 2025, the women's soccer squad did indeed announce its new moniker: Boston Legacy F.C.

11

WHAT'S IN A NAME? OTHER TEAM AND LEAGUE ISSUES

Introduction

Sports teams and leagues can face crises that aren't strictly sports-centric. These can include all the issues that confront most organizations, such as accidents, service disruptions, or accusations of racism or sexism. But a big one that's unique to sports is pressure to change the name of a team, particularly regarding sensitivities to Native Americans. We have a post here on that — on how the team now known as the Cleveland Guardians (formerly the Indians) expertly rolled out its name change.

It's a good example of crisis communications and response being about *preventing* crises by handling such challenges well in the first place. The team clearly spent a lot of time and resources on the issue. It also wisely involved the fans. It knew it was a sensitive subject and had to be addressed gingerly. That's the approach communicators should take when dealing with such a momentous issue as a team's name change.

Two other posts concern the confusion that arose over ticketing when the COVID-19 pandemic first hit and the furor that erupted when 12 of Europe's biggest soccer clubs tried to form a new league.

Communicators would do well to study the communications history of the COVID-19 pandemic. Many companies and organizations were challenged by having to reach out to employees and others to communicate their response and how the situation would affect their work lives. The federal government was criticized for its changing messages regarding what people should do to stay safe. The government failed to communicate that its understanding of the science would evolve, and its recommendations would evolve with it.

There's a lesson in that: Crisis communicators should relay what they know and often that their understanding of the situation may change. They will have to provide updates when needed.

As for the issue raised in the COVID-19 post in particular, one crisis scenario sports communicators must be ready for is a service disruption. Imagine a ticketing problem at your stadium. Sports fans will be furious. As the communicator, you'll have to know what operational person in the organization will have the facts for you to relay to your stakeholders. You'll have to know how you'll communicate those facts. You'll have to know what position (and attitude) the team's front office will take.

For crisis communicators, the lesson from the 2021 European Super League episode is that, even when trying to do something positive or promotional (such as introducing a new sports league), thought must be given to how the public will react. Your organization might think the future holds nothing but love and roses; other people may see things differently. Because leaders often live in a bubble, part of your job as a communicator is to put yourself in the place of those outside your organization and try to determine how they'll react.

Sports Fans Face Refund Confusion Amid COVID-19
First published April 16, 2020

Our first post about communicating the COVID-19 pandemic noted at least two canceled music festivals weren't planning to provide refunds, which we said would probably lead to another round of crises. The refund issue is now raging in the worlds of sports and recreation. Some companies are handling it better than others.

Many of those refusing to refund rely on the idea that the events are postponed rather than canceled. None exemplifies this more than Major League Baseball, especially for those with season tickets. It's pretty clear to everyone that MLB can't play a full season, yet the league deems missed games as being merely postponed. In terms of refunds, that's similar to a rainout.

The MLB page on this notes that on March 15 the Centers for Disease Control and Prevention (CDC) recommended restricting events of more than 50 people for two months. So the opening of the 2020 baseball season, scheduled for March 26, was pushed back.

"The clubs remain committed to playing as many games as possible when the season begins," the MLB page says.

As for individual teams, the Los Angeles Dodgers' FAQ at its website, for example, says, "In coordination with MLB, the Dodgers will provide more information about our plans, including our ticket policy for impacted games, as soon as it is available."

We're pretty certain that, for a lot of fans, that's not good enough.

Another company that's run into issues on the COVID-19 refund front is ticket-resale outfit StubHub. The company boasts about its FanProtect policy that provides cash refunds of tickets to canceled events. Yet in the wake of the coronavirus, and according to a refund policy dated April 10 on its site, it is instead offering a credit of 120 percent of the value.

A lot of people are unhappy. On April 2, a Wisconsin man seeking class-action status sued StubHub for the alleged retroactive cancellation of the FanProtect cash-back policy. (Ticketmaster is facing a new backlash for changing its policy to offer refunds only for officially canceled events.)

Another related industry are gyms. Some have been quick to stop charging members once they were ordered to shut down. For example, Equinox told its customers by March 17 they wouldn't be billed while its gyms were shuttered. "Your membership will be put on freeze at no cost as of the day the club closed," it wrote.

Planet Fitness also froze memberships. "We have proactively frozen all memberships on your behalf, and you will not be charged any fees during this time," it wrote. "We will keep you informed and let you know when your club is ready to reopen, and look forward to serving you in a clean, sanitary, and judgment-free environment. Can't wait to see you back in the club soon!"

Not all gym operators have been so cooperative.

On April 3, the attorneys general of New York, Pennsylvania, and the District of Columbia wrote to Town Sports International — parent of New York Sports Clubs, Boston Sports Clubs, and other gyms — about continuing to charge fees even though its gyms are closed and about its unclear refund policy.

According to the letter, the company at first said members could cancel their memberships only in person, when the gyms were closed, or by certified mail. As late as a March 31 email to members, the company was still vague about how they could cancel or freeze memberships and how credits would be issued.

Apparently the company is getting the message. On April 8, it posted a member letter announcing all memberships are frozen at no cost and advising on how to cancel. But now Town Sports is reportedly considering bankruptcy.

From a crisis communications point of view, sports teams and related organizations should recognize what Equinox and Planet Fitness already have: People are facing economic hardship due to COVID-19 — millions have lost their jobs — and shouldn't have to wait many months to get their money back.

Companies that don't see this are metaphorically blind. Sports teams and related companies should understand the goodwill that would come from refunding tickets immediately — and communicating that effectively.

Postgame

The COVID-19 pandemic obviously presented companies and organizations with operational and communications challenges. Things were especially confusing early on, including for sports venues.

StubHub in late 2021 reached a settlement with consumers in 10 states and Washington, D.C., for $20 million. This money was to be divided among the ticket holders affected by the cancellations. StubHub also was forced to make clearer its refund process and to refrain from changing its rules for its own benefit.

As for Town Sports International, the company went on to file for bankruptcy in September 2020. It was bought out of bankruptcy, much shrunken in number of gyms, by multiple investors. Many of its localities were transferred to New York Sports Clubs and its brands. But the situation was costly. In January 2023, nearly 2,000 New York Sports Club members began to receive restitution checks after the company was sued by New York Attorney General Letitia James for unlawfully charging customers during the COVID-19 gym shutdowns.

The onset of a pandemic is an extraordinary event, but it's also without question a crisis that needs to be communicated. Such "natural disasters" should be on the list of potential crisis scenarios.

Euro Soccer Commits Costly Error
First published April 29, 2021

Normally, not being prepared in soccer might mean you weren't paying attention to the coach during practice or you didn't warm up properly before the game. But for 12 of Europe's biggest clubs, "failure to prepare" was recently taken to a whole new level. And it's a good lesson for crisis communicators.

On April 18, the sports world erupted when it was announced that a dozen of the world's most prominent soccer clubs had decided to break away to form their own "Super League." The concept, as laid out in their announcement, was that the best would be playing only the best and that that "would help football at every level," according to Super League Chairman and Real Madrid President Florentino Pérez. His quote also pointed out that these powerhouse teams had a "responsibility" to "respond to the desires of the fans."

There was only one problem: They could not have been more

wrong about the desires of the fans.

The announcement was immediately and overwhelmingly met with outrage among the football faithful of Europe. The fans saw this as a scheme to help the rich get richer while the smaller clubs would suffer in obscurity from no longer competing against the big-name clubs.

The fans' response was so passionate and one-sided, in fact, that it raises the question: Could the organizers of the Super League really have underestimated so massively the ensuing wrath of the game's supporters? It hardly seems possible, but that's what happened. The people behind the ill-fated breakaway venture clearly were not prepared for the public backlash, as evidenced by their plans completely imploding just two days later. Teams that joined almost immediately backed out.

While there is plenty of blame to go around, one obvious and unflattering reality of this doomed venture is the "ugly American" factor.

The most prominent English teams to commit to the Super League are American owned: Liverpool (John Henry), Arsenal (Stan Kroenke), and Manchester United (Joel Glazer). Even prior to the now-infamous coup, supporters of these clubs roundly resented the foreign ownership and saw the Yanks as, at best, interlopers and, at worst, greedy, uncaring, and naïve to the ways of European football. With their push to start a new, more profitable league, these men did nothing to improve those negative perceptions.

The league's astoundingly quick collapse was all the proof anyone needed to see that these organizations either completely misread how their maneuvers would be publicly received or, worse, thought they could just bully their way through.

Ownership response varied. Stan Kroenke's son Josh defended his family's governance of Arsenal, while Joel Glazer wrote an open letter of apology to Manchester United fans. Neither tack proved effective, as thousands of angry Arsenal fans protested outside their stadium chanting, "We want Kroenke out," while frustrated Manchester United fans broke into the club's training facility carrying "Glazer Out" banners.

Even JPMorgan Chase apologized for arranging financing for the new league and misjudging fan response. "We will learn from this," a company spokesman said.

The result will go down as one of the greatest miscalculations in modern sports history and will also be the ultimate case study for any company that wants to know what not to do in a public-facing crisis. It certainly is evidence that you must be prepared for any negative fallout of your actions.

Postgame

The quick implosion of the proposed European Super League in April 2021 was one of the most astonishing blunders in sports-business history. Much of crisis communications involves gauging public sentiment. The organizers here failed miserably.

And yet, in October 2022, they appointed a new CEO and said the league would relaunch within three years. In December 2023, the European Court of Justice ruled it would be contrary to European law to ban clubs from joining a European Super League. In December 2024, A22 Sports Management, the promoter that originally launched the league, submitted a new proposal to UEFA and FIFA for what it's now calling the Unify League, which it says would have 96 participating clubs. The concept, at least, is still alive.

The lesson here is that any group that seeks to alter a sport whose competition structure is so ingrained in the hearts and souls of the masses, in this case the European masses, ought to learn from these mistakes. Anticipating public resistance and having a sound communications plan in place would be critical.

Cleveland Hits the Ball Out of the Park on Name Change
First published July 29, 2021

The Cleveland Indians professional baseball team, like similarly branded clubs, has been pressured for years to change its name, which many Native Americans view as racist. Last week, it unveiled a new moniker with a campaign aimed at anticipating blowback. It wasn't just good PR, but good crisis communications.

Baseball loves stats, and the team's July 23 announcement that it would switch its name to the Cleveland Guardians had a lot of those. The organization was eager to show it had put a lot of effort into the project, which was a smart move.

To wit, it had surveyed 40,000 fans; conducted more than 100 hours of teammate brainstorming sessions and 140 hours of interviews with fans, community leaders, and front-office staff; and gathered 1,198 appellation possibilities, which it narrowed to 14.

The new name comes from the "Guardians of Traffic" statues on the Hope Memorial Bridge near the team's ballpark. Cleveland unveiled a new "Guardian Fastball" logo, yet the press release emphasized continuity in colors, typescript, and its "C" symbol, which it adopted after dropping its controversial Chief Wahoo logo in 2019.

As part of the campaign, the team set up an information-rich web page, which includes a video with fans championing the new moniker. It also released a two-minute video voiced by actor Tom Hanks, and rolled out a number of tweets on the issue — it clearly wasn't trying to bury the news.

As far as we can tell, there's been little pushback, though there has been some. People even seem to like "Guardians," though Cleveland may face litigation from a roller-derby team with the same name. The forward-thinking and skillful unveiling deserves at least some credit for avoiding an onslaught of criticism that could have become a crisis.

Cleveland has been more agile at the name-change process than the fumbling professional football team formerly known as the Washington Redskins. Both clubs said they would investigate the question around the same time, July 2020. In December, Cleveland said it would make the shift and, obviously, conducted intense due diligence to do so.

Washington owner Dan Snyder resisted calls to replace the team designation for two decades. Less than two weeks after the squad said it would investigate the issue last July, it announced a temporary change to the generic Washington Football Team until it picks a new name, which it still hasn't.

Washington was goaded into action largely by pressure from corporate sponsors such as Nike, Pepsi, and especially FedEx, which has the naming rights to its ballpark. During that time it was also dealing with its perennially bad performance and a sex-harassment scandal, which has since resulted in it being fined $10 million.

Other organizations are implicated in the questionable-name issue. What say you, Atlanta Major League Baseball team? Kansas City National Football League team? Anyone?

Postgame

Changing the name of professional sports teams to express sensitivity toward indigenous people is itself a sensitive and controversial subject. Cleveland's baseball team, now known as the Cleveland Guardians, showed how to do it right. The team took the process seriously and rolled it out expertly. It even resolved the lawsuit from the roller-derby team, allowing both to use the "Guardians" name.

In its first season with its new name, the Cleveland Guardians (the baseball team, not roller-derby squad) won the 2022 American League Central Division championship, but went on to lose to the New York Yankees in the American League Division Series.

The Washington Football Team, mentioned here, finally rebranded as the Commanders in 2022. Yet the name change didn't affect the culture. Owner Daniel Snyder never successfully extricated himself from the mess he'd created during his two-plus decades at the helm, and ultimately sold the team to a group led by Josh Harris in 2023.

Interestingly, the name changes have some pushback from indigenous people. In the summer of 2023, a group called the Native American Guardians Association, or NAGA, started separate petitions to switch the names of both the Guardians and Commanders back to the old monikers. NAGA said it believes the names weren't originally meant to be derogatory, but rather nods of respect and admiration.

Brooklyn Nets Sort of Apologize for Bad Season
First published April 18, 2024

We tend not to think of problems that crop up in the everyday course of an organization's business as a crisis in the strict meaning. Think of a company having a bad quarter: not good, but not really a crisis in the crisis communications sense. Yet we have an interesting example of someone addressing a similar performance issue in sports.

On the night of Wednesday, April 10, the Brooklyn Nets, then with a dismal 31–48 record, were about to play their final home game for the season, against the Toronto Raptors, at Barclays Center. Before the start of play, Nets shooting guard and small forward Mikal Bridges addressed the crowd from halfcourt.

"On behalf of my teammates and the Nets organization, we appreciate you guys coming out this year. I know it's been a tough year, but we appreciate you guys hanging on with us," he said, according to a report by Erik Slater in ClutchPoints. "We'll be back next year."

What Bridges did was unusual. Sure, a player or manager might address the team's ghastly performance in the locker room or at a postgame presser. But from halfcourt before the game? And about the whole season?

Then there's the substance. As we say, it would be like a company asking forgiveness for a down quarter. In sports, a disappointing game or even season isn't necessarily something you draft talking points for. Maybe *six* bad quarters or seasons (that could be seen as a slowly unfolding crisis).

Both ClutchPoints and the New York *Daily News* called what Bridges said an apology (the *News* called it "a sincere apology"). It wasn't exactly an apology, but it was close.

We're pretty certain Bridges further ingratiated the team with fans — gave the Nets some goodwill, some credit in the "Credibility Bank." But that's what motivated Bridges: Despite the squad's disappointing play this year, and not making it into the postseason, the fans have stuck by it. Bridges spoke before a sold-out crowd.

After the game, he explained why he did what he did. "You know, just the season ending like this while there's a lot of basketball going on left. I know it's not fun for them, it's definitely not fun for us," he said, adding that the Nets have "been surprised [at fan support despite] how poor we've been playing all year. But it just shows the true fans and how much they really care."

Sure, some fans *won't* care about Bridges' "apology." As we say, they'll see it as more of a performance issue: "How about playing better?" But it was a worthy attempt. And at least the Nets beat the Raptors that night 106–102.

Postgame

Alas, the two (away) games the Nets had left in the 2023–2024 season didn't shower the team in glory. They lost to both the New York Knicks and the Philadelphia 76ers, ending with a 32–50 record. At a press conference, Mikal Bridges reflected on how difficult the season was for both the Nets and himself. He said it even affected him mentally. "It was really tough just personally," he said. "I got a couple gray hairs." Unfortunately, the Nets didn't fare better in the 2024–2025 season, maintaining a losing record. Fortunately for Bridges, he was traded to the more-successful and more-popular New York Knicks before that season started.

A Tale of Two Olympic Apologies
First published August 1, 2024

It was the best of Olympic Games opening ceremonies, it was the worst of Olympic Games opening ceremonies, it was the opening ceremony of wisdom, it was the opening ceremony of foolishness. But mostly, it was the opening ceremony of apologies. Here we examine two, which are instructive concerning corporate mea culpas.

A major mistake occurred at the July 26 opening extravaganza of the Paris Olympics when the South Korean team was introduced as the

North Koreans. This upset the South Koreans. "This absurd gaffe occurred because those in charge of operations failed to be attentive," said Lee Kee-heung, president of that country's Olympic committee, according to South Korean newspaper *Hankyoreh*. Lee said he would demand an apology.

He didn't have to wait long. The International Olympic Committee issued a statement the next day revealing that IOC President Thomas Bach spoke by phone with Republic of Korea (aka South Korea) President Yoon Suk Yeol and "apologized sincerely for the mistake," which the statement said was caused by "human error, for which the IOC is deeply sorry."

So, pretty straightforward: An organization blundered and it apologized for that blunder.

Compare that to the second, more controversial situation. The opening ceremony included a tableau of people, including drag artists and dancers, assembled along a bridge over the Seine. At the center of the group was French disc jockey and lesbian activist Barbara Butch.

Many people took this to be a depiction of Leonardo da Vinci's *The Last Supper*, and a blasphemous one at that, with DJ Butch and the drag queens and others representing Jesus Christ and his apostles. Conservative religious groups objected. For example, the French Bishops Conference of the Catholic Church said the scene was a "mockery and derision of Christianity."

Thomas Jolly, artistic director of the ceremony, denied that interpretation and said the scene was meant to represent a pagan feast. In fact, Dionysus, the Greek god of wine (among other things), was featured heavily in it. "My wish isn't to be subversive, nor to mock or to shock," Jolly told the Associated Press.

Still, given the backlash, an official response was in order. "Clearly there was never an intention to show disrespect to any religious group," Paris 2024 spokesperson Anne Descamps said at a press conference. "If people have taken any offense we are, of course, really, really sorry."

That was it in terms of apology. Given the disagreement over the facts, the apology was much different from the Korea situation. This is an important concept in corporate apologies: Facts come into play and the apology may be less forthright if the accused organization feels it's not as culpable. No doubt, the debate about the interpretation of the tableau will continue.

MLB Listens to Players, Fans on Hated Uniforms
First published October 3, 2024

This week saw the resolution of a situation that highlights the importance of listening to your stakeholders, in this case professional athletes and their fans. We speak of the great baseball-uniform fiasco, which brings together — unhappily — MLB, the players union, Nike Inc., and Fanatics Inc. You can think of it as the "New Coke" of sports.

For spring training this season, Major League Baseball debuted lighter and thinner Nike-designed uniforms. Alas, players and fans immediately blasted them as having, among other ills, a poor fit, too-small lettering, and non-custom-fitted pants. The jerseys were also sheer enough to reveal heavy sweat stains.

In April, the MLB Players Association sent a memo to its members declaring the outfits would be altered. It's unclear how certain that was, but the league responded by saying it would work with Nike to see about that.

On Monday this week, MLB made it official. It said it would revamp the attire to return to the older designs, including pants customization, increased letter sizes, and the heavier fabric. It said it collaborated on the switch — which won't be fully implemented until the start of the 2026 season — with the union, Nike, and manufacturer Fanatics.

The league announced it was also ditching the new Nike-designed, multicolored uniforms for All-Star Games and was returning to the previous practice (stretching back to the 1930s) of having the players wear their regular team attire during the mid-season game.

This was a double-lede story with some outlets emphasizing the regular-season uniforms and some the All-Star garb. Either way, there was jubilation (and relief) throughout the sports land. The *New York Times*-owned Athletic called it "a total reversal" and "a triumph for public outrage." *Sports Illustrated* reported it as "the moment most MLB fans have been waiting for."

"MLB *finally* got the hint," wrote Phil Hecken, editor of Uni Watch, a website that covers — you guessed it — sports uniforms. Hecken referred in particular to the All-Star uniforms, which he called "clown costumes."

Sportico Deputy Editor Eben Novy-Williams called the hated duds (in two senses) "a rare design miss for Nike." He reported that most of the blame was being placed on that company because it "refused to address the issue as it was taking root in club houses and on social media." Bad crisis response, especially as the athletes really did turn to their social-media platforms to protest.

"At its core, what has happened here is that Nike was innovating something that didn't need to be innovated," the players union said in its April memo, according to an article that month by Novy-Williams. The memo also said the sportswear giant's response to the controversy was "Nothing to see here. Players will need to adjust." Nike doesn't seem to have commented on the latest announcement.

In absolving Fanatics (in which the union owns equity), the memo implied that Nike didn't reach out for player consultation on the designs. "Fanatics recognizes the vital important [*sic*] of soliciting player feedback, obtaining player buy-in, and not being afraid to have difficult conversations about jerseys," the memo said, according to Sportico.

"New Coke," of course, refers to Coca-Cola's 1985 reformulation of its ubiquitous soft drink, which made it sweeter. The new formula was met by almost universal derision, causing the company, three months later, to bring back the old recipe as "Coca-Cola Classic." The company dropped New Coke altogether in 2002. As fount of wisdom Wikipedia puts it, "The story of New Coke remains influential as a cautionary tale against tampering with an established successful brand."

In other words, listen to your stakeholders.

12

SEE YOU IN COURT: LAWSUITS

Introduction

Almost all crises nowadays have a legal dimension, and litigation communications is considered a subset of crisis communications. But the two are different. Legal disputes tend to unfold more slowly than crises.

Whether a lawsuit will garner a lot of press interest can depend on how well known the parties are and the issues raised. Litigation involving a star professional athlete would likely draw *a lot* of attention.

Litigation communicators work closely alongside attorneys. As our post on the U.S. women's soccer team shows, legal and communications strategies must mesh — and certainly not conflict. A reasonable legal strategy can be a terrible media strategy; a legal approach that doesn't take into consideration public perception can lead to huge reputational harm.

An important factor in litigation communications is the power imbalance between lawyers and PR pros. Too often this dictates that the attorneys hold sway. But communicators must insist that public image be an essential part of the legal strategy. One role of the communicator is to listen to the developing legal strategy as Joe Public might respond to it. Lawyers aren't usually focused on that; they're focused on winning in the legal arena, especially in the courtroom.

Communicators must defend their concerns about reputation. Brett Favre's ongoing legal problems, as highlighted here, show how bad things can get when you don't defend yourself in the court of public opinion while legal action is ongoing.

Sports crisis communicators should familiarize themselves with the basics of litigation communications. That includes how to find what you need in a court docket and how to behave in a courthouse (don't talk to jurors!). It also means knowing the mileposts of a litigation that will most pique reporters' interest in covering it.

As a general overview of civil litigation (especially in federal court), those mileposts are:

- the filing of the complaint (which starts the lawsuit)
- the motion to dismiss the complaint
- the answer to the complaint (discussed in the second Favre post here)
- the motion for summary judgment (in which one or more parties asks the judge to decide the case without the need of a trial)
- the trial itself

The filing of the suit and a trial — though trials are rare — would garner the most attention from reporters.

U.S. Soccer Scores PR 'Own Goal' With Legal Strategy
First published March 26, 2020

The claims made recently by the U.S. Soccer Federation (USSF) in its argument against the men's and women's teams being paid the same might have been considered strong... that is, if they had been made prior to 1999. Instead, they provide yet another example of a legal tack that is a terrible communications tack.

The strategy employed by the USSF's legal team in the lawsuit brought by the women players for higher pay is as shockingly oblivious to public perception as one could imagine. Public relations professionals around the world collectively cringed upon hearing the contention that the women's national team should not be paid as much as the men's team because they're not as strong or as fast as the men and don't have to deal with as much scrutiny during road games.

This raises an important question that lawyers in 2020 constantly have to struggle with — how can I present my best argument without being considered insensitive and tone-deaf by the public?

In a sense, there's a long history to this case.

In 1991, the United States Women's National Soccer Team (USWNT) won the first official Women's World Cup. But women's soccer in the U.S. attained an unprecedented level of superstardom when the 1999 team led by Mia Hamm, Brandi Chastain, and Julie Foudy defeated China in an unforgettable overtime shootout that took place at the Rose Bowl in California in front of over 90,000 fans.

The U.S. Men's team has largely not shown any major progress in the last 20 years and bottomed out when it failed to qualify for the 2018 World Cup. The very fair public perception is that the U.S. Women's team is consistently the best in the world, while the U.S. Men's team has yet to rise to the level of its European and South American counterparts.

Last year, the USWNT successfully defended its 2015 World Cup victory. Certainly no easy task when it was the favorite and the main target of every other nation in the tournament. Immediately following the celebration, talk turned to members of the team fighting for equal pay with their male counterparts. It was more than talk: They sued. It's presumably at this point that USSF's legal team began to, in earnest, develop a defense strategy.

Lawyers, as we know, are trained to present the facts, feelings be damned. But as we've seen time and time again recently, that rote delivery of facts can be perceived by the public as obtuse and even callous. This is exactly how USSF's case played out to the masses. In particular, it was the arguments in a March 9 court filing that caused major blowback. Those reacting negatively included advertisers; Volkswagen said it was "disgusted." The heat got bad enough that the federation's president, Carlos Cordeiro, decided to resign on March 12 and issued an apology as well.

His replacement, fittingly, is Cindy Parlow Cone, a member of the legendary 1999 Women's World Cup champion team. Cone apologized for the sexist language ("Last week's legal filing was an error"). The federation brought on an additional law firm and, when it filed a new court brief March 16, the press coverage noted the "different tone" (it praised the women players).

Even in the earlier filing, along with the misogynistic "men are stronger than women and bear more responsibility" line of defense, the USSF lawyers presented more straightforward assertions about the men's team competing in more lucrative tournaments, having higher ratings, and generating more revenue than the women's team. All valid points if they can be proven. These perfectly legitimate and less offensive arguments, however, were buried in the public narrative by the headline-grabbing sexist points.

While the original USSF lawyers should have foreseen this backlash, if the federation itself wants to understand where it went wrong, it need only look inward. Neither former President Cordeiro nor the board did anything to stop their lawyers from causing damage to their public perception in this hotly debated legal battle.

Unfortunately, as we're seeing, many firms have been slow to make the adjustments necessary to build a successful case in both actual court *and* in the court of opinion.

Postgame

In February 2022, the U.S. Soccer Federation agreed to pay $24 million to settle the pay-disparity suit brought by the women players, with $22 million going directly to those who were plaintiffs and $2 million to an account to benefit players in their post-careers and for philanthropy. The terms of the settlement dictated that U.S. Soccer will pay men and women at an equal rate, including for friendlies and tournaments, as well as the World Cup.

The United States Women's National Soccer Team continues to be a powerhouse, though it had a disappointing performance at the 2023 World Cup, where it didn't make it to the semifinals. It did, however, win (and host) the inaugural 2024 CONCACAF W Gold Cup and win the gold at the 2024 Summer Olympics in France.

Its fight to be paid as much as the men's team spurred congressional action as well. In January 2023, President Joe Biden signed into law the Equal Pay for Team USA Act, which ensures equal compensation for U.S. women competing in international events.

On Brett Favre's Welfare Scandal
First published September 29, 2022

Talk about a reputational challenge. The heat keeps turning up on ex-NFL quarterback Brett Favre. As part of a larger scandal, he's alleged to have pressured Mississippi officials to turn over $8 million in welfare funds for his pet projects, including a volleyball stadium at his alma mater. And yet Favre seems to be doing nothing to defend his rep (such as it is).

The crisis, simmering for years, could scorch the former gridiron star, especially in his home state (Mississippi), where he's been a favorite son. That good standing may not stand. Conversely, some say he has no good rep to defend. For example, during his career he was banned from drinking alcohol and was fined for not cooperating about a sexting allegation against him. His postretirement image has been sort of clownish.

Favre hasn't been criminally charged in the welfare scandal, as some others have, though he's one of many defendants in a civil suit the state brought in May.

Still, for Favre, the pocket continues to collapse, especially with the trickling out of damning text messages. In 2019, he was working with then-Mississippi Governor Phil Bryant to build the new volleyball facility at the University of Southern Mississippi, where his daughter played the sport. Favre was raising money for the project, but now it's come out how he allegedly did that, and it isn't pretty.

Favre kept pushing the governor even after he told the ex-pro that misuse of the welfare funds could be illegal. Favre has denied knowing that such funds would be used. That's hard to square with the texts.

Favre has reportedly repaid $1.1 million (though not the interest) given to him for promotional appearances he never made. With regard to that plan, in 2017 he texted the leader of the nonprofit that distributed millions in federal welfare dollars, "If you were to pay me, is there anyway the media can find out where it came from and how much?"

That's not a good look.

Is Favre tarnishing his 20-year NFL career? The public scrutiny isn't going away. SiriusXM has suspended his NFL show and ESPN Wisconsin has done likewise with his biweekly appearances, according to CNBC. A spokesman for the Pro Football Hall of Fame told *The New York Times* he's fielded about a dozen calls from people asking Favre to be booted from the institution.

And it doesn't appear Favre or his lawyer have said much, other than denying he knew about the welfare funds. In terms of crisis response, that's a factual question that should be answered with facts — marshaling them is a major part of crisis communications. And yet maybe he simply doesn't have a more in-depth answer to the allegation.

A Favre Filing and a Lawsuit Answer's News Value
First published May 11, 2023

Legal communicators should understand enough legal procedure to know a litigation's "mileposts" at which journalists will be most eager to write about the lawsuit. One that usually doesn't get much attention is the filing of an answer to the complaint. We have an example of one that did get some notice and for obvious reasons.

In May 2022, the Mississippi Department of Human Services sued retired NFL quarterback Brett Favre and almost three dozen others, accusing them of misappropriating welfare funds. Last month, Favre lost his bid to get the case against him dismissed. That meant he had to respond to, or answer, the complaint, which he did on May 5.

Typically, answers are dry documents that don't offer reporters much in the way of juicy tidbits to write about; they regurgitate the facts and allegations in the complaint, which the defendant either admits to or denies. Yet, for certain cases, journos will work overtime to find something to spill ink over.

Communicators should keep the answer filing in mind as a possible "media moment" (as with other lawsuit phases). At least one reporter, Wes Bruer of CNN, thought the Favre document worthy of writing up. This is probably because Favre is famous and his answer seems to be somewhat more substantive than is typical.

Bruer was able to lead his article with Favre's denial of the allegations. He also mentions that the document states, in the standard legalese of an answer, that "Favre 'lacks knowledge or information sufficient to form a belief as to the truth of the allegations' that he conspired to defraud MDHS."

Answers often include "affirmative defenses," which can cause PR headaches. Lawyers plead these defenses, even if there's no evidence to support them, because they can't add them later and the legal team hopes through the process of discovery to find evidence to support the claims.

Bruer writes: "The answer to the complaint lays out 21 affirmative defenses, where Favre's attorneys question the statutory basis against the allegations, otherwise claiming that Favre acted in good faith and that 'If there was a civil conspiracy in MDHS complaint, MDHS was a co-conspirator.'" Some might chafe at that last statement, though Bruer didn't make much of it.

Other than that, the article goes through the usual admissions and denials and the ex-pro's requests for a jury trial and for the case to be moved to a different district.

The filing of the document hasn't gotten a lot of coverage, but that's the point. An answer usually doesn't, but legal communicators should be ready in case one does.

Postgame

For sports stars, especially those with household names, virtually anything they convey — whether it be verbal or written — can be fodder for the media. Pro Football Hall of Famer Brett Favre is no exception. The Mississippi case put Favre so under the microscope that even a typically innocuous response to the complaint was scrutinized by the media.

His efforts to defend himself in court, as well as in the court of public opinion, haven't been going as well as he'd like. The MDHS went on to accuse him of failing to comply with discovery requests to turn over all the text messages he exchanged with others in the alleged welfare-fund scam. He also sued fellow retired NFL players Pat McAfee and Shannon Sharpe for defamation over their comments about the allegations against him. He dropped the suit against McAfee in May 2023, and that November a judge dismissed the case against Sharpe.

To compound matters, longtime football fans will recall that this isn't the first time Favre has gotten into trouble because of his text messages. In 2010, his lone season with the New York Jets, sideline reporter Jenn Sterger accused him of sending (two years earlier) inappropriate texts, voicemails, and photos. Favre admitted to sending the voicemails, but not the photos, and was fined $50,000 for not cooperating with the NFL's investigation. Regardless, this established what is now a pattern, one that has the fabled quarterback scrambling to avoid further blemishes to his reputation.

13

TAKING IT TO THE CLEATS: POLITICS AND POLICY

Introduction

Politics have always been a part of sports. Think of the career of baseball great and first Black MLB player Jackie Robinson. Lots of people wish sports could be completely isolated from politics, but this has never been so and never will be.

Sports crisis communicators will have to deal with political situations, protests, and conflicts. They may stem from players, fans, or outsiders, but they will occur. Crisis communications teams must be ready to respond.

Policies should be in place outlining the organization's views on getting involved in politics and responding to political disputes. A policy means knowing what the guardrails are in terms of addressing political (and social) topics. Because of the sensitivities, thought must be given to how the involvement will affect various stakeholders and interest groups. Will the political stances invite strong negative reactions from certain quarters? How is the organization prepared for that?

 Much of this entails being clear on what your positions are and what you will say to defend them. Should the team disagree with, say, statements a player made, but want to defend his or her right to express those opinions? Generally, free speech should be safeguarded, but play interruptions by political protesters don't need to be. These can raise difficult questions for leagues and teams. It's important to discuss these matters, and how to respond, before they arise.

A classic, though recent, example came from NFL pros who protested police brutality and racism by "taking a knee" during the playing of the national anthem before games. Fans were deeply divided over this, and players, teams, and leagues were pressured to either defend it or condemn it. One of the posts here addresses that, especially the spotlight on the NFL itself. While NFL players kneeling hasn't been nearly as prevalent recently, it could easily become popular again as political landscapes shift. Other political issues will crop up as well.

Communicating political topics can be akin to longer-term issues management, but our post on the Los Angeles Dodgers and its plan to honor a controversial gay-rights group shows they can also flare up quickly. As you will read, the team's decision-makers were caught off guard and consequently endured a public-facing dilemma that could have been mitigated with a solidly prepared PR plan addressing the potential pushback.

Another sports-crisis scenario concerns how to deal with political protesters at events, including games. Here we include a post about a protester at a FIFA press conference. Political protests also raise questions of safety. Crisis communications statements should relay what the league or team is doing to ensure all those impacted are safe.

Partisan politics present great difficulty. Firm leaders, including team leaders and others, should be counseled about the damage political diatribes can do to an organization. Statements, including tweets, should be vetted. But the organization must also be prepared for the fallout should the leader just not be able to restrain herself.

More generally, in the freewheeling sports cosmos, communicators have to deal with strong personalities — owners, managers, players — who too often don't think before they spout off. Obviously, the best way to handle that is to have policies in place to prevent the negative event happening in the first place. But communicators can't police the speech of everyone.

Instead, they often have to clean up the mess. That can involve a heart-to-heart with the speaker involved and finding out if that person regrets the statement or stands by it. If regret, an apology will be in order. If he or she is resolute, facts will have to be gathered to defend what was said. Or the organization may decide to distance itself from the utterance.

These are the kinds of challenges and choices crisis communicators often face.

Finally, our post on how Dick's Sporting Goods navigated the restriction of gun sales shows a sports-adjacent company dealing successfully with a difficult political issue. When the decision is reached to take a bold action, the planning must involve careful consideration of how it will be communicated. Criticism is inevitable. Communicators should be prepared to respond to that, too, usually by emphasizing the talking points decided around the issue in advance.

Dealing With, and Preparing for, an Unexpected Protest at a Live Event
First published July 20, 2015

FIFA's crisis-management team must be pretty worn out. Today, FIFA officials held a press conference in Zurich to announce that the election for its next president will take place February 26. But that news got sidelined after a British comedian ran onto the stage and showered current FIFA president Sepp Blatter in fake money. The stunt raises the issue of how to deal with such protests during live events.

Overall, Blatter handled the situation with composure. Once the protester, Simon Brodkin as his character Lee Nelson, was dragged away, the FIFA executive went to the podium to condemn the display as having "nothing to do with football." The press conference then resumed after a brief pause to clean up the fake money.

Today's event brought more negative attention to FIFA, or the Fédération Internationale de Football Association, the soccer governing body that organizes the World Cup. The group was shrouded in scandal in May when several of its officials were arrested in a $150 million corruption prosecution. Blatter has since said he will step down.

Activists and publicity hounds commonly use surprise ambushes and disruptions to promote their causes or themselves. Corporations should have a crisis plan in place to handle such situations.

During an April press conference, Mario Draghi, president of the European Central Bank, was showered in confetti and paper by a protester shouting, "End the ECB dictatorship!" Also in April, protesters invaded an activist-shareholder conference to complain about low pay at fast-food restaurants (though one of their targets, hedge-fund manager Bill Ackman, wasn't on that particular panel).

Crisis communicators should work with company representatives to identify situations that could attract protesters and then practice ways for the representative to manage the negative situation.

The most important thing is to remain calm. Getting riled up will only turn the situation into a bigger story and make you look worse. The more composed you are the better you look in the long run and in news coverage.

Of course, staying calm involves preparation. Giving thought to the possibility of such protests happening is important. It's also essential to know what the security arrangements are for the event.

Humor can be used to redirect attention following an unexpected outburst. Politicians are well known for this tactic. President Obama constantly uses zingers, like his "You're in my house" quip from June when a heckler interrupted him during a speech in the White House. Or when a shoe was thrown at Hillary Clinton during an event in Las Vegas, she laughed it off by asking, "Is that part of Cirque du Soleil? My goodness, I didn't know that solid-waste management was so controversial." The audience laughed and the speech moved on.

Live events, including press conferences and trade shows, are essential for organizations to announce news and to grow their brand. If protesters attempt to hijack them, the best approach is to acknowledge the moment and move on. The goal is to keep people focused on your talk or your news and not on activists trying to make their own headlines.

Postgame

The story lost its legs rather quickly after the surprise brouhaha took place. Unexpected protests at live events are not talked about as much as they should be.

Simon Brodkin, the English standup comedian who threw money at former FIFA President Sepp Blatter, was released from the custody of Swiss authorities. He was charged with trespassing, but wasn't indicted and the charges were dropped.

Brodkin still performs comedy, while Blatter, who finished serving an initial suspension for his involvement in the FIFA corruption scandal, was handed a second ban by the association for financial wrongdoing that will keep him away from professional football until 2027, when he will be 91 years old.

A more recent example of how a live-event interruption can be handled effectively occurred in 2023 when climate-change protesters disrupted the U.S. Open semifinal tennis match between American teen sensation Coco Gauff and Karolína Muchová. Despite the match being delayed for nearly an hour by a protester who'd glued his bare feet to the floor, Gauff regrouped, won the match, and deftly handled questions about the incident in a postmatch press conference. While admitting she wished the protest hadn't happened during her event, she showed empathy by acknowledging the problem of climate change and also pointed out that some tennis tournaments were more actively trying to take measures to help the environment.

NFL Teams' Protest Statements Display a Variety of Response
First published September 28, 2017

Early on in President Trump's administration, we, like many others, commented on the challenge companies and organizations face in having to respond to his wrath — Twitter or otherwise. This past week, it was the National Football League and its teams' turn. The variety of their reactions, as detailed in their statements, is instructive to ponder from a crisis communications point of view.

A handful of players had been kneeling during the national anthem before games to protest police brutality and racism, causing a major backlash. During a rally on Friday, September 22, and in weekend tweets, Trump declared that players who don't stand for the anthem should be fired and that people should walk out of the stadiums over the protests.

This was an assault on the players, the league, and the teams, and it called for a response. That response was reportedly planned (somewhat and hastily), with the NFL as a go-between for the teams to learn what their competitors were doing.

In the end, more than 150 players, coaches, owners, and managers participated on Sunday and Monday by kneeling either before or during the anthem, by standing with locked arms, or by sitting out the song altogether and remaining in the locker room.

NFL spokesman Joe Lockhart said the planning and demonstrations showed that the league, owners, players, and players union could, in *The Washington Post*'s words, "work cooperatively in a crisis." Political commentator Charles Pierce quipped that, with his comments, Trump "managed to unite labor and management in a way once thought unimaginable."

Nearly every team issued a statement (some, such as the Dallas Cowboys, seem to have only commented in press conferences). Some of the responses came as early as the day after Trump's rally, some as late as this Tuesday morning (Pittsburgh Steelers owner Art Rooney II).

What to say posed a challenge because many fans have criticized the protests to the point that they said they have stopped attending or watching the games. And, of course, dealing with Trump is always sensitive; we've written about that before in terms of responding to his tweets and his travel ban. Also, some owners donated to Trump's campaign.

Some statements were direct in their response to the president's comments. Others were more evasive; the owners of the Los Angeles Chargers and the Jacksonville Jaguars said only that they agreed with the statement issued Saturday by NFL Commissioner Roger Goodell, who, without mentioning Trump, said, "Divisive comments like these demonstrate an unfortunate lack of respect for the NFL." (After Sunday's game, Jaguars owner Shad Khan commented more fully.)

Some of the most forceful reactions came early on. "It's unfortunate that the president decided to use his immense platform to make divisive and offensive statements about our players and the NFL," Green Bay Packers CEO Mark Murphy wrote. New York Giants owners John Mara and Steve Tisch: "Comments like we heard last night from the president are inappropriate, offensive, and divisive."

Many teams praised their players and their charitable work, and some said outright that the owners or managers supported their right to free speech. "We respect their demonstration and support them 100 percent," tweeted Baltimore Ravens owner Steve Bisciotti.

"Every day I see the genuine dedication and hard work of our players," said Philadelphia Eagles owner Jeffrey Lurie. "And I support them as they take their courage, character, and commitment into our communities to make them better or to call attention to injustice. Having spoken with our players, I can attest to the great respect they have for our national anthem and all it represents."

Some sought to comment on the situation while barely touching the hot-button issue of the actual protests. The press release issued by New England Patriots Head Coach Bill Belichick (famous for his vagueness) was particularly evasive. None of the team statements mentions the word *racism* or *race*, other than the New Orleans Saints saying the team serves its community "without care of race, creed, or sexual orientation."

Of course, individual players and their union also responded to Trump's attack and much more bluntly than the teams.

Eric Winston, free-agent offensive tackle just released from the Cincinnati Bengals and current president of the NFL Players Association, called Trump's comments "a slap in the face to the civil rights heroes of the past and present, soldiers who have spilled blood in countless wars to uphold the values of this great nation, and American people of all races, ethnicities, genders, and sexual orientations who seek civil progress as a means to make this country, and this world, a better place."

Now, that's a protest.

Postgame

Even after the 2017 kneeling episode, the league was reluctant to speak on the spat between its players and the president. Tensions escalated in June 2020 during the George Floyd protests. New Orleans Saints quarterback Drew Brees reiterated his view that kneeling for the anthem disrespected the American flag. But then he quickly apologized for that statement. Trump would go on to tweet about the situation, insinuating that Brees should not have apologized.

The NFL finally broke its silence over these comments with a speech by Commissioner Roger Goodell, who said, in regard to the league not listening to its players earlier and not encouraging them to peacefully protest, "We were wrong." He added: "I personally protest with you and want to be a part of the much-needed change in this country."

While all the consternation about players kneeling during the national anthem did leave an indelible mark on everyone from both sides of the argument, the passage of time and football fans' lust for the game ultimately restored order. The television ratings for Super Bowl LIX, which took place on February 9, 2025, in New Orleans between the Philadelphia Eagles and Kansas City Chiefs, were historic. The game averaged 127.7 million viewers across television and streaming platforms, making it the most-watched broadcast in the United States since the moon landing in 1969!

CEO Takes Us Behind the Scenes of Gun-Sale Crisis
First published October 17, 2019

Ed Stack, the CEO of Dick's Sporting Goods, has a book out in which he brings us inside the company's decision to severely restrict gun sales — a move that brought upon it, and Stack, a major backlash. He presents useful insight into how a company deals with a crisis.

In *It's How We Play the Game* and a fascinating interview with the *Harvard Business Review*, Stack lays out how Dick's Sporting Goods addressed the communications issues.

The catalysts were the mass shootings at Sandy Hook Elementary School in Newtown, Connecticut, on December 14, 2012, and at Marjory Stoneman Douglas High School in Parkland, Florida, on February 14, 2018.

After Sandy Hook the retailer pulled assault-style weapons from its shelves without much fanfare; it addressed the issue only when it got flak from gun enthusiasts. It continued to sell assault-style weapons in its Field & Stream stores.

The big change came after the Parkland shooting. The company decided to no longer sell assault-style weapons or high-capacity magazines or to anyone under 21 years old, including at Field & Stream. "I felt that we needed to stand up and say something," Stark told *HBR*.

More recently, it's gone further, removing guns altogether from first 10 stores and then 125 (Dick's Sporting Goods has more than 700 locations plus its Gulf & Stream and Golf Galaxy brands). It sold eight Field & Stream stores, which are hunting focused. "We continue to have the whole hunt business under strategic review," Stark told *HBR*.

Stack said his initial preference was to simply release a statement about what Dick's Sporting Goods planned to do after Parkland. His advisors convinced him the issue was bigger than that. One reason he agreed was a lesson he learned from the company's quiet approach after Sandy Hook.

By not speaking out, he writes, "We opened the door to others with their own agendas to interpret our actions to the public. We lost control of our own narrative."

That's a pretty good lesson in crisis communications. So the company came up with a communications plan. On February 28, two weeks after the Parkland shooting, it issued a press release and sent emails to employees, customers, and vendors. Stack also did two TV interviews, with George Stephanopoulos on *Good Morning America* and Chris Cuomo on CNN. Afterward, he got more than 400 interview requests, he writes; he declined all except NBC.

The backlash came soon enough from customers, vendors, and employees (about 65 quit). "We had a number of people who were really upset, who sent emails and letters and phone calls," Stack told *HBR*. "They were pretty descriptive on how they thought about us and about me in particular. What we were surprised about is the outpouring of support that we received from the public about our decision."

Stack is open about the difficulties with vendors. "Our suppliers were not happy with us," he said. "We had a number of pretty spirited conversations with them, and a number of them decided not to do business with us anymore." But the company never caved in to them.

On March 2, Stack tweeted out an acknowledgement to both the company's supporters and critics.

The important point for crisis communicators is that Dick's Sporting Goods prepared for the backlash. It also prepared for the financial hit (and lowered its guidance), which was massive. The damage was pretty close to expectations, according to Stark: at least $250 million. (It cut costs and emphasized areas it had neglected, such as student sports, and was able to then raise its guidance.)

As part of its losses, Dick's Sporting Goods destroyed $5 million worth of rifles.

Postgame

Dick's Sporting Goods continued its promise, removing guns from more than half of its locations. Ed Stack retired as CEO in 2020, but remains executive chairman. His account shows how companies can navigate politically controversial actions. The restricting of gun sales that he implemented, along with a carefully crafted communications strategy and fiscally sound recovery plan, proved to be successful.

Dodgers Try to Dodge a Bullet
First published May 25, 2023

We live in incredibly polarized political times. When pursuing anything that even touches on politics, organizations must proceed with extreme caution — and readiness. The Los Angeles Dodgers baseball team gives us yet another example of an organization not doing that, and then having to reverse course.

Up until May 17, the team planned to bestow its Community Hero Award on the L.A. chapter of a group called the Sisters of Perpetual Indulgence. The pregame ceremony was to take place on the team's annual LGBTQ+ Pride Night on June 16. The sisters, founded in San Francisco in 1979, use street performance and humor, with members wearing garb that includes nuns' habits, to protest bias.

Catholic organizations, including the Catholic League and CatholicVote, objected. U.S. Senator Marco Rubio (R-FL) wrote to Major League Baseball Commissioner Rob Manfred questioning whether the team was being inclusive by "giving an award to a group of gay and transgender drag performers that intentionally mocks and degrades Christians."

On May 17, the Dodgers tweeted that, "given the strong feelings of those who have been offended by the sisters' inclusion in our evening," it would now *not* honor the group.

Naturally, bowing to the backlash caused a backlash. The Los Angeles LGBT Center said the team "caved to a religious minority that is perpetuating a false narrative about L.G.B.T.Q.+ people," and demanded it reinvite the group or cancel the event altogether. LA Pride, organizers of the LA Pride Parade, and the American Civil Liberties Union of Southern California, said they would now not participate in Pride Night.

The New York Times' Scott Miller wrote on May 18 that the force of the blowback caught the Dodgers "off guard," and that it was "working internally on potential compromise solutions."

Why the team was caught off guard is a mystery. States are passing anti-drag legislation. The team had the recent example of Bud Light, which still finds itself embroiled — and experiencing sales declines — after it had trans activist and social-media influencer Dylan Mulvaney do an Instagram promotional spot. Again, any politically controversial move will make one constituency or another unhappy.

On Monday this week, we got the results of the internal machinations. The Dodgers, "after much thoughtful feedback from our diverse communities," announced it had apologized to the sisters and reinvited the group to the event. The sisters accepted. The team said it viewed the incident as a learning experience, that it would "continue to work with our LGBTQ+ partners to better educate ourselves."

The team deleted the tweet in which it originally announced it was rescinding the invitation.

Postgame

Protesters gathered outside Dodger Stadium on June 16 to object to the Sisters of Perpetual Indulgence receiving their Community Hero Award, which they did before the game "with few fans yet in their seats," according to NBC News. The protesters held "stop anti-Catholic hate" and "God will not be mocked" signs, but the demonstration resulted in no disturbances or arrests, NBC said.

Sports today have no shortage of examples that speak to legendary UCLA basketball coach John Wooden's famous quote, "Failing to prepare is preparing to fail." The Los Angeles Dodgers were no exception when they were caught off guard by uproar from both sides of a thorny issue.

Pride Night celebrations at arenas and stadiums across the country have become somewhat routine over the past few years, but the Dodgers underestimated the polarizing nature of a group they invited to the 2023 edition of their LGBTQ+ fete. Given the heightened political climate we live in, that's not entirely surprising. What *is* surprising is how unprepared the Dodgers were for the unintended consequences that arose from the religious right. The team really didn't seem prepared to defend its decision.

14

ORGANIZATIONAL CULTURE: SEXISM, RACISM, AND HOMOPHOBIA

Introduction

People don't often remember this, but a sports organization is a workplace. Teams and leagues need to follow the same rules as other companies and organizations. That includes creating a safe work environment and not engaging in discrimination. This goes for whether we're talking about the players on the field or the workers in the front or back office. This chapter highlights posts we've done on sex, race, and sexual-orientation discrimination.

While sports are rightfully lauded for bringing people of all walks of life together, these biases still exist in both the professional and collegiate ranks. Prejudiced views and stereotypes are often still applied with regard to personnel decisions for coaches and players alike.

Sexism is a huge problem in sports. As women become more involved, whether as players, executives, or sideline reporters, men still in thrall of the old-time sports-bro ethos find their views increasingly challenged.

Sexism in sports is expressed in various ways, from belittling the contributions of women to out-and-out bias in terms of hiring, promoting, or firing. One example is the pay dispute in U.S. women's soccer (see chapter 12 on lawsuits).

Sexual harassment, a type of sex discrimination, is also unfortunately rampant in professional sports. Teams and leagues are often accused, and rightfully so, of not taking sex harassment seriously enough. This is especially true in the NFL (see the post in this chapter on the Washington football team now known as the Commanders). Sports organizations must institute policies against sex bias, including sex harassment, and communicate those policies to internal and external audiences. The public and fans need to know that the leagues, teams, and players are sincere.

As noted in a post below, we found that the Dallas Mavericks responded admirably to a sex-harassment scandal in 2019. Yet (as we note in the update after the post) it did a less-stellar job responding to a later incident. The New York Mets provided another positive case, and we have a post on that. The Mets episode underscores the importance of showing that you're taking action in answer to a negative situation.

The Astros post emphasizes another crisis communications lesson: the importance of gathering information at the start of a crisis and not using information unless you're sure it's accurate. Rather than speculate, it's better to issue a more general comment and note that you'll speak further when more is known.

Alas, it's not uncommon for organizations to have to release follow-up statements fixing earlier misinformation. This harms the organization's credibility and reputation. That's the exact opposite of what crisis communicators want to accomplish. And sports fans aren't known for their shyness in criticizing players, teams, and leagues.

Unfortunately, racism also has long been a problem in professional and collegiate sports. As conveyed in the post on Robert Sarver, then-owner of the Phoenix Suns and Phoenix Mercury, accusations of racism (and other infractions) often spur internal investigations by outside law firms. Communicators should be prepared to speak out when the initial complaints are lodged (or news articles published) and when the report is issued. These situations are often ugly to confront, but that's why it's called "crisis" communications.

The best approach is to be prepared for such negative events, to admit wrongdoing when in the wrong, to defend oneself when in the right, and to keep your stakeholders informed of what's going on.

It was interesting to see affected organizations in the Sarver situation respond appropriately to the release of the internal report (prepared by a law firm) into his workplace behavior. All organizations should be aware that audiences, including sports fans, will expect them to speak out. Still, other observers — including NBA players LeBron James and Chris Paul — continued to criticize Sarver's punishment as too lenient.

Another post here concerning a team leader centers on Bob Huggins, the legendary men's basketball coach at West Virginia University. This is another instance of a sports organization being blinded by a star's fame and prowess (in this case, a star coach). Leagues, teams, and college athletic departments are too often reluctant to speak out against, contradict, or discipline someone seen as essential for their success.

In the long run, concern for reputation is more important. A communicator should be one person at the table arguing for the organization's long-term interest, including its reputation. How these negative situations are communicated is essential to that.

Another post, on European soccer, raises a sticky issue for sports crisis communicators: how to deal with bad behavior from fans. Obviously, racism and other "isms" are not to be tolerated. But a team's fans are an important stakeholder group (maybe *the* important stakeholder group). Any messaging criticizing them must be done with care. That means paying close attention to the wording used. For example, it can make sense to point out that only a small minority in the stands were involved in the bad behavior.

In any event, this is why it's so important to plan for, and to draft statements ahead of, crises your organization is likely to experience. You have time to think carefully about what you would say and how you would say it. Yes, when the actual crisis unfortunately hits, the language will have to be tweaked to address the specifics. But by having the draft statements at the ready, you're starting out on third base (okay, maybe second base). Or to use a soccer analogy, it's like having a player with a fresh set of legs ready to come in off the bench.

The blog posts on "Huggy Bear" and Red Sox player Jarren Duran highlight that homophobia is also a problem in sports (see also our post on the L.A. Dodgers and the Sisters of Perpetual Indulgence in chapter 13 on politics). But we also have a happier post on the coming out of pro football player Carl Nassib, which really became a nonstory.

Mavericks Tried to Move the Ball Forward With Sex-Scandal Response
First published January 10, 2019

Bloomberg Businessweek recently ran an article on the Dallas Mavericks basketball team's sex-harassment scandal last year. The piece highlighted an essential element of crisis response: action. You have to show your constituencies you're *doing something* to respond to the crisis.

The Mavericks' situation began in February when *Sports Illustrated* published a story alleging the team's corporate office had a culture that ignored sex harassment.

The Mavs got in front of that, putting out a statement before the piece was published on February 20. It said such behavior violated its policies, that it only learned of the behavior in the previous few days, and that the main person accused had left the company three years before.

It said it would increase its training. Most importantly, it hired outside counsel to conduct an investigation into both the individual and its wider culture. The Mavericks also said it fired another employee involved in a domestic-violence incident he hadn't disclosed.

One negative: The team's statement didn't name either employee. The first was former CEO Terdema Ussery — hardly a minor "player." The team had investigated allegations against Ussery as far back as 1998, according to *Sports Illustrated*.

Less than a week after the *Sports Illustrated* story appeared, the Mavs announced it hired a new CEO, Cynthia "Cynt" Marshall, who had been chief diversity officer at AT&T.

The December 20 *Bloomberg Businessweek* article was a (sort of) profile of Marshall. It noted that some people were skeptical about hiring an African American woman for the job. "Whether [owner Mark] Cuban's motives were cynical or not, the optics of a very public white male billionaire asking a woman of color to clean up his mess aren't great," the magazine wrote.

On May 3, Marshall gave an update on her "100-day plan" to improve the team's culture, and on July 12 the team announced it was establishing an advisory council for its diversity and inclusion efforts. The council is co-chaired by Dallas ex-Chief of Police David Brown and includes a wide variety of community leaders. A Mavericks fan named Meegan Trotter is also on it — because she wrote to Cuban complaining about the team's reputational crisis. Nice move.

Marshall brought in counselors for employees, opened a hotline for reporting incidents, and hired new employees, including a new compliance officer. Add this to the other things — hiring Marshall in the first place, creating the 100-day plan, launching the independent investigation, and establishing the advisory board — and all this shows a lot of action.

Do such maneuvers — especially the advisory board — meet with distrust from some quarters? Sure. But, as the Bible says, the critics you will always have with you. When confronted with a crisis, you have to show you're *doing something.*

The lawyers the Mavs hired for the probe (who interviewed 215 current and former employees) put out their report in September. It was a bombshell, with tales of harassment winked at by management. No company relishes a report whose table of contents includes the entry "The Condom Incident."

The document's 13 recommendations were fairly typical for such things (better incident-reporting procedures, better training), though one suggestion was focused heavily on Cuban, who was accused with Ussery of protecting and even encouraging perpetrators (Cuban himself was not accused of harassing anyone).

Bloomberg says that the recommendations overlapped with Marshall's 100-day plan and that NBA Commissioner Adam Silver told his board of governors all teams should follow the suggestions.

That shows the Mavericks are moving the ball forward toward making a difference.

Postgame

With all its activity, the Mavericks organization seemed to be moving in the right direction when, in September 2019, it was slammed with yet another allegation of inappropriate behavior. The team's director of player personnel, Tony Ronzone, was accused of sexual assault by a woman who wasn't a Mavericks employee. The alleged incident took place inside a Las Vegas hotel room that July during the NBA Summer League. Team owner Mark Cuban said he didn't learn of the situation until two months later. The HR department was notified shortly after, yet Ronzone wasn't disciplined in the following months. It wasn't until 2021, when the Mavericks alleged, according to media reports, they learned of "new information," that he was fired for his alleged actions back in 2019.

In March 2022, yet another incident of a sexual nature was alleged against the organization in a lawsuit filed by former GM Donnie Nelson, who claimed he was fired for reporting to the team that his nephew had been sexually assaulted and sexually harassed by a Mavericks employee in 2020. Nelson and the Mavericks settled the litigation in October 2024. Terms weren't disclosed.

Astros Whiff in Responding to Exec's Tirade
First published October 31, 2019

For any organization, there is of course never a good time for a crisis to erupt. But if you're a Major League Baseball franchise, the absolute worst time would be right before your team is about to begin play in the World Series. This is precisely the predicament the Houston Astros found themselves in almost two weeks ago.

Here's a timeline of what happened, with an emphasis on the mistakes the team made, which should be lessons for all crisis communicators.

Saturday, October 19

The Astros became the American League champs by eliminating the Yankees. In the postgame celebration that ensued in the clubhouse, Assistant General Manager Brandon Taubman yelled the following, several times, in the direction of three female reporters: "Thank God we got Osuna! I'm so [expletive] glad we got Osuna!" The Astros acquired pitcher Roberto Osuna last year while he was serving a 75-game suspension for violating MLB's domestic-violence policy.

Monday, October 21

One of the reporters who was the target of Taubman's vitriol, *Sports Illustrated*'s Stephanie Apstein, wrote an article about this incident. *Sports Illustrated* gave the Astros the opportunity to comment before it published the story, but the team declined. This ill-advised decision set off a sequence of poorly handled communications between the Astros' PR staff and the media.

Instead of a "no comment," the Astros should have told *SI* words to the effect of, "We take accusations like this very seriously and are currently looking further into the matter." Instead, the team issued its own statement later in the day calling the article "misleading and completely irresponsible" and accused Apstein of attempting to "fabricate a story."

It seems that, despite more than a few witnesses who corroborated Apstein's assertions, Taubman convinced Astros upper management that he was only supporting a player and that his comments "were also not directed toward any specific reporters."

Tuesday, October 22

Sports Illustrated stood behind its story and issued its own unwavering statement, at which time Taubman acknowledged his comments were "unprofessional and inappropriate." Though this seemed like a step in the right direction, he actually doubled down by adding that his comments were misinterpreted. MLB said it would investigate the incident.

Wednesday, October 23

In his first public comments on the situation, Astros General Manager Jeff Luhnow claimed that "we may never know" Taubman's intent, thereby attempting to reduce it to a he-said-she-said matter.

Thursday, October 24

Despite saying the day before he would "withhold further comment" until MLB concluded its probe, Luhnow announced that Taubman was fired. The Astros also apologized to Apstein, whom, just three days earlier, they falsely accused of fabricating the story.

This sudden turnaround of course raises the question: *Where did the Astros go wrong with their initial public statement?*

Luhnow acknowledged what was already painfully obvious — the team responded with a classic knee-jerk reaction and had not conducted a proper investigation. Instead of thoroughly examining what transpired that night, the Astros only heard Taubman's version of the facts as well as only one other witness who was also a team employee. Luhnow appropriately refused to say who in the organization wrote the original statement, but did admit that he saw it before it was released.

Though the Astros' desire to clear this matter up quickly was understandable, their rush to judgment was inexcusable and costly. The franchise will likely have to re-answer questions of why they signed Osuna in the first place. MLB Commissioner Rob Manfred said his office is now investigating because of concerns regarding the Astros' initial statement that accused *Sports Illustrated* of making the whole thing up.

When issues like these arise in your organization, always keep in mind that, while responding *quickly* is important, it's not more important than responding *correctly*.

Postgame

On January 13, 2020, after the incident recounted here, Brandon Taubman was placed on MLB's ineligible list. After the conclusion of the 2020 MLB season, the former Houston Astros assistant general manager applied for reinstatement, which was accepted, although

Taubman hasn't expressed interest in returning to baseball. One reason MLB gave for the acceptance was that it didn't find he participated in the team's sign-stealing scandal. It also said Taubman atoned for his actions with the female reporter as well as volunteered at a domestic-abuse center and attended therapy. There's a lesson: Taking action like that goes a long way toward repairing a reputation. As of 2022, Taubman was reportedly working as a chief information officer for a Houston-based real-estate company.

Washington NFL Team Confronts Harassment Claims
First published July 23, 2020

Amid the crisis over its name change, the Washington, D.C., NFL team formerly known as the Redskins is facing sex-harassment accusations similar to those made in 2018 against the NBA's Dallas Mavericks. The D.C. team's response has been lackluster and missing some important elements.

On July 16, *The Washington Post* reported that 15 women who formerly worked for the team said they were sexually harassed during their employment. All but one spoke on condition of anonymity, citing nondisclosure agreements they signed. The *Post* said the team declined to release them from those pacts so they could speak freely (a mistake in this day and age).

Owner Dan Snyder, who is not implicated in the behavior, refused to speak for the story. The team provided a statement to the *Post* in which it said it hired D.C. attorney Beth Wilkinson and her firm, Wilkinson Walsh, to conduct an independent investigation into the allegations. "The Washington Redskins football team takes issues of employee conduct seriously," the team said, according to the *Post*.

On July 17, Snyder put out a statement of his own. As commenters noted, he didn't say much. "The behavior described in yesterday's *Washington Post* article has no place in our franchise or society," he wrote. "This story has strengthened my commitment to setting a new culture and standard for our team."

Snyder said that on completion of the independent investigation, the team would implement changes suggested by Wilkinson. This was a mistake. Shortcomings in the team's operations are apparent — including allegedly a too-small human-resources department. Snyder should address these problems now, in part so that when the law firm's recommendations are announced, he can point out that many of them have already been implemented.

Snyder and his wife reportedly also wrote a memo to team employees.

The NFL issued its own statement on July 17. "These matters as reported are serious, disturbing, and contrary to the NFL's values," it wrote. "Everyone in the NFL has the right to work in an environment free from any and all forms of harassment." It said it would decide whether to take any action after the internal review is completed.

Snyder is certainly coming under fire. Two recent headlines: "Dan Snyder Still Doesn't Get It" and "It's Time for Incompetent Dan Snyder to Sell the Washington NFL Franchise."

Snyder received unsolicited advice from billionaire Mark Cuban, owner of the Mavericks, which had its own sex-harassment crisis after a 2018 *Sports Illustrated* exposé. (For comparison, the Dallas team released a statement on the matter before the *SI* piece even came out.)

Cuban said on SiriusXM Radio that Snyder must come out now to recognize, and apologize for, mistakes he's made, according to a July 19 *New York Post* story. "That's painful," Cuban said. "I made a lot of mistakes. And that's the only way this is going to get resolved."

Cuban, who said he cried when *Sports Illustrated* published its story, gave $10 million to women's groups and apologized publicly (the NBA didn't punish Cuban but said he should have paid more attention to his team's culture, according to the *New York Post*).

The sex-harassment crisis comes on the heels of the Washington team dealing with its name change. After many years of criticism from Native Americans and others, the team announced on July 13 it would retire the Redskins name and logo.

It has yet to choose a new moniker.

Postgame

Shortly after the Washington Football Team, now the Washington Commanders, began its investigation into the harassment claims, the NFL took over the probe. On July 1, 2021, the league released a brief summary of its findings, which included instances of bullying and intimidation and an overall lack of respect for women in a workplace that was deemed "highly unprofessional." The ownership and members of the front office were found to have not paid attention to the negative environment. The team was ultimately fined $10 million.

The investigation never produced a written report. Asked why the findings weren't publicly released, NFL Commissioner Roger Goodell said the league wanted to withhold the names of the women who had come forward. Many people felt a report still should have been issued, and, frankly, not doing so displayed a lack of transparency (a lack that is not good when responding to a crisis). In December 2022, a congressional committee put out its own report saying the NFL "buried" the one lawyer Beth Wilkinson had done.

That same year, the league had appointed former U.S. Attorney Mary Jo White to conduct yet another investigation into the Washington team's conduct. It released White's 23-page report in July 2023, and fined owner Dan Snyder $60 million for the improprieties concerning the team's workplace culture. Those actions were preceded the same day by NFL team owners approving Snyder's sale of the Washington squad for more than $6 billion.

(See chapter 18 for Andrew Brandt's discussion of the Washington Commanders probes.)

The Mets Connect on Crisis Response
First published January 21, 2021

The New York Mets on Tuesday fired its new general manager after ESPN reported he had sent harassing texts and lewd photos to a female journalist. It's a good example of an organization responding quickly — though not perfectly — to a crisis.

The Mets hired Jared Porter as GM only last month. A major theme of the story is that it needs to improve its vetting process. Another is that this happened as the team — under new ownership — is trying to move beyond missteps of the past.

ESPN published its story Monday night. It relates accusations against Porter for what he did in 2016 when he was with the Chicago Cubs. Mets President Sandy Alderson gave a statement to ESPN in which he said he was first hearing of the accusations. He had spoken to Porter and was reviewing the facts.

"Jared has acknowledged to me his serious error in judgment, has taken responsibility for his conduct, has expressed remorse, and has previously apologized for his actions," Alderson wrote. "The Mets take these matters seriously, expect professional and ethical behavior from all of our employees, and certainly do not condone the conduct described in your story."

The Awful Announcing sports blog criticized this statement as falling short and the team for sending the same comment to other media after the story came out. The *New York Post* called the statement "a little lame." But this seems unfair; the team acknowledged what it knew and said it was investigating further. Can you imagine if it refused to comment to ESPN? It is true, though, that it should have tailored an updated statement for the other media.

By Tuesday morning the team decided to fire Porter, which was a laudably quick crisis reaction. "We have terminated Jared Porter this morning," new Mets owner Steven Cohen tweeted at 7:55 a.m. ET. "In my initial press conference I spoke about the importance of integrity and I meant it. There should be zero tolerance for this type of behavior."

Alderson, the team president, held a press conference on Tuesday in which he discussed the original statement and the firing decision. "The statement that we sent out last night was crafted largely before we had a chance really to read the story," he said. "At about 7:30 this morning, Steven Cohen and I had a conversation at which we agreed that the only course of action here was to terminate Jared, which was done in the next 45 minutes."

According to Awful Announcing, Alderson also disclosed identifying information — since scrubbed from the video — about the accuser, who is anonymous. That was a throwing error.

We have another recent, less noticed, example from the sports world of a company reacting to a sensitive crisis. Ralph Lauren Corp. announced it was ending its sponsorship of golf pro Justin Thomas after he responded to a missed putt by uttering a homophobic slur.

Although Thomas quickly apologized, the fashion company acted and put out a strong statement. "We believe in the dignity of all people, regardless of age, race, gender identity, ethnicity, political affiliation, or sexual orientation," it wrote.

The Associated Press pointed out that last year Ralph Lauren was designated by the Human Rights Campaign as the "Best Place to Work for LGBTQ Equality."

Clearly, companies and organizations are becoming more sensitive to incidents like these. Crisis communicators should take heed.

Postgame

In June 2021 after an investigation, MLB placed former Mets General Manager Jared Porter on the ineligible list, with the ban continuing at least through the 2022 season, due to his behavior with the female reporter. While Porter has largely faded from the scene, the episode is another reminder of the problem professional sports have with misogyny and harassment of women. Still, it showed that even a big, high-profile organization like the New York Mets can respond quickly and agilely to a crisis. It's an example to emulate.

On the Noncrisis of Carl Nassib's Announcement
First published June 24, 2021

If a big goal of crisis management is to avoid a crisis — and it is — then it's fitting to celebrate such successes, especially when they come about at least partly because of deft communications. Las Vegas

Raiders defensive end Carl Nassib's announcement that he's gay — the first active NFL player to come out — is such a case.

Nassib's Instagram announcement Monday, June 21, was low key. "I just wanted to take a quick moment to say that I'm gay," he said. Nassib added that he hoped for the day when this wouldn't be noteworthy and also that he was giving $100,000 to The Trevor Project, which seeks to prevent LGBTQ+ youth suicide.

Responses from those concerned made it a noncrisis — we might have had a different outcome only a few years ago.

"I was proud of Carl when he led the nation in sacks, but I'm even more proud of him now," James Franklin, Nassib's coach at Penn State, tweeted. The Raiders said, simply, "Proud of you, Carl." The NFL tweeted similarly, "The NFL family is proud of you, Carl."

NFL Commissioner Roger Goodell issued a brief statement that echoed Nassib's own: "The NFL family is proud of Carl for courageously sharing his truth today. Representation matters. We share his hope that someday soon statements like his will no longer be newsworthy as we march toward full equality for the LGBTQ+ community. We wish Carl the best of luck this coming season."

Compare this to just a few years ago, in 2014, when Michael Sam was the first openly gay player to be drafted into the NFL. He ended up never playing during a regular season, and whether his disclosure had to do with that is controversial; it was still a year before the U.S. Supreme Court ruled that gay marriage was legal.

This week, Sam himself put out a congratulatory tweet about Nassib's news. "Carl Nassib thank you for owning your truth and especially your donation to the @TrevorProject," he wrote.

It wasn't all happy news. Joy Behar was roundly criticized for a homophobic joke about Nassib's announcement she told on *The View*.

But, other than that, something that would have been seen as a potentially sticky situation just a few years ago came off as a nonevent — or even a cause for celebration. The NFL itself may have helped: Just last year it released a PSA called "National Coming Out Day PSA" in which both "out" former players and current stars encouraged current LGBTQ+ players to not hide their orientation.

Another sign of change: In the 24 hours after Nassib's Instagram video, his was the best-selling jersey on the Fanatics e-commerce site.

Happy Pride Month!

Postgame

Pro football player Carl Nassib's announcement that he's gay turned out to be a big nothing. It shows how much times have changed. But that didn't mean it wasn't a communications issue for his then team, the Las Vegas Raiders, and the NFL, among others. After all, there are football fans who, for religious reasons or otherwise, oppose homosexuality. All in all, the communications were handled well.

In this post from 2021, we noted that Nassib's announcement may have met with more opposition had it been made a few years earlier. Since then, we've seen renewed attacks on gay rights and on LGBTQ+ rights more generally. All sports organizations and participants must be prepared to respond to such attacks when they are affected by them. That goes for other social issues such as racism and sexism.

In 2022, Nassib returned to his previous team, the Tampa Bay Buccaneers, before retiring in September 2023. After seven seasons in the NFL, Nassib said he wanted to focus on his company, Rayze. On its website, the outfit describes itself as a "mobile platform that uses positive social media to simplify the way we give back in the form of volunteering and donations." A fitting mission statement for a man who inspired so many by publicly acknowledging he's a gay professional athlete playing in the most rugged and popular sport in the U.S.

Ugly Soccer Racism Gives Rise to Attractive Crisis Statements
First published July 15, 2021

Adding to the anguish of England losing the final of the European soccer championship Sunday was the racism spewed on the three Black players who missed their penalty kicks. If there's any consolation in the situation, it's the quick slew of statements from politicos and others who condemned the ugliness.

The fervor around the match was understandable. England hadn't made it to the final of a major tournament in 55 years, according to *The New York Times*. So the loss was agonizing. But the bile aimed on the three young players through social media was vile.

Yet the responses came fast, furious, and strong. It's both a crisis communications lesson and an indicator that, more than ever, this discrimination won't be tolerated. Corporate communicators would be well advised to take note of the prompt action.

"We could not be clearer that anyone behind such disgusting behaviour is not welcome in following the team," tweeted the Football Association, governing body of English football. Prince William, president of the association, also spoke out. "It is totally unacceptable that players have to endure this abhorrent behaviour," he tweeted. The Union of European Football Associations weighed in.

Prime Minister Boris Johnson was also angered. "This England team deserve to be lauded as heroes, not racially abused on social media," he wrote. "Those responsible for this appalling abuse should be ashamed of themselves." (He and Home Secretary Priti Patel were criticized for their statements because of their previous equivocal messages regarding those who boo players taking a knee to protest racism.)

London Mayor Sadiq Khan went further, demanding the platform companies take action (creating a crisis for Facebook and Twitter). "Those responsible for the disgusting online abuse we have seen must be held accountable — and social-media companies need to act immediately to remove and prevent this hate," he wrote.

Others also called for such action, including Arsenal, for whom one of the three targeted national-team athletes, 19-year-old Bukayo Saka, plays. (Four people have been arrested for the abuse, the BBC reported today.)

Perhaps most poignant were the heartfelt words of England Manager Gareth Southgate at a press conference. "They should be, and I think they are, incredibly proud of what they've done," he said of the team. "For some of them to be abused is unforgivable really."

Many U.K. papers ran a photo of Southgate consoling Saka after he missed his kick.

Postgame

In August 2021, the Metropolitan Police in the U.K. — which faced its own accusations of racism in how it dealt with crowds outside the stadium — announced it had arrested 11 people in connection with the online racism. Twitter said it removed 2,087 racist tweets concerning the final, the vast majority of which came from U.K. accounts.

While efforts such as this have begun to curtail racism in European soccer, more recent events have proven there's still a ways to go.

In 2023, one of the world's brightest young footballers, Brazilian Vinícius Júnior, who plays for one the most successful clubs in Europe, Real Madrid, was the target of racist taunts spewed by rival fans. Júnior called out La Liga, Spain's top men's professional football division, for not doing enough to curtail racism in what he called "a country of racists."

Júnior received a significant amount of high-power support from other star players, politicians, and soccer officials, but league president Javier Tebas opted to go on the defensive and accused the player of attacking the league without fully understanding what it had been doing to combat racism. The approach didn't go over well.

Sarver Suspension Sires Sober Statements
First published September 15, 2022

The responses by interested parties to the National Basketball Association's one-year suspension of Robert Sarver, owner of the Phoenix Suns and Phoenix Mercury, are notable for their seriousness about the serious situation. Sarver was suspended on Tuesday, and also fined $10 million for his alleged workplace behavior.

The story broke in 2021 when ESPN did an exposé. At the time,

Sarver denied wrongdoing. "I categorically deny any and all suggestions that I used disparaging language related to race or gender," he said.

The NBA hired New York law firm Wachtell, Lipton, Rosen & Katz to conduct an internal investigation. After interviewing more than 300 people, the firm wrote up a 43-page report, which the league released Tuesday, saying Sarver "engaged in conduct that clearly violated common workplace standards."

In addition to general yelling and bullying, Sarver was found to have used sex-related comments in addition to a racial epithet at least five times "when recounting the statement of others." He also treated female workers unequally and exposed his genitals to male employees, according to the report.

"Regardless of position, power, or intent, we all need to recognize the corrosive and hurtful impact of racially insensitive and demeaning language and behavior," NBA Commissioner Adam Silver said in the statement announcing the actions.

The report said the Suns' HR department was ineffective; employees didn't feel comfortable reporting misbehavior (it also found misconduct by other Suns workers). This is an important warning to people working in crisis response and communications: Systems must be in place to prevent crises from spiraling out of control.

In its comments, the Suns took the recommended approach in such situations and focused on changes already made. "The NBA's findings concerning the organization focus, for the most part, on historical matters that have been addressed in recent years, including through meaningful enhancements to our workplace compliance program," it said.

Sarver's tone with regard to Tuesday's announcement was quite different from last year. "While I disagree with some of the particulars of the NBA's report, I would like to apologize for my words and actions that offended our employees," he said, according to ESPN. "I am sorry for causing this pain, and these errors in judgment are not consistent with my personal philosophy or my values."

Although the fine of $10 million is the maximum allowed, not everyone was happy with the outcome (a bit of backlash has begun).

"It's barely a slap on the wrist and shows us the league truly doesn't stand for diversity, equity, or inclusion," a former staffer who spoke to ESPN for the 2021 story told the sports publication.

Postgame

The same month the report was released, Robert Sarver announced he would sell both teams. The following December, billionaire Mat Ishbia, CEO of United Wholesale Mortgage and a former walk-on basketball player at Michigan State University, agreed to buy majority stakes (including all of Sarver's) in the teams for a record $4 billion.

As for Sarver, the NBA said his one-year suspension would remain in place until September 2023, though he disputed that was possible given that he was no longer an owner. On his way out the door, he reportedly attempted to make a kind of financial amends by giving a $20,000 individual bonus to a few hundred team employees. It was also reported that he would donate $5 million to the team's charity — moves that at least demonstrate a certain amount of willingness to help restore his tattered reputation.

Huggy Bear's Slur Puts WVU in a Tough Spot
First published May 18, 2023

Bob Huggins, the men's basketball coach at West Virginia University, did a radio interview during which he used an anti-gay slur and also managed to disparage Catholics. This put the school in a difficult position. We think it ultimately handled the situation well, though others disagree.

WVU issued a brief statement that same day, May 8, saying Huggins' remarks were "insensitive, offensive, and do not represent our university values." It said the school and its athletics department would review and address the incident.

Huggins, 69, also issued an apology the same day for his "completely insensitive and abhorrent phrase." He wrote: "As I have shared with my players over my 40 years of coaching, there are consequences for our words and actions, and I will fully accept any coming my way."

The school, in Morgantown, had a dilemma as to what to do. Huggins, who's coached the West Virginia Mountaineers since 2007, is a beloved local figure — he's nicknamed "Huggy Bear." At the same time, it's not unusual for someone to be fired for a foul such as this, and debate arose about whether he should be. Morgantown Pride, a local LGBTQ+ group, called for him to be let go.

There were other complications. Huggins' rep isn't pristine. In 2005, he unceremoniously left his coaching gig at the University of Cincinnati partly due to his DUI arrest. In 2020 he had former Cincinnati Reds announcer Thom Brennaman — who had been fired for using the same anti-gay slur — speak to the WVU team about accountability. Some said Huggins didn't learn from Brennaman's bad example.

What to do? What to do?

WVU's full response came two days later, on May 10. It put out a long statement saying what actions the school would take. And it was a lot. Huggins' annual salary will be reduced from about $4 million to about $3 million and his contract will now be year-to-year rather than multiyear. The saved money will support LGBTQ+ and other marginalized communities. A three-game suspension was imposed. And Huggy Bear will undergo sensitivity training.

The school also informed him that any similar future incident will result in his firing.

Some people think the punishment is too lenient. One benefactor has said he will switch his donations from the athletics program to the school itself. But, in this age of cancel culture, we think WVU took the situation seriously and imposed heavy corrective measures. Huggins has to know he must now be on his best behavior.

The incident shows the difficulty of deciding how to respond to a blow to one's reputation. But it doesn't always require the ultimate punishment.

Postgame

Only a few coaches in the history of American college sports have risen to the level of deity that Bob Huggins did at West Virginia University. Nobody breathed the rarefied air of Mountaineer basketball quite like Huggins. He had as much leeway as just about any big-time coach could in being able to withstand self-inflicted controversy.

But three such episodes in the space of two months ended up being a different story.

Huggins proved he had enough clout and was beloved enough to keep his job after making anti-gay and anti-Catholic remarks on a radio show. But before his team, or his reputation, had a chance to re-bound, he was *again* arrested for driving under the influence, in June 2023. This appeared to be just the type of "similar future incident" WVU referred to earlier in the year. At this point, it looked like even Huggins knew it was time to move on. A statement attributed to him announcing his resignation was released the next day.

About two weeks later, with the last remnants of Huggins' reputation dwindling away, his lawyer sent a letter to the university contending that his client "never communicated his resignation" to anyone at WVU; he said the university wrongfully relied on a text sent by Huggins' wife to conclude that he quit. This was nearly a month after the letter of his resignation was widely reported. The university emphatically disputed this and reiterated that it had moved on and that there was no chance for a reunion with Huggins.

Jarren Duran Shows Apologizing Isn't That Hard to Do
First published August 15, 2024

During a tense moment of play, Red Sox All-Star outfielder Jarren Duran called a fan a homophobic slur. He quickly apologized in a pos-itive way that makes us wonder why so many people find this so hard to do in a crisis. We say this even though Duran's effort didn't prevent him from being punished.

It was Sunday, August 11, and the Red Sox were playing a home game against the Houston Astros. The Sox were down 10 runs in the bottom of the sixth inning. Duran was at bat. In came a 94-mile-an-hour cutter that he swung at and missed.

A fan, hoping to provide helpful advice to Duran, yelled out that, instead of a baseball bat, he needed a tennis racket. The batter apparently didn't appreciate the advice, and responded by telling the fan to shut up, using both an expletive and the aforementioned homophobic slur.

According to *Sports Illustrated*'s account, Duran didn't utter this loudly, but it was picked up by the TV microphones. So, a hot-mic situation. Awful Announcing's X account has a clip of it, including the offensive language — you've been warned.

About five hours after the game ended, 27-year-old Duran released an apology. It's worth quoting in full because it's a good example of an apology made without excuses.

"During tonight's game, I used a truly horrific word when responding to a fan," Duran wrote. "I feel awful knowing how many people I offended and disappointed. I apologize to the entire Red Sox organization, but more importantly to the entire LGBTQ community. Our young fans are supposed to be able to look up to me as a role model, but tonight I fell far short of that responsibility. I will use this opportunity to educate myself and my teammates and to grow as a person."

It's hard to find fault with that apology. It names the offense and apologizes to the right people. Yes, the "grow as a person" bit is a cliché, but it indicates he wants to try to avoid a repeat performance, which is important in these apologies. The only thing he didn't do was offer some recompense, such as to a charity.

The Red Sox released its own statement and apology, noting the team had "addressed this incident with Jarren immediately following today's game." Apparently, that wasn't enough. On Monday, it suspended him for two games without pay and said it would donate the saved salary to PFLAG (Federation of Parents and Friends of Lesbians and Gays). There's that recompense.

The Red Sox scrambled to determine its crisis response, already working on it by the end of the game, according to MassLive's Chris Cotillo. The effort included calls with Duran's camp and MLB officials. When the player met with journalists on Monday and apologized again, "Red Sox President Sam Kennedy and Chief Baseball Officer Craig Breslow lingered a few feet behind the scrum of reporters," Chelsea Janes wrote in *The Washington Post*. The high officials' involvement shows the team took the matter seriously.

Alas, Duran appeared before the press throng wearing his unofficial "uniform" for this season: a T-shirt bearing the words "[Expletive] 'em." Some suggest his sartorial choice at this time puts into question his sincerity.

Postgame

More light was shed on Jarren Duran's situation in April 2025 when he revealed the extent of his mental-health struggles. On a Netflix documentary series that followed the Red Sox, Duran said that at the lowest point of his up-and-down career, he attempted suicide. He said he took the failed attempt "as a sign I might have to be here for a reason." The 2024 season was in fact his best, and Duran's decision to share his struggles seems to be an indication that he is now in a better place.

Duran also conveyed the meaning behind his colorful turn of phrase: "On [the tape on] my left wrist, I write '[Expletive] 'em' because it's me telling my demons, 'You're not going to faze me.' And on my right wrist, I write 'Still alive' because I'm still here and I'm still fighting."

PART THREE:

COLOR COMMENTARY

INTRODUCTION

The summer of 2020 was a time most of us would like to forget. While the world was experiencing unprecedented lockdowns and limitations on everyday activities due to the COVID-19 pandemic, it became necessary for businesses to get creative and find new ways to not only operate, but to market themselves to remain relevant.

It was in this atmosphere that the *Crisis Communications in Sports* podcast was created. With a descriptive title and a straightforward tagline/mission — to "break down the communication breakdowns" in sports — we set out to offer our take on the most pressing, interesting, and challenging communications crises of the moment.

Too often, we come across the mishandling of public-facing crises that commonly plague sports. Whether it's from a poor read of a situation, a resistance to sound advice, or just a tone-deaf public statement, sports at the highest levels are fraught with PR pitfalls that can be minimized with sound approaches. Our goal is to shine a light on these strategies and techniques in every episode of *Crisis Communications in Sports.*

We interviewed some of the most significant and well-respected figures from sports media to gain their perspectives on how and why things went wrong publicly for an athlete, a team, a league, or anyone else across the sports landscape. With their insight and our experience, we present intelligent takes that result in practical advice for our fellow sports PR pros who make their living trying to devise winning strategies to sway the court of public opinion. We also delve into some areas that aren't strictly related to crises, but nonetheless are fascinating about the business of sports.

The following chapters contain the transcriptions of some of the most compelling conversations we've had with these luminaries. The interviews have been edited for clarity. We hope they'll serve both to inspire and to provide some of the critical tools necessary to succeed in the often complex arena of sports PR.

15

MARY CARILLO:
"IF YOU REALLY WANT PEOPLE TO LISTEN TO YOU, YOU HAVE TO WIN"

Podcast Interview Recorded
September 24, 2020

When we spoke to sports-broadcasting legend Mary Carillo in the fall of 2020, the world was still in the throes of the COVID-19 pandemic. Professional sports had returned, but with tight restrictions and unfamiliar settings that included no fans in attendance. We asked Carillo about some of the specific noteworthy incidents that had recently occurred in and around the game of tennis, the societal challenges facing young athletes, how the role of media in sports has changed, and the challenges of social media. Over the course of her decades-long, illustrious career, Carillo has seen and experienced athlete-media interactions across multiple generations, and she was kind enough to share her invaluable insights with us.

Mary, I want to ask you about an incident at the U.S. Open that we were monitoring here because we were looking at different sorts of crises that pop up in the sports world: the Novak Djokovic incident where he accidentally hit a linesperson with a ball in the throat. Our take on it here was that he missed the boat by not addressing the media in person immediately afterwards. His apology on social media was sincere and genuine, at least that's the way I took it, but what was your take on that? Do you also feel that he would have been better served to have spoken to the media directly?

Not even a question. I mean, what he did was absolutely wrong. He'd already been agitated the game before. You could tell he was in a prickly mood. It was terrible luck that he hit a lineswoman in the neck with that ball, but he knew immediately that he was out of there. I mean, there was about a 10-minute situation with him up at the net speaking with the referee. But my take on that was that the referee was just letting Djokovic air out. He was just letting him have his say. But it was over and Novak knew it as well as anybody. But then he blew off the press conference. We showed video of him getting into a car and driving away. It was such bad form.

And as much as there was plenty of contrition in the statement he made hours later, and by the way, I covered the Italian Open this past week, and he was asked about it multiple times. The fact is he should have done it right away — he's the No. 1 player in the world, for God's sakes. And I think the reason he was so uptight was because he knew, in the absence of Federer and Nadal, of course he should win the U.S. Open again. Of course he should get within breathing space of those other two in titles. So it was bad form. I'm hoping that he goes into the French Open without having to go over this again and again, but had he given a press conference that day, right away, he wouldn't be dealing with all this stuff now. [*Editor's note: In 2023, Djokovic did surpass Rafael Nadal to become the men's all-time leader in career Grand Slam titles.*]

That's exactly what we felt. That wound up overshadowing the apology, because instead of the storyline being what the apology was on

social media, it was about the fact that he blew off the media. Which again, as you said, he is a top player, he just can't really do that.

Jim, the fact is there was a TV presence, obviously, but the media — everyone had to Zoom and do all this stuff. And it was hard getting into some of the pressrooms, the virtual pressrooms, anyway. So you've got the media who are, and they're all over the world, all hours of the morning and night for these press people, a lot of whom are good friends of mine. They couldn't believe that the guy blew off a big — I mean, it became one of the biggest incidents of the 2020 U.S. Open. [*Editor's note: See chapter 6 for our blog post on the Djokovic incident.*]

Mary, speaking of the U.S. Open, and Naomi Osaka, who is one of the biggest stars in the game, she has been really the star of the summer in the tennis world for her activism and really bringing a new voice to activism as a leader. Can you tell us a little bit about what she's been doing and how the tennis world is taking notice?

What you have to understand about Naomi Osaka is that she's shy. One of the things she wrote this summer when everything was happening, and she became very involved in the Black Lives Matter movement, and she was genuinely horrified by everything that was going on. One of her early tweets said, "I'm done being shy." Now, if you're a shy person, that kind of declaration is bold, and it means that you are totally stepping away from your comfort zone. And then Naomi continued to do that. She and her boyfriend went to Minneapolis to march peacefully in protest of what happened there [the police killing of George Floyd]. She just kept reacting to the news and coming out. There's another player, 16-year-old Coco Gauff, who did much of the same thing.

And so Naomi shows up at the U.S. Open, and every time she walked on the court, she had a mask with another name of a victim of violence, a person of color who was a victim of violence, either with the police or something else. And I think it was one of the driving forces of her title win. She said in the beginning, when she first walked out and she had the name on her mask, she said, "I brought seven of these, and there's a lot more I could have brought," basically.

She has been a revelation. It's how much she has grown in the last several years. I mean, she's been a good player, a really good tennis player, for a long while. But now there's a wholeness to her person. And she understands that if you really want people to listen to you, you have to win. If you are an athlete — it's like LeBron, right? — if you are an athlete and you want to show your personal power, it means you have to be a winner. That's when people pay attention to you. She's done a remarkable job.

And people are certainly paying attention. I mean, one of the things that I noticed when I was reading up, Serena has been around forever, since the '90s. And on the men's side, you've had the big three who have won 56 Grand Slams. I mean, they've been it. And they have all had a certain type of stardom and a certain type of leadership. And it seems like Naomi is shifting away from that. What is the reaction from insiders about a star wielding leverage differently?

It's interesting, this summer when Naomi especially started speaking up and after Coco Gauff had given this impromptu speech in Florida celebrating her grandmother who had been her own kind of pioneer back in the day, I called up Billie [Jean King] and I told her, boy, this is like they're taking the baton from you, you know? And Billie said something so interesting, and I wonder if you guys agree with it.

Billie said that while it used to be that an athlete would hesitate to speak his mind politically or culturally or anything, going back to Bill Russell and Muhammad Ali and the '68 Olympic guys who put up their fists, their gloved fists, she said now athletes, and especially people of color, will be rewarded for that. Nike wants that. Gatorade wants that. Powerade wants that. She said there has been this tectonic shift of plates now, if you are an athlete and especially if you're a winner. We go back to that, right? Your sponsors, advertisers — they want to know where you stand and they will celebrate where you stand and re- ward it. It's the antithesis of what happened to Colin Kaepernick four years ago. Isn't that something?

Absolutely. I mean, going back 30 years, Michael Jordan's "Republicans buy sneakers, too," everything has changed. If you're coming from an authentic place, and just saying, "I'm shy and yet I feel compelled in my position to speak out," that's so authentic that that's what brands want. And I'm curious — tennis has always been a relatively conservative sport. Do you see some players feel obligated or feel the impulse to go out of their comfort zone to speak, and say, "If I want to get the Nikes and the Gatorades, I can't just go by my play on the court, but I have to be taking a stance"?

Well, as conservative as tennis has been, as white as it has been, we still had Billie Jean King. We still had the late, great Arthur Ashe. I mean, activism has had a role in my sport for a long while, and I'm very proud of that. Those are two of my biggest role models in my life. I mean, Arthur Ashe had to decide for himself at a pretty young age that he wanted to go to South Africa to play tennis there, and Blacks didn't want him to go, whites didn't want him to go, you know, why would you go there? Why would you support apartheid? And Arthur's decision, which was very thoughtful and very measured, he said, I want Black children to see a Black man live in freedom and have all — and again, he was excoriated on both sides, but he knew what he needed to do for him. He knew how big that message would be.

So again, we've got to go back, and Billie Jean King changed everything. And she wasn't just fighting for women to have equal rights, she was fighting for everybody. She hated the amateur days. She railed against it. She wanted tennis to go pro. She fought for it. Then she fought for a women's tour. Then she fought to create a women's tennis association. I mean, she has been fighting the good fight with arrows in her back for more than 50 years now!

There have been tennis players who have tried to right the wrongs of the sport. And you know, obviously Venus Williams famously at Wimbledon years ago shamed the All England Lawn Tennis Club into giving men and women equal prize money, and the next year it was equal. They had been the holdouts. So I think there's been so much unease, disruption, violence in the year 2020 that these young players almost had to speak out. They almost had to say, this is so wrong, this is my life, this is, I don't feel safe, you know?

And it makes a good point, too, because I think there's a lot of players now, young players in team sports as well, who may not feel . . . the way you said even Osaka had to overcome her shyness. I think there's a lot of players now who maybe just are not comfortable talking about social-justice issues, maybe because they're young or they just want to play ball. What advice would you give to either a tennis player or a person on a team sport, a young player who's trying to find their voice and rather just stick to what's going on on the court, on the field of play, as opposed to having to find their voice and speak out publicly?

Tennis players travel the world. I mean, they go everywhere — you have to be woke in some sense. You have to understand when you land in a country, this is what's happening in this country. This is what's happening right now in England or Australia or wherever you go. And, of course, tennis players should have a sense of history about how they got there, about how, when they arrive at a tournament to get their credential, the locker room is full of food, and the stands are full of fans. They have to be more aware of all of that, to my mind. I just think that, when people rail against athletes speaking out, I've always had an issue with that. Why shouldn't athletes speak out? Why shouldn't we hear from them? Especially athletes of color in the NBA, in the NFL. I mean, they are living entirely different lives than me, you know, a white woman of a certain age with children and a grandchild. I don't know what kind of life they've been living, leading. More than anything, people have to be aware. They have to be present. They have to understand the moment that they're living in, and then they have to decide what to do with their voice.

And I have to tell you, Jim, I remember it was an anniversary, it was during a U.S. Open, Jennifer Capriati was a kid, she was a teenager, and it was an anniversary, I think, of Title IX [which prohibits sex bias in education, including sports]. And I asked her something about it and she said, well, I don't know what that is. And so I quickly explained it to her. And after that interview, people were coming up to me and saying, "Can you believe Jennifer Capriati doesn't even know Title IX helped create her?" And I said, "Hold on a second. It happened when she wasn't even around yet." The fact that Jennifer Capriati doesn't know what Title IX is, we should celebrate that. She didn't have to deal with all that. Getting on me like, boy, you should have nailed her harder on that. Nailed her? How great is it that Jennifer Capriati didn't have to know about Title IX? Didn't have to know that legislation had to happen.

You got to keep in mind some players, frankly, and this is true of all athletes, because I've gotten to cover a lot of them, sometimes the only thing mature about an athlete is the sport they play. They grew up being tennis balls with feet, okay? And you have to allow for that. They didn't go to high school. They were homeschooled or they weren't schooled at all. You know, like, that's okay. You just have to understand who these people are.

Tennis introduces us to stars at a younger age than anything else. Same with the Olympics. And you've covered many Olympics. And as we just said, NBA players coming one year out of high school are also in that situation. Do you see a difference with a younger generation, feeling more comfortable addressing this, or more comfortable because they grew up with it, knowing how to develop their own voice?

Well, social media has changed everything. Let's go there for just a fraction of a moment. I mean, the stuff, whether it's Twitter or Instagram or Facebook, athletes now, no matter how young they are or how educated they are, whatever, they can immediately reach out to their base immediately.

And their base can find them earlier. These high-school players, in basketball at least, with 500,000 followers following their junior-year math class.

And so there are benefits and drawbacks to the immediacy of all that. Like Sonya Kenin, who won the Australian Open this year. I have been watching Sonya Kenin videos from the time she was 5 years old. I mean, there was all this machinery backing this young, cute little blond Russian — American, but from Russia. So I have been aware of her forever. And it turns out she's a really good player and a very nice kid.

The drawback for people like us in the media is that these athletes don't really need us anymore! They've got their own platforms. They want to put out their message. They want to give their take of what happened, and boom, they put it right out there. It's their own spin. They don't need to hold a press conference anymore. They don't need to ring up *The New York Times* or the *New York Post* or wherever. They get to decide, "This is what I want to say about that." And they show us where they are all over the world, and in bikinis and playing with their kids, and, "Look, I'm a family man."

So social media, yes, to my mind, has absolutely changed everything in trying to cover a sport. And a lot of it is good. I love the fact that I can, I mean, I follow tennis on Twitter like crazy. I read 20 different newspapers a day, and I follow a bunch of tennis players and, Oh, God, Nick Kyrgios is starting a Twitter fight with some other dude. Oh, my God, this is crazy, you know?

So, turning that around on you, how has that changed your job? In the broadcast booth, do you have more leeway to say, "Well, I just saw on Instagram they had a kid"? Or do you now feel the need from producers to work more of what those players are offering to the world into your broadcast?

Oh, absolutely. I mean, again, if it's verifiable, certainly we move on it immediately. We at Tennis Channel, for instance, we showed Twitter stuff all the time, and a lot of it's nonsense. A lot of it is like, are we really giving this airtime? Really? Because some people think it's adorable? To me, some of that stuff gets cloying. But yeah, it can be a big help. And it's interesting when a player decides, "Alright, I'm going to set the record straight, this is what really happened." I want to hear their take on it. It's not the Bible or anything, but yeah, I want to hear what you got to say.

Do you think players, because they have their own platform to give out a mea culpa or respond to something, are less comfortable responding to questions from the media? Do they say, I don't need you, I have my website or I have my Instagram?

That's how I feel. Some players continue to be very respectful of the media, and it's much appreciated. But a lot of players would rather send out their own message, send out their own whatever they're sponsoring. They could throw that out there. Yes, there's all kinds of ways that athletes in any sport can get out the message they want to send without filtering it through the press.

So, Mary, I want to ask you a little bit more about how social media has changed your job, specifically thinking of the recent spate of broadcasters who have had some missteps on-air, caught on hot mics, saying things that clearly shouldn't have been said and were taken to task for it. How has the job changed for you over the past 20, 30 years, as far as do you find yourself censoring things that you want to say more? Are you constantly in your head thinking, "That might be taken the wrong way," and then five minutes later it'll be all over social media. Or do you just kind of free flow with it?

First of all, I have to tell you, Jim, I don't curse. I mean, almost never — every now and then if I'm home and something dumb, if I've done something stupid. One of the reasons I don't curse, first of all, I think it's kind of lazy, and I think I can be more imaginative than just using a curse word, but —

Well, maybe not even just a curse, but maybe a point of view that may not be politically correct nowadays or something like that.

But as far as cursing goes, I don't want to slip up on the air because I don't want to react to a big moment and say, holy . . . whatever. But I can't say that I have done anything to moderate my opinions, my voice. I know there are hot mics, and I know I'll say something that will go viral. Like, I'm aware of that potential.

Were you as aware of it years ago, though, or was it not even a thought? You didn't have to worry so much about that then.

No, but look, I'm one of the few people who get to cover tennis who has not won Wimbledon. Let's face it, you know [*laughs*]. I used to get letters from students from Syracuse or other broadcasting schools and they'd say, "Oh, Mary, I'm majoring in communications, I'm minoring in English, I do a radio show every week, and bah, bah, bah. But tennis is my sport. I love your sport. How do I get your job?" And invariably I'd say, "Alright, first win Wimbledon" [*laughs*].

So the reason I get to cover tennis and other sports is, but especially my sport, I wasn't a champion — if anyone has ever hired me, it's because they know what they're getting. I'm very devoted to my sport, I'm a real nerd, I do my research, I have my own distinct voice. So for me to temper it would mean that I'm not doing what I was hired to do. So, no, in my personal case, I don't know that I've really tamped down anything that I've been saying for the last 40 years. Because to my mind, that's how I pay down my mortgage. That's why anyone would feel like hiring me.

But there have been certainly instances. A famous incident that happened years ago in tennis, there was a guy named Doug Adler who worked for ESPN International, and he was a former player, he knew his stuff. He was calling a match involving Venus Williams and there was a moment in the match where Venus came in, she attacked on an approach shot, and then she's got this big old wingspan at net and she ends up winning the point.

And Doug Adler said something like — the phrase that got him fired — he said, "That's guerilla tennis." Now, he didn't mean *gorilla* the animal, he meant g-u-e — *guerilla*. And it went viral. Somebody posted it on Twitter and it was a moment in a match, and I know Doug, he didn't mean it. He didn't mean that Venus Williams was a gorilla, good God. It went viral and the next day he was taken off this tournament and then he was fired. And he went to court, and it was a long, involved, and expensive process for him. And ESPN ended up writing him a big check because he was able to prove — one of the things that he was able to prove was there was a cool Nike commercial years ago, where it's the streets of San Francisco, and all of a sudden, car doors open up and Andre Agassi and Pete Sampras put a net across the street and they start playing in the street. And Nike called it "guerilla tennis." So *they* called it that.

Anyway, there's a great danger, obviously, and again, Twitter loves creating that stuff. And there are people who cling to that and throw it out there, especially if they don't like a certain announcer. They're looking for reasons to go after somebody. That is a great danger. I continue to call matches the way I think I've always called them and hope that people understand my intention. There's a consistency, I think, to your body of work. It's like when players — if I say something very critical about a player, and I'll do time in the penalty box with that particular player, or her father or her agent, but I know that eventually I'll probably get out because there's a consistency. I'm not picking on somebody. I'm picking on that moment.

You're being fair. And I think you make an excellent point that your body of work over time speaks for itself. So it's not a case of this is someone they're hearing for the first time who they're going to judge right away. You're going to get the benefit of the doubt because you've earned it.

That's the hope.

16

KERY DAVIS:
"I TELL OUR PEOPLE ALL THE TIME: WE'RE IN A FISHBOWL"

Podcast Interview Recorded
November 10, 2020

Few people in the sports sphere have as diverse a background as Howard University Athletic Director Kery Davis. He has accomplished some remarkable achievements that have resulted in the Washington, D.C., university being front and center in some very public-facing stories. Most notably, in 2020, he helped secure the commitment of a five-star basketball recruit — a rarity for a historically Black university. This came just one year after NBA superstar Steph Curry announced his financial support for a new men's and women's golf program at Howard. Prior to his role as the school's A.D., Davis spent 17 years overseeing HBO Sports' acclaimed boxing program. During that time he helped facilitate some of the greatest and most-memorable fights in boxing history.

What was it like going from that world, as a sports-television executive, to being an athletic director of a prominent college? I imagine that it came with a lot of challenges and circumstances that might be interesting to learn about.

You know, it's interesting. I had a preconceived notion of what I thought the job of an athletic director was. I sort of thought it was like being the general manager of a basketball or baseball or football team. So you sort of get to play around with pieces, move them around. I always wanted to be president of the Knicks [*laughs*], so this felt like a good step toward that. But what I found is it was really a lot more of being an educator. It was about the relationship with the students, from a role-model standpoint and from a mentoring standpoint.

It's a huge part of the responsibility of being an athletic director. I went in with a sense — I'm a huge competitor — and I went in with the idea of, we're going to win, we're going to turn things around, we're going to go to the NCAA tournament every year, we're going to challenge everyone in football. As it turns out, the first thing you have to do is make sure you graduate your students and make sure you get your students to the next place in life. And you're a positive influence on that. And so I still have the drive to win, but I also now look at the overall development of our student-athletes. That's my priority.

You've got a background as an incredibly successful, high-profile sports-TV executive, which is the path less traveled to your position. How has your background helped you with these milestones you've reached? How has that helped you navigate and capitalize?

I loved my experience there. Those 17 years I spent at HBO were part of the best years of my life. And the reason why I loved the fabric of the company is because they set no limits for themselves. If you could dream it, if you could think about it, we could try to figure out a way to make it happen. I remember I was talking to a promoter named Murad Muhammad. His name is not important for this conversation, but we were talking about Roy Jones Jr., and we were saying, Okay, you know what, let's figure out a way to do something special for Roy in

New York. He wanted to play in the Garden, and I said, "I don't know if we'll sell enough tickets at the Garden, but let's do something different. Why don't we play Radio City?" A boxing match had never even occurred at Radio City. And we just started dreaming, "Wouldn't it be cool if we could get Whitney Houston to sing the national anthem, and some New York rappers to bring them into the ring?"

And six months later, Roy's fighting at Radio City, Whitney Houston sang the national anthem, and Method Man walked him into the ring. That's who HBO was, that was the fabric of the company: Have big visions. If you swing and miss, okay, you're going to swing and miss sometimes.

We wanted to do the Mayweather–Pacquiao fight for years. We swung and missed a few times. That's okay. We tried to do it with Jerry [Jones] and Jerry World [AT&T Stadium, home of the Dallas Cowboys]. We wanted to be the first event. We thought like that. And so that's one of the things that I think I've brought to Howard, which is: Let's not think in the box, let's not be thinking, "Oh, we're an HBCU, this is our lane, this is what we should do." No. You've got something that you can't buy, which is a great brand. So let's think great. Let's think we can become the next Duke. Let's think we could become the next — we could overtake Georgetown in this city. That's how I look at the world. And so I think that's the biggest strength that I bring from HBO. The other thing I bring is, and Jim would know this, I made zillions of deals with difficult people — whether it was Don King or Bob Arum or Al Haymon. These are not easy people to deal with.

I wasn't going to name them [*laughs*].

I will! And sometimes I have really good feelings about all of those gentlemen. You know, some more than others [*laughs*]. But there was also that feeling, again, that I always felt like, as long as we're talking, we can make a deal. And so that's another thing I bring to the table. Let's try to close deals, if you will, whether the deals are for recruits or whether the deal is a network or whether the deal is at a power company. Whatever it is, that's sort of been, I believe, my strength in coming here.

That actually leads us to the most significant thing that we've all heard about with sports at Howard University. This past summer, getting a commitment from Makur Maker, a top basketball prospect, a top high-school prospect in the country, blue-chip prospect, however you want to look at it. For different reasons, usually the top basketball prospects in the country end up at places like Duke and Kansas and Kentucky and North Carolina. Unfortunately, it's very unusual for someone of his stature to go to one of the historically Black colleges and universities. So just tell us what that was like — the significance of it, maybe for you personally and professionally, what it was like for the university and the impact it's had?

One of the things that I envisioned from the day I took this job was the idea that we could get, quote-unquote, five-star recruits interested in Howard University. Howard's such a great brand that I think we can get in any door. Now, you're right in competing with Kentucky and Kansas and Duke or whatever for these top players. They have so many advantages, from facilities to resources with regard to strength and conditioning and nutrition and all of those things, and the niceties. But we felt that there were some things that Howard had that other universities couldn't match, and how can we sell those things? And so that was our game plan.

So I read an article, written by Jimmy King, and the thrust of the article was, "What if the Fab Five had gone to Howard instead of Michigan?" [*Editor's note: The Fab Five, of which Jimmy King was a member, refers to the 1991 University of Michigan men's basketball team, considered to be one of the greatest recruiting classes.*] And trust me, we use that article in every conversation we've had with a blue-chip player since, because it breaks down the benefits of what would have happened had the Fab Five gone to Howard. I'm sure they had a great experience in Michigan — they went to two Final Fours, etc. But Michigan was not family for them. Yet they would have had that same influence at Howard with regard to media exposure. Because if the Fab Five would have come to Howard, every television network in the country would have been right behind them. The money would have also followed them in terms of benefiting the resources, if you will, improving the resources, that would have all happened. So we talked about, this is a step that we think we can take, and here is the data that shows what can happen if you do.

And so we approached Makur, and we actually had another five-star player who also visited, by the way, named Josh Christopher. So we had two of the top 10 players in the country on our campus for a visit on back-to-back weekends. And we said to them, "Here's what's going to happen if you choose Howard. You're going to get a tremendous amount of media attention that you can't buy because it's going to be a huge story. And it could be the start of something, the start of a rock rolling downhill, if you will. This could be the start of a movement.

And wouldn't it be great to be the foundational elements of that movement?" And so we gave him a 30-plus-page presentation, both of them. Here's all the ways you will benefit by going to Howard. From a marketing standpoint, a brand-building standpoint, still a great education, as good as you can get anywhere in the country. And it was effective. And Makur had the vision that he saw this as an opportunity for him. And I think he's seen the result. I mean, he's been on the *Today* show and *Good Morning America*. And he announced it on ESPN. Trust me, if he would have gone to Kentucky or UCLA, *none of that would have happened.*

Kery, you raise a great point about this global brand and the work you're putting into the department to culminate in a five-star recruit choosing Howard. And as you mentioned, the announcement really made a lot of news. I saw that it had over a billion impressions on social. That's millions and millions of dollars of exposure for Maker and for the school. But can you walk us through after that crowning achievement of getting the recruit that you knew was going to come eventually — what ripples have that billion impressions and that major decision created for you in the few months since?

We've probably had close to $2 million in donations to our basketball program since his announcement. We're still in negotiation with ESPN right now to televise all of our games. Fox — we're playing Notre

Dame on our campus this year, and that was done before Makur arrived — but Fox is putting that on their broadcast network. Those are things that would not have happened. As a university, those are benefits that we've ascertained because of him. So we understood what the impact would be for us.

With a typical recruit traditionally signing, let's say, in their junior year, and then you have the senior year — especially with such a high-profile recruit — sort of lock in those major games, lock in those tournaments or TV deals, has this just been that much more of a whirlwind? Trying to go in this sporting environment, which is up in the air to begin with, and you're holding the rock now?

That's a very astute question and it's probably the biggest disappointment from that standpoint is that we're doing this in a COVID era. If not for COVID-19, we would have also sold out our building. I mean, we've had so many ticket requests. And what we have to tell people pursuant to the District of Columbia gathering restrictions, we can't have fans. So that's incredibly disappointing. You know, NBA scouts would have been flocking to our games. They can't come. We would have had all these media companies. That's not happening. I will say, though, we are shooting a documentary, we have an all-access documentary following the team right now which will air in real time, like the all-access program that Duke had. But you're right, we lost out on some opportunities due to COVID-19, unfortunately. But still, I'm not complaining about all the benefits we did receive.

You raised an interesting point that transitions to a question we've been discussing here for a long time. The NCAA is currently redefining how a player can use their likeness. And having a player, certainly your highest-profile player to date, coming in at this time, having endorsement opportunities. Where does that stand, and was that part of your presentation or consideration when Maker was signing?

It was part of the conversation, but it was speculative because we knew name, image, and likeness wouldn't be here this year. So if we're lucky enough for him to stay *two* years [*laughs*], he will certainly have the benefit. I sit on the NCAA Basketball Oversight Committee. And so one of the things that we've spent a lot of time discussing, besides COVID and the reopening of basketball, is the name, image, and likeness legislation that's coming through the NCAA for next year. I think it's going to be a hugely impactful item for basketball and maybe across all sports. This may not stop at basketball. I'm looking at volleyball programs and women's softball programs, which are utilizing the opportunities that these young people can have to sell their image and likeness going forward in the future.

Right now the NCAA doesn't have its hands around it. They really haven't defined how they're going to shape this yet: Is this going to be something you say, okay, student A, hire a lawyer, hire an agent. You go do your thing and just leave us out of it? Or do you want the universities to in some way have some control over it so it doesn't get out of hand? How is it going to be orchestrated and implemented? We all know that's something we want. These young people should be able to benefit from their name, image, and likeness, but we also don't want it to be just a facilitation for schools to cheat. We don't want the booster from the Chevy dealership handing Makur $250,000 and say, you know, go to Kentucky instead of Howard. So the NCAA is really trying to get its arm around it. I do believe next year we will have legislation, though. Or we will have provisions in place which govern it. I can't really tell you what they'll be.

Do you think that the NCAA is working on — they're obviously trying to hold it and work on their time frame to figure out these questions that they've been cutting their teeth over for decades. State legislatures are working on a very different time frame with different end goals. Do you think that the NCAA can control that time frame or be forced into a corner as they're sort of looking for the perfect solution, while 50 states are looking for something else?

I don't think the NCAA will have the privilege of being able to work on their own time frame. I don't think they will have that opportunity. I think the circumstances of what's happening in many states —

California and New York, etc. — is going to dictate them moving their time frame up a little faster than they probably wanted to. That being said, I also don't believe you can allow good to be the enemy of perfect. So I think that they will try to get their best solutions possible. It'll probably be some kind of work-in-progress. There'll be some provisions for it in 2021, and then, it'll probably be looked at again in '22 once we see what happened in '21. So I think it'll be fine-tuned. But I don't think we can wait. I don't think the NCAA can wait two or three years to implement a strategy with regard to NIL. [*Editor's note: See chapter 10 for our blog post on NIL.*]

Makur is facing a very interesting situation in that there was such great feeling and vibes about him choosing Howard for all the obvious reasons we discussed. But he has a pressure on him, I think, and tell me if you disagree, that is very different from other top basketball recruits, in that someone like Zion Williamson — it's no surprise and no pressure for him to leave Duke after one year. It's expected, it's understood. Makur is in a situation where he may feel some internal pressure, maybe external pressure, too, to continue to set the trend and stick around at Howard for a little bit longer than just a year, so that he could maybe help recruit younger guys or just rebuild the program. I just wanted to find out what your thoughts are on that subject.

I think Makur is — I think his intention right now is to be a professional basketball player. That's what he wants. And so I think wherever the best opportunity for him to achieve that goal, whenever that comes, that'll be the time he takes advantage of it. So for example, if after this year he doesn't look like he'll be a first-round pick or a lottery pick or whatever, maybe he does come back and stay a second year. But his goal, and he's made it very clear, and this is the goal *we* want for him, is to be a professional basketball player. So I wouldn't put a time frame on it, although we're expecting him to be in the lottery next year [*laughs*].

I think it probably took a lot of pressure off him to be very upfront

and honest about it and to just kind of say, "Listen, if I'm a one-and-done guy, if I have that ability and I could be a top pick in the NBA, I'm going to do that. Would I love to hang around and help Howard, sure, but I have to be realistic."

Well, Jim, I would say this another way: The pressure's on us. I think it's important for him to be a first-round draft choice next year or a lottery pick, hopefully. Because if that happens for us, then that will show other five-star kids that you can get there from Howard. You don't have to go to Duke, you don't have to go to Kentucky. That will be as big a recruiting tool as if he stayed [*laughs*]. So either way, for us this is a win, if you will.

I just wanted to shift gears a little bit to a sport that I know is very near and dear to your heart as well, and that's golf. Most people probably saw, close to a year and a half ago now, Steph Curry stepping up and funding the golf program at Howard, essentially restarting it after 40 years. I imagine that there's a lot of things you go through, Kery, that are incredibly gratifying, but I can only imagine, just knowing your love of golf, how much that meant to you. So tell us a little bit about it — I mean it's a great story, it's a feel-good story in general. But what was it like when that was all unfolding?

This has to go back to my interview with Dr. Wayne Frederick, the president of the university. He's also an avid golfer like myself. And in our very first meeting, we talked about starting a golf team, starting a golf program. But with the financial position that we were in as a department, I was like, okay, well, where's the money? So it was tough for us, but we had our eye on the ball and our intention was always to start a golf program.

When the opportunity — and many people have heard the story — Steph Curry premiered a documentary on our campus. During that documentary, one of the young people who had approached me about starting a golf program — he was a senior in high school when I started at Howard — he had started a club team at Howard. And so he approached Steph at the end of the documentary and said, "Hey

Steph, why don't you stick around tomorrow and let's play a round of golf?" And Steph said, "Well, hey, are you on the golf team?" He said, "Well, no, we actually don't have a golf team. I play on the club team."

And that started a conversation between the two of them. Lo and behold, Steph's manager calls us and says Steph would like to become involved with Howard golf. And so at first we were talking about: How can we truly fund a club team? But when we started talking about the history of golf at Howard, Steph's manager called me back and said, "You know what? This is such an interesting story. Steph wants to fund a Division I team. Let's do it." I'm like, "Really?" [*Laughs*] I have to tell you, I was almost in tears.

And I have to tell you, he has been the most incredible, steadfast partner. Again, we're in an unlucky situation — this should be our inaugural year right now. And the fact that we're dealing with COVID and the golf team's not even on campus, but we hired a great coach. We hired a coach who was an assistant coach at Stanford when they won a national championship. He was head coach of Michigan State. And he was recommended to me by the head coach at Stanford, who's a friend of Steph's. And so when I called him, I actually didn't even think he'd be that interested. But the places he had been and he said, "Hey, this is a dream job. I can build a powerhouse at Howard. Let's do it." And so he's been a great addition to our program. And Steph has stayed with us.

I'm not making an announcement here, because it's already been a public release, but Steph is playing in a TNT event on November 26th or seventh, whatever Black Friday is, and with him, Charles Barkley, Peyton Manning, and Phil Mickelson. And a significant part of the proceeds for that event are going to our Howard golf program. In addition to the money that Steph gave us, he's adding to our endowment program for golf. [*Editor's note: "The Match" event in 2020 raised $6.4 million for HBCUs.*] So he has been a steadfast partner. So we're thrilled to have him. This is more than just him starting, he's a contributor. I don't speak to him every day, but I probably speak to his manager a lot, and the people in his company a lot. And they're great teammates.

A theme of this whole conversation has been strategically setting expectations, right? Whether it be the expectation is, we're going to get a five-star recruit because we're selling a brand that's a lot bigger than a one-and-done storyline. But conversely, you've gotten a lot of media off the bat for a team that hasn't really started yet. And how do you set expectations internally in your league, in the media . . . Hey, we're starting something from scratch and we may have the best basketball player on the planet behind us, and we may have an incredible amount of generous funding behind us, but we are starting something and we have to set some building blocks here.

That's a good point. And one of the things, if you were doing this interview with Coach Blakeney, I've heard him say this a thousand times: We won four games last year. So we're *starting* from there. So that's our starting-off point. Our starting-off point is not No. 1 in the conference. Even in the preseason conference polls, we weren't picked in the top four teams. Because other than Maker, we were a very young team. I think we'll surprise some people — I'm holding hope.

So we've had to temper expectations everywhere we go. And I think that, again, this is where COVID is helping us, because we would have sold out every game, and I think people would have come to the gymnasium expecting us to now beat Norfolk State by 30. Well, guys, Norfolk State's pretty good [*laughs*]. And so, you know, we're not going to beat them by 30 just because we have Makur. I'd be happy with a one-point, triple-overtime victory [*laughs*]. But I think that COVID has actually helped us do that a little bit. Yeah, there'll be a lot of attention on us, and I think we'll win our share of games, but I think that Coach Blakeney is very good at telling everyone that this is a first step in our process. Let these — even if Makur is not here a year from now — let these nine or 10 new recruits blossom. Maybe we have to add two Makur's next year, maybe Nojel [Eastern] plays next year — that's the kid from Purdue I was talking about. Let's let those pieces come together and let's give Coach Blakeney an opportunity to really build this program.

Part of what plays into your program for basketball, and of course for golf, is the school's brand and the fishbowl of where it's located in Washington, D.C. And over the past four years, there has certainly been an elevated focus on what's coming out of D.C., the rhetoric that's coming out of D.C. Even starting way back when with kneeling. And it's crazy that you made your social-media team make noise, that you put the cheerleaders kneeling on social. And from there, how has that been a part of your department's day to day, week to week — every news story can't be separated from that?

You're absolutely right. Part of the DNA of Howard is the cultural and social impact that the school has. Back in the '70s when SNCC [Student Nonviolent Coordinating Committee] and Stokely Carmichael were running, were taking over the "A" building, the administrative building — it's always been a cultural, political, social hotbed, if you will. That's why they call it the Mecca. Our graduates have gone on to do tremendous things, a lot of them in that area. We have the vice president–elect is a Howard graduate. Elijah Cummings, who just passed away this past year, is a Howard graduate. Andrew Young, David Dinkins, the first Black mayor of New York City — all Howard graduates.

So we're used to being in that fishbowl. That's who we are. So that's the easiest part for us to handle. Because also with that comes a target. One of the things that I talked about last year was that we had a financial-aid scandal at the university. It wasn't a whole lot of money. But there was some fraud and mismanagement, etc. The school dealt with it, and the school dealt with it quietly, and then when it became public, that this university had dealt with it, it became a big story on CNN and *Washington Post*, etc., etc. Columbia had the same exact issue that we did. *Columbia* — not Saint Agnes Prep — one of the top schools in the country had the same issue. They got nowhere near the media attention that we received at Howard.

And I tell our people all the time: We're in a fishbowl. So if you go out and you do something stupid, like I tell our students, if you make a bad choice, that's going to reflect on all of us. *However*, if you do something great, we will also get the benefit of that, too. Like the

Steph Curry story, like the Makur story, like the Kamala Harris story. So it's a good and bad that comes with it. We take it, we live with it, it comes with the territory, so to speak. But we acknowledge it and we understand it.

Editor's note: In September 2024, Makur Maker began playing for the Al–Ittihad Jeddah Club in FIBA's West Asia Super League.

17

JAY HORWITZ:
"ONCE THEY CATCH YOU IN A LIE, YOUR CREDIBILITY IS DONE"

Podcast Interview Recorded
December 10, 2020

Few places in the world can match the media frenzy generated by the professional sports teams in New York. Over the years, the city has been the ruin of countless athletes, coaches, executives, and owners. Any PR professional who can thrive at the highest level in that cauldron, decade after decade, commands great respect. And perhaps nobody deserves more respect than longtime New York Mets PR guru Jay Horwitz.

The venerable Horwitz joined the Mets in 1980, and when we caught up with him in 2020, he had just released a new book, *Mr. Met*, detailing his career. We asked him about how he navigated his way around all the infamous events and crises that took place in the organization, especially the very public and less-than-glamorous ones that transpired in the mid to late 1980s.

Speaking with Horwitz is akin to taking a master class in frontline, high-profile sports PR. It was apparent throughout that the root of

Jay, you are widely known, especially to people of my generation who grew up in the New York area, as a PR extraordinaire, just someone who was omnipresent for four decades on the New York scene. And you have a great new book out called *Mr. Met*, which I'm excited to be reading, *even as a Yankee fan.* I'm still excited to learn about it because I just associate you with an era, especially in the '80s when the Mets were really surging. What was it like back then when the Mets were coming in, from the early to the mid '80s, when they really started to turn things around and become the team that we all knew in '86. What was the feel back then?

Well, it really all started in 1983. In October, we hired Davey Johnson as the manager. Davey was a kind of a guy who didn't really care what he said. He was very outspoken. You know, Davey was a multi-millionaire. He was a real-estate guy, flew his own plane. So he just spoke his mind. He was the perfect manager for the team. My first three years here, we weren't relevant. And when we added Davey and Darryl Strawberry, Keith [Hernandez], Gary Carter, Doc [Gooden], Ron Darling — it became not knowing what to expect when we got to the ballpark. A lot of these guys had really big personalities. They appeared not only in the sports pages, the front page of the paper. It's well known some of the guys did get into trouble with drugs and alcohol, so it was like a thing when you came to the park, you never knew what to expect. They kept me on my toes all the time. And it was, like, '84 to '90. We took over New York and we were the talk of the town and just kept you on your toes as soon as you got to the ballpark — a lot of times driving home from the ballpark — you get a call about one of our guys.

One of the things that you sort of inherited a little bit, I guess, was a problem with Keith Hernandez and the cocaine issue, which happened back when he was on the Cardinals. But he did actually get summoned to testify at some point when that story was breaking. And there's a great piece in the book about how you chose select reporters to speak to, and without follow-up questions, and how that was the right solution for that particular issue and that Keith went on to play well and the writers were satisfied. Could you tell us a little bit about what that was like?

Yeah, one thing why I was able to exist in the locker room for 40-plus years — you have to walk the line. You have to let the players know that you care about them. I never regarded myself as a suit. So when Keith came back from Pittsburgh, the night before, we were in San Diego and he got four hits right before they got on the plane. So we just thought the best way to do it, when he came back — Arthur Richmond, who was a traveling secretary at the time, got us a suite in the hotel. The guys came up, they asked some questions, Keith said what he had to say. And from then on, for the rest of the year, Keith and I talked, he would say, "Hey guys, I addressed the issue. I don't have to keep going over and over it again."

The thing is that, all those guys — you know, from Darryl and Keith and Doc — the reason they're still so popular is they never ran from anything, they addressed their problems. And we just thought the best way with Keith was not to run away from it, which he didn't want to, but we addressed it once and then we would get questions and reporters would ask questions. I would a lot of times step in and say, "Hey guys, he answered that question already," to kind of let Keith or the guys know I was in their corner and I had their back. And it was an important thing for me — how to get along with this group of guys.

Can you take us back to ramping up to that initial press conference and meeting with the media in the hotel? I mean, how did you go about picking who was going to be there? What was the forum going to be?

It was basically the beat guys. I don't remember who was there, but it was the beat guys who traveled with us — at that time, would have been Joe D'Urso from *The New York Times*, Dan Castellano from *The Star-Ledger*, Marty Noble from *Newsday*. Maybe Mike McAlary. Or just the people who traveled with us. So we told them, this is the format and we made Keith available. We took it away from the ballpark so it wouldn't be a distraction to the game. Then when he got back there, he addressed it once, he said his thing, and that was that. It was just — the whole thing was to not hide anything. The one thing I learned early, working in New York, if you hide or don't tell the truth, you get caught.

I'll give you one quick story. We had a player who went on to have, hopefully, a Hall of Fame career, Jeff Kent. We were in St. Louis. Jeff used to travel with a gun. He used to practice on a gun range when he went to different cities. At that time there were no charters, so we went through a public security thing and they got his gun. We explained [why he had it and what he used it for]. And we told the press about what happened, instead of waiting for it to leak out, or, "Jeff Kent arrested at St. Louis airport." So we told the truth. Early on, I found out that you can't — there's just too many media people there, and me as a public relations guy, once they catch you in a lie, your credibility is done. You're done. I mean, maybe you get away with it in smaller markets like Kansas City or Detroit or whatever. But once you get caught with a lie in, like, New York, Chicago, L.A. — you're done. So I always try to just tell the truth and have the player's interest at heart, but get the story out there.

What happens when you have to juggle the interests between the player, the team, and *your* credibility? And sometimes there are three different angles that might not necessarily meet up.

Well, I mean, you have to have an open dialogue with the ownership. During my time, through the years with the Wilpons, they trusted me. They had a good sense about me. So we would talk about it. We had, at some points in time, a crisis committee. We would talk about certain things. But the thing is, maybe you don't tell all the truth, sometimes you get most of it out there. And I think the players knew, I think ownership knew, that I had the best interest of the organization at heart. I mean, I couldn't have existed there for 40 years if there was a feeling that they didn't trust me with stuff.

But I just try to, again, walk the line between being what's good for the player and being what's good for the organization. I mean, go back to the Keith thing. It might have been even better for the organization if he didn't speak — or, why prolong the story? — but they agreed with my suggestion: Just do it in a controlled setting, get it out there, do it once, and control it the rest of the year after that.

You actually just mentioned something, Jay, that's kind of music to our ears. You said that the Mets had a *crisis committee*, which is brilliant and which we're always preaching to people. What prompted that? I mean, aside from maybe a need [*laughs*], but how did you guys decide, "We need to designate certain people to decide what's going to happen if a crisis occurs"?

Well, we had somebody from the legal department, somebody representing ownership, somebody representing marketing and communication — I was in there. But a lot of times, it's all well and good, but since I was on the road most of the time, if stuff came up, I would maybe call the lead person on a committee, tell them what I was going to do, and he ran it by the other people. But we had [to deal with] long-range stuff. You can talk about problems that come up, but it was just a way to talk it out with somebody in legal that might have a different view than me. And just to hear it out, just to really talk around about long-range problems, just to have sounding boards to get other people's opinion. So your opinion wasn't the only opinion.

What would sort of fall into your lap that you felt you could handle by yourself and what did you feel was the red line that would have to be crossed in order for it to have to be brought up to that crisis committee?

I'll give you an example. Say, we're on the road in Chicago and Darryl Strawberry was taken out of the lineup for an injury, I would just let the people know in New York — we're telling the people what happened, so they're not surprised when the ownership or the general manager listens to TV that night and Darryl Strawberry is out of the lineup.

I mean, we had some curfew problems on the road, where I would let people know so they weren't surprised at what happened. Just try to keep the people who had to be in the know, in the know. The worst thing in the world for me is if somebody above me heard about a problem with the team before they heard it from *me*. And so I try to prevent — to keep the people who ought to be in the loop, in the loop. So they knew what was going on with the team.

How did that change over time? Obviously now they say that most trades in Major League Baseball happen without GMs even getting on the phone. It's all texting. And in this crisis committee, did it evolve over time to where it's more of a constant text thread, emails, or was it still giving a phone call, and then we're going to meet?

It was mostly by phone. The thing is now, nothing — with Twitter and Instagram and all the other things — nothing's a secret anymore. It's all got to be by text or by phone or by word of mouth. I mean, something happens, you have to pick up a phone and call somebody. And if you signed a big free agent now, it's never going to be quiet, you have to be out there. I stopped writing press releases about 10 years ago, whenever Twitter came in. Either the agents, or reporters like John Heyman or Buster Olney, Ken Rosenthal, they'll break stories all the time. There's no such thing as a secret anymore. I mean, it's just kind of been a little passé. It's got to be by word of mouth. The thing is, the ownership people have to trust the PR person that is on the road that he'll have the best interest of the team at heart.

It's interesting because your career has spanned since the days of the typical tabloid newspapers into the social-media age. What was that like for you? Was that a big adjustment, or did you embrace it at first, or were you skeptical?

I embrace it, but the thing is, we just started to do player seminars in the spring, when with the advent of social media, you just have to be aware who you go to a restaurant with, who you ride up an elevator with. Look what happened with the swimmer Michael Phelps — he took some of his friends, posted a picture of him doing drugs. You might go up in the elevator, put your arm around somebody who's not your wife, your girlfriend. That'll be on social media.

So the last couple of years, I just — we just preached at the Mets, "You got to be aware of your surroundings. Don't take anything for granted. If you tweet, try to stay away from controversial stuff. You can make 50 percent of people happy. Fifty percent of people aren't happy. So just try and be conservative with your tweet and just be aware of your surroundings." But really, nothing's a secret anymore. A lot of times a club will listen to Jon Heyman and Ken Rosenthal, Buster Olney, to find out what's going on, what's going on in the baseball world, because they call the agents, they call the GMs of the other clubs. So yeah, that's a tool to find out what's going on.

One of the really interesting things in the book, Jay, was there's sort of a fine line sometimes between taking what could be a little bit of a negative and playing off it for a little bit of energy instead of it just being a total crisis. So one thing I thought was interesting in '86, which was obviously the big World Series year for the Mets, there were during the season a few different scuffles that had gone on. And I think it was Ray Knight and who was it . . . ?

Ray and Eric Davis.

And Eric Davis when he slid hard into third and punches were thrown. I thought it was really interesting that you said you liked the notion of the fighting Mets sort of thing, and that you kind of turned that negative into a little bit of a positive because it was sort of an edgy feel that fed into the Davey Johnson Mets.

The rest of the National League hated us. I mean, we were boastful, we had the players to back it up. And that particular game Eric Davis slid in hard to third base. And when he got up, Ray Knight clocked him. A couple of times during the year, we got into beanball fights and George Foster got hit early in the year. That's why Mike Tyson, before he became Mike Tyson, chose us to come out and take BP [batting-practice] pictures with Darrell and Doc and Ray and Kevin Mitchell. It was just that particular fight was the example of why we were so good. We didn't back off from anybody. We were boastful, but we had the talent to back up the boast. But that particular game, it ended with [pitchers] Jesse Orosco and Roger McDowell in the outfield, [catcher] Gary Carter at third base. So we just keep fighting to the end and we alienate a lot of people along the way. And we had the people to back up the boast.

And to your credit you found a way to embrace it and make it a positive. That was the swagger of that team. And it worked.

It was the swagger. That particular game was. Yes, sir.

So a couple of the other scuffles that happened, I think this was the same year, was the Keith Hernandez–Darryl Strawberry thing. So now you have an in-team situation where they're taking the —

That team picture, I didn't program that [*laughs*]. I think it was spring of '80, whatever it was. To make a long story short, Darryl was under the impression that Keith had said some things about him in the winter, which might have hurt him getting an MVP. And I don't know what was right or wrong. So in the middle of our team picture, in the middle of the field in Port St. Lucie, they exchanged blows and they started a fight, which they broke it up, and I said I was happy because that team picture got publicity all over the country [*laughs*]. I got congratulatory notes from all the fellow PR guys saying, "Way to get PR, national PR, for a team picture," which was usually a boring event. So I tell guys, "Well, I asked the guys to fight to help me get the good PR out of it" [*laughs*].

Might as well take the credit!

Right.

I'm kind of interested in learning how you would balance your responsibility, especially when the Mets were good. But it's also New York. How do you balance your responsibility to the beat reporters versus national reporters? When you were talking about which reporters they're relying on now, the Heymans and everybody, they're all national. So we know that when there's a story, good or bad, that's when national swoops in. How do you balance that?

Well, the whole thing is really going back to not lying and telling the truth and knowing that, the market that we're in, that you can't lie. I mean, I think how I existed was I was credible. The players knew that I had their backs. When I used to go to Keith or Darryl, after a problem, they knew I had their best interest. Like in the '86 World Series — Dwight didn't have his best two games, he lost both games, gave up a lot of runs, and they [Boston] won the games. And I said, Doc — after one of the games in Boston [Game 5] — I said: We have to go to the bullpen where they had their pressroom and talk. He knew I had his interest at heart. I didn't want him to walk out of there without talking to the writers.

So they knew when I would ask him to do something unpleasant that I still, even though it was unpleasant, I still had their best interest. Whether it's local guys or national guys, for a PR guy to be successful, you have to establish that trust with the players, and, again, keep in mind I work for the organization. So I mean, I had to keep in mind: Look, it would be a bad thing for the organization if one of our star players walked out of the room in that kind of an atmosphere without talking to the writers. So just a question of having the trust of the players, not lying and just try to walk the fine line between telling the truth and not losing your credibility with the beat guys. Ten years ago, we used to travel 10, 12, 14 beat guys on a regular game, and you get to the playoffs, it's like a hundred. So once they find out you lied, you're a dead person.

Cities like Boston and Philadelphia have passionate fan bases. But they don't really get that in New York City you grow up either a Yankee fan or a Mets fan, and you're fighting the other team before

233

you even fight anyone outside your city! What was it like for you be-ing the "Met PR guy" in an era when they had some success, and then the Yankees had success, and it was always back and forth? I always got the impression you sort of relished in being the Met guy, almost kind of being like the younger brother fighting up in weight.

I love the competition. I'm in the business of getting back pages in the papers, getting guys on the radio. It used to gall me — in one particu-lar sequence, I think when we signed Carlos Beltran, they signed Randy Johnson the next day. I could have my facts screwed up, but I took it as a competition. I try to find interesting stuff about the play-ers, promote human-interest stuff. But it galled me when the Yankees would get back page after back page, and I always took an offense to it — in my position, that I can't give up. I mean, Mets fans were always, I think, the working people of the city. The Yankees have won X amount of championships. We won two World Series, they won 27. So people will say, "Well, we don't play against the Yankees," but we do. We compete against the Yankees for time, and papers, on the radio, on the talk shows. So I took it as a personal battle to try and win the battle as much as I could.

18

ANDREW BRANDT: "THE NFL, THERE'S JUST DRAMA EVERY DAY"

Podcast Interview Recorded November 3, 2022

Daniel Snyder's 24-year tenure as owner of the Washington Commanders (formerly the Redskins) was one of the most acrimonious in American sports history. By the early 2020s, after more than two decades of failure on the field and fan frustration, the team was hit with accusations of sexual harassment in the workplace. This was in addition to a drawn-out and highly publicized battle over Snyder's resistance to changing the franchise's name, which was deemed by many to be racist.

We spoke to the esteemed NFL journalist and native Washingtonian Andrew Brandt during the 2022–2023 football season about the statements and strategies being used by the team, the league, and other owners to address these crises.

With over 25 years of experience in professional football, including as a team executive, Brandt has vast knowledge of the industry. He has appeared regularly as a business and legal analyst on ESPN, providing his unique perspective on the NFL, player negotiations, policy questions, and player finance. Brandt writes the Business of Football column for *Sports Illustrated*, hosts his own NFL podcast called *The Business of Sports*, and is the executive director of the Moorad Center for the Study of Sports Law at Villanova University in Pennsylvania.

Andrew, we're going to take you back a few weeks ago to when the NFL's fall owner meetings were occurring, and Indianapolis Colts owner Jim Irsay came out and said, "I believe there is merit to removing him" — *him* being Daniel Snyder — as owner of the Commanders. Now, that was a jaw-dropping moment for most people, probably was for you, certainly was for us as communication professionals, because that just doesn't happen in the NFL ranks, right? Owners don't ever do that to the other owners. So you knew that it was going to grab a lot of attention. And that certainly seemed to be a planned tactic, which we'll get into in a minute. But first I just want to ask: What effect do you think that had as far as the public narrative?

I think the first thing I should say personally is I'm born and bred in the heart of Washington, D.C., and a diehard Redskins fan growing up. This has been my team, and not only my team, but my family, my friends. I grew up within probably two miles of Daniel Snyder. We are peers, we are contemporaries. I never knew him growing up. My 10 years in the league at the Packers, I did see him at meetings. You know, there were a couple hellos in there, but I was not kind of at the status where he would talk to me [*laughs*]. As I was a vice president of a team and he was way above that. So there's a little background for you.

And they were — and we can talk later about whether they still are or not — a jewel franchise. There's no question: Back in the day, and of course in my childhood and my early adulthood, we had Joe Gibbs and we had this owner named Jack Kent Cooke, who was kind of

treated like royalty in the D.C. area, and the Redskins were a galvaniz-
ing force in a city that's more polarized than ever, but it was
polarized even back then — he brought that team, brought Republicans, Democrats, all races, genders, all together.

So I start there because I think it's sad, for me as a fan, for me as a
Washingtonian — I know people that interact with Daniel Snyder —
it's sad that we've come to this. So then you get into the history decades before he changed the name, decades of what has been reported
copiously by ESPN, by *The Washington Post*, by *The New York Times*, by
others, as a hostile workplace, especially for women, over a couple
decades. I host a podcast, as you know, called *The Business of Sports* —
I had some of the women affected by that culture on my podcast last
year, and the lawyers representing them, and it was just bad. Just talking about how you could never look Snyder in the eye, and if you
somehow talk to him, you've got to call him Mr. Snyder, no matter
who you are. Women that were told never to wear flat shoes, only high
heels. Women that were told never to wear pants, only tight dresses.
Just kind of that whole thing.

Now we have a penalty, a year ago, July 4th weekend, 2021,
$10 million fine and one-year suspension. And it kind of went under
the radar. You talk about crisis communications? The NFL put that out
on Friday of July 4th weekend. So we didn't — "we" meaning the
media — everyone just kind of really didn't notice, *until*, as everyone
remembers a year ago, the Jon Gruden emails came out, and then
everyone's like, well, wait a minute. . . . Now the focus, the spotlight,
goes back to Washington as part of these emails going into Washington, and this is what was going on. . . . And then Congress gets interested and then, another investigation. [*Editor's note: The investigation
into the Washington team revealed that longtime NFL coach Jon Gruden
sent emails to Washington General Manager Bruce Allen that contained
racist, misogynistic, and homophobic slurs.*]

But I think where we come out of this is, what's going on, right?
The NFL had this investigation that culminated a year ago, then
slipped it under the radar on July 4th weekend. And then it comes out,
we sort of recognize like, wait a minute, there's no report! There's a
$10 million fine, there's a year suspension, but it's based on an oral,

not written, report. And Beth Wilkinson, the attorney in Washington handling it, maybe wrote down notes because she interviewed a lot of people. But those notes are in a drawer somewhere. So a lot of this kind of just makes you scratch your head before we get to the current situation — like, wait a minute, why does this guy continue to have kind of a free rein? And the NFL, it seems, protected him throughout all this.

And believe me that tactic of going on 4th of July weekend is of course something that is utilized a lot in our world, very purposeful, burying bad news. But another interesting fact is that some NFL communications people were reportedly within earshot when Irsay did this. I got the impression that maybe Irsay was nominated by a handful of owners who said, "Listen, you're going to be the one to deliver this shot. And here's what we want to say. . . . We want to put this out there." Did you get the sense that that might be the case, that this wasn't just sort of an emotional outburst on Irsay's part?

Well, again, what happened in the recent weeks, we had the big ESPN article that talked about Snyder having dirt on the other owners, Snyder basically saying if they try to take him out, he's going to take the whole ship down with him. Yeah, it just seemed like all of a sudden now we have an owner speaking out. Because in that article by ESPN, there were no on-the-record comments. No one came out publicly against him, *nor* publicly for him with their name attached to it, which I thought was interesting.

The Irsay thing made news because you have — I don't know if the right word is *code* — but having been around the NFL a long time, the membership has this sort of: You don't bash other owners. It's the most exclusive fraternity in the world. You don't get into all that. And Irsay went there.

You probably know better than I do how that would happen because it could have been an orchestrated plan. But it also could have been a rogue owner, like he is, not caring that this is not protocol, not caring that this is not the formality, the way they do it. But as we get into the heart of this from my viewpoint, I think Irsay knew, and knows, what I've been saying all along: The NFL owners are not going to vote him out. It's not going to happen.

Never has happened.

Everyone asks me that. No, it's not happening. Like, "Why? He's such a bad guy." I'm like, no. A few reasons. Number one, they don't want to have that precedent. It could come back on them. What are the skeletons in their closet? Number two, and more importantly, Snyder has proven to be one of the more litigious people in the country, and they'd be tied up in lawsuits, not months, but years. And in that time he wouldn't leave.

So what I suggested, as you referenced, is kind of a different plan. And we have evidence of this in the NBA in the last month. What's so amazing is that Robert Sarver, the owner of the Phoenix Suns, had the similar behavior we talked about with Snyder, right? Bad treatment of employees, especially women. And he got the *exact* same punishment from the NBA commissioner, *the exact same.* A one-year suspension and a $10 million fine. It's almost like copy and paste. That's what he got. So what happened? No, they didn't vote him out. There was what I viewed — I have no inside knowledge on this, Jim — I viewed it as a coordinated campaign, that other owners took sidebars with Sarver. We saw the vice chairman come out and say, "I'm not going to be here if Sarver is still here." We saw PayPal, the sponsor on the jerseys, say, "We're not going to be here if Sarver is back." And then, of course, LeBron James and Chris Paul tweeting. And there had to be moves from the commissioner as well. So, what happened, as everyone now knows, Sarver is selling. Is that happening with Snyder? *I don't know, I really don't.* I think before we get to the news of this week, it's naïve of us to think that no one's come to him before and said, "Hey, maybe you should take the money and run." So what's different this time? And that's where we sort of pivot to right now. I'm not sure. There's probably a couple theories out there. [*Editor's note: See our blog post on Sarver in chapter 14.*]

I liked how you talked about the different tactics that the NBA might

have used to get Sarver out of there without an actual vote. And you mentioned how Chris Paul and LeBron James decided to step up and tweet out and basically try to influence the situation with the NBA. I'm curious, because as you know, the Commanders don't really have a Chris Paul— or LeBron-level player with that type of influence. So do you think it would have to start more with a Tom Brady or a Patrick Mahomes to actually move the needle?

It wouldn't have to be only a Commanders player. It'd be nice if it was, but that's career suicide, right? I get that. I just don't think it's going to happen like it is the NBA. It's just, as you know and as everyone knows listening, it's just a different league with different progressive attitudes. So I don't see that happening with a Brady, with an Aaron Rodgers, with a Mahomes, with a Josh Allen. It's just not going to happen. So in the NFL case, who are the likely influencers of Daniel Snyder? It's going to be the commissioner, it's going to be other owners, some that he really trusts more, like [the Dallas Cowboys'] Jerry Jones. It's going to be sponsors.

And then, I'll just get to the news, Jim. I know a lot of people are hopeful that this news, that he has retained Bank of America for potential transactions, means he's going to sell. I'm kind of in the camp where I'll believe it when I see it. Here's a couple of things that could be going on with B of A. They are the debt financer for the NFL teams. A lot of owners engage them for different things. It could be they're being engaged to survey the market and see that, yes, someone out there will pay — pick a number: 4, 5, 6 billion dollars — use that to go back and finance a stadium, because that's been a problem for him. It could be he wants a minority owner, who could be a minority or a woman, which would help him public relations–wise. It could be that he wants to show the world he's thinking about it, but not really do it. It could be a lot of things. So we'll see. [*Editor's note: Snyder sold the Washington Commanders in 2023 to a group led by private-equity investor Josh Harris. The price was $6.05 billion, a record for a North American sports franchise.*]

That was the speculation yesterday because it seems so odd that he would reverse course, and you knew whatever it was, it had to be calculated. It was very purposeful. I mean, down to the wording — he didn't use the word *sale*. The words were carefully chosen in that statement. But it was interesting that they did decide to beat everyone else to the punch and put the statement out themselves. I suppose that was smart to control the narrative and put that out there.

One thing I did want to ask about as well, before we move off of this part of it, is: As far as the investigations that have been going on, the one that's getting the most attention now, probably even more so than the one by the House Oversight Committee, is the Mary Jo White report that we're expecting. And the two things I wanted to ask you about is, one, I think it's safe to assume, unlike the report that we referred to earlier, that this will not just be oral, that it'll be written. And then two, how damning do you think this could be? What we've heard from all the spokespeople for the Commanders is: deny, deny, deny. It's just been total "Stick to that script. We'll be vindicated. The rest of the world has it wrong. We're right." If that doesn't turn out to be the case for them, how harsh do you think this is going to be and how are they going to backtrack?

Well, I'm not sure I have read the statements from Washington as deny, deny, deny instead of more what I see them as saying all the time is "Look at all the changes we've made in the past two, three years — that's all old news." And that's not going to cut it. You can't just say that's old news — and they hired a new president, he's a minority, they hired a coach who's a minority. They've done all this stuff. They have a woman leading one of the divisions. But so what?

You're so right. Mary Jo White's investigation will be public. I'm not sure public — it will be written. But hopefully it'll be public, too. In no way on God's green Earth it's going to be private and oral again. [*Editor's note: The NFL released former prosecutor White's report in July 2023.*] It's going to restart the discussions about further discipline and the push towards selling again. If what we just heard kind of fades in the woodwork while he's thinking about transactions, this will rev it up again. So she's looking into a lot of behavior we talked about.

In the Wilkinson report — which there is no report — we hear about bad behaviors, the things I talked about, the women I talked about being talked to like that. But it *seemed* that Snyder was above it, even if he tolerated it. But now we see reports that he was in it. And allegedly, *allegedly*, groping a cheerleader, pushing her towards his limousine, and maybe even some sexual assault on his plane years and years ago.

So if those things come out, you know how the media is: She'll write a 150-page report and we'll see those two paragraphs out there big time. So that's what we're going to look for. And then it goes past Sarver and Snyder tolerating a hostile workplace, then it gets into action. And then, here I go again, they're not going to vote him out. But then it's even more of a pressure campaign.

With all these investigations, and whether he's going to sell the team or not, I'm curious, from your perspective, how do you think the NFL might navigate this going forward from a communication stand-point?

Well, as I always say, there's a new crisis in the NFL every week, so we turn away from the one that was just happening [*laughs*]. I wouldn't call it crisis; I call it drama. The NFL, whether intentional or not, there's just drama every day. Now, a lot of it this time of year is on the field, it's about how the teams are doing. And the Bucs and Packers and Rams are stinking up the joint this year, and that's a story. And the new teams like the Eagles. So, I think the NFL hopes and knows we're going to move to other things. And I don't know if they're going to do any lead communications about this Snyder stuff. I think that's all going to be team. I think from a *team* point of view, I think they put out the statement and then I don't think we're going to hear about it for a while.

So there actually is a little bit of precedence with the Commanders in the past couple of years when they were dealing with the whole name change, how FedEx and Pepsi and Nike really kind of wielded their power a little bit and kind of did help move that forward so that the name change could occur. Do you think it would take that type of

combined effort from some major, like Fortune 500 companies that are sponsors, to then take this to the next level and force his hand to sell the team?

Yeah, I mean, you're right, the name change went on and on forever and you did hear about FedEx and [CEO] Fred Smith getting in his ear about that change, which I think has led, as much as anything, led to the name change. I think that could happen. But I think now we're getting a little into psychology — I just think his whole identity is wrapped up in being the Commanders' owner. That's why I keep saying I'll believe it when I see it. I just think he's not going to cede control of this franchise unless he absolutely, positively has to. Would that come from sponsors? Perhaps, and other owners.

You know, we haven't talked a lot about the stadium situation. As I cover on *The Business of Sports*, we've got massive, massive stadium subsidies going on around the league. Buffalo's getting $850 million from the state given to the owners. Tennessee, they're going to give over $1 billion in public subsidy to get that stadium built for the Titans owners. And Daniel Snyder can't get a stadium built. And he's got three legislatures to bid against each other — District, Maryland, and Virginia — and he can't get any public money. This is a problem. And I know the owners don't like that. I think he's not getting public money because of *him*. Everyone loves the team. So I'm not sure how that would translate into pushing him out, but it's certainly something owners talk about.

This gets to the point you mentioned earlier about burying bad news on a holiday weekend — again, smart tactic in a lot of ways, a tactic that's used often in our world. But do you think that they could even *try* that this time around, to bury the results of the Mary Jo White report? Or for that matter, any other damning news against Daniel Snyder at this point? Or is it just so far gone that it's just going to be a headline no matter when they release it?

I think both of what you said is going to be true. It's that, number one, it's impossible to bury this one. But number two, it'll come out when they need it to come out. So, you know, *bury* is a relative word. It could be the morning of an NFL Sunday. That could put a spotlight on it, from like 9 o'clock to 11 o'clock in the morning. But at 1 o'clock, the games start, and no one's talking about Mary Jo White's report by 1 o'clock. Or on a Monday, and the game starts at 8 o'clock.

There's a couple schools of thought on that, right? Because if you do it during the season, you could say, "Well, it's going to detract from the season." But on the other hand, to your point, people want to focus on the games, so it could still get lost a little bit. And then if you wait until the season's over, at that point I guess you could say, "Well, people are in baseball mode," or something else at that point and they're not worried as much about football. But they'll have an interesting decision to make, and rest assured, it is going to be a conscious decision of when that news gets out.

I think you're right. I think, as you said, she's been working on it a while and it can be done. There's a saying, in the NFL meetings, or probably a lot of corporations: The commissioner won't call a vote unless he knows the result of the vote. So they're not going to call out a report until they know the result of the report and strategically aim it that way.

Editor's note: See chapter 14 for our blog post on the Washington Commanders probes.

19

MICHELE TAFOYA:
"HER APOLOGY WAS SORT OF HASTILY THROWN TOGETHER"

Podcast Interview Recorded
November 29, 2023

Questions and opinions about journalistic integrity began flying when NFL personality Charissa Thompson, host for Fox Sports and Amazon Prime Video's *Thursday Night Football*, very casually mentioned in an interview that she had sometimes made up reports early in her career as a sideline reporter for Fox. To dissect that issue in the best way possible, we spoke to Michele Tafoya, one of the most respected NFL sideline reporters of the past 25 years. Tafoya, a veteran of both *Monday Night Football* and *Sunday Night Football*, covered 327 national primetime TV games, regular and postseason combined, which is the most ever for an NFL sideline reporter. She helped us break down the details of Thompson's admission, why it was so significant, and why it, somewhat surprisingly, didn't result in any official repercussions.

Now, Michele, when you first got wind of this, I'm sure several thoughts popped into your mind, but what would you say was the most instinctual reaction you had?

Well, the first thing that she says is "I didn't get fired the first time I said this" — I'm not sure if I'm paraphrasing. "I've said it before and I didn't get fired." So she understands that when she said it the first time, it potentially *might* have gotten her fired. And now she's going to say it again because she thinks, "Well, it didn't get me fired the first time, so I'll say it again." So I think that knowing that she had a sense that what she did, in making up these reports and admitting to it, may have been something fireable.

I want to say at the outset that I know Charissa a little bit, and I found her to be a lovely person. I like her a lot, and I think she's very talented in her current roles. I think she's very good at them. But what she admitted to is something you just can't do. In any business, when you make stuff up, there's going to be a consequence. I don't care if you're a financial planner. I don't care if you're a sideline reporter, whatever. But in particular, when you are presenting yourself to the public on a televised game — you are a journalist when you're transferring information that you supposedly have gleaned to the audience. That's journalism.

And so to suggest that it was okay to just, "Well, no one's going to blame me if I just say, yeah, he wants to stop the run," where the blame comes in is, he may very well want to stop the run, but you can't put those words in a coach's mouth and report that, and suggest that that's doing the job. I would make a thousand other suggestions as a way to handle that scenario of not being able to get to the coach or not having the information you want on time.

And one thing I do want to underscore that you mentioned, and thank you for pointing it out, obviously, we're not, as we never do on the show, we're not tearing anyone down. By all accounts, from what we've heard you say, and other people that Charissa has worked with, she is a nice person and was just a little misguided on this front and thinking that this wouldn't be a big deal, I suppose. And you can

probably chalk it up to, early on in anyone's career, they might not have the confidence and security they have when they get a little bit older. So somewhat understandable, not to make excuses, but again, we're looking at it from the end result, and what really happens as kind of a learning lesson.

Right. I think that's important to recognize. People are saying, "Oh stop piling on" and "Charissa, hang in there." It's not about the person. It's about the act. It's about the admission and what I think I'm afraid it does, because so often sideline reporters have been belittled as unnecessary sort of accessories on a game, when in fact there are times they are *crucial* role players in the transmission of information that the guys up in the booth can't get and that even sometimes cameras can't get. So she sort of propagated that idea that, "Well, it's not really that important because they all say the same thing anyway." Not all coaches say the same stuff.

Not only did she say that she made some of this stuff up, I think a lot of people had a problem with the tone, right? So if you read and listen to a lot of comments from people who are upset, they thought she just sounded nonchalant and maybe a little oblivious or had an oblivious attitude about the whole thing, which, once again, I think upset them the most. Was that aspect of it a big part that bothered you?

I did think it was a lack of judgment, and I thought, "Did I hear that right?" Listen, just the admission of it and suggesting that it's "I can get away with this" is sort of a nonchalance, like you said. So it's kind of this "I've gotten away with it. I'm okay to say it. I'm in this group. I'm kind of talking to the frat boys," if you will — and sorry to generalize, but that's kind of what the aura was — "and so I'm just going to say the truth." This is tough because it was an honest admission, but it was an admission to a very, very bad use of judgment during a telecast. And we don't know how many times she did it. It's kind of like an accountant saying, "Well, I didn't really have the numbers, so I just went with what was in my gut." You can't do that. And there's so much mistrust in the world today as it is that it's sort of given people more ammunition for, "See: You can't trust what anyone in the media says."

Exactly, and that actually leads me perfectly to my next question. To what extent do you think the collateral damage is? And probably just in general across all news and media. But I think specifically what I'm thinking is obviously most sideline reporters are women who are working so hard to break into male-dominated sports. What do you think this does to their efforts?

Well, some people have argued, "Look, it only hurts Charissa and it doesn't hurt everyone." And there's a certain part of me that agrees with that. But the more that I've seen people posting about it and saying, "Hey, look, you're no Woodward and Bernstein here, it doesn't really matter, don't take this so seriously," I would say to them you have no idea how hard all of us have worked to not only gain our positions, but sustain them, gain the trust of the people we work with. Not only our producers and co-workers, but the coaches, the players. I mean, it takes often *years* to establish trust with certain coaches or owners or GMs or whomever you're working with. This is a hard-fought trust that you have to earn.

And so now, Charissa's sort of become this meme of "According to so and so, he had to have his arm amputated at halftime." I'm sure you guys have seen that meme when Joe Burrow got injured and they said Charissa Thompson said he had his arm amputated at halftime. So it does impact, I think, how people view the role, and particularly those who have always looked down upon the role. It just gives them more ammunition for that. Now, I would say to anyone who's in the role, just keep doing what you're doing. Do it with integrity. Keep building on it. It has to be done. There have been plenty of times where that role of the sideline reporter has become a *major, major* role in a broadcast, and I can detail those, but let me just tell you, that comes with a lot of hard work.

With something like this happening, are you concerned that this could impact the existence of the role? There's definitely a group of

people out there that think it's disruptive and invasive. You can even find people saying, "Why would you even interview Gregg Popovich?" Because sometimes he doesn't even give you anything. So do you think this situation gives credence to the naysayers at all?

In their minds, it probably does. I was discussing this with my former producer Fred Gaudelli. He's a Hall of Fame producer who produced *Monday Night Football* and *Sunday Night Football* when I was on it. We just had a conversation about this the other day. There was a time, I don't know if you guys remember this, probably 15 years ago, where some of the networks decided to dispense with sideline reporters. And they paid for it. There was a guy named Bill Simmons, a sports commentator, who was like, "These people are worthless. Why are they even down there? They give you no substantive information." And then there was a Chargers game where both Philip Rivers and LaDainian Tomlinson got injured, and no one had any information because there was no sideline reporter at the game. And Bill Simmons, the same guy that said we were worthless, said, "Where's the information? Why don't they have a sideline reporter there?" And I was like, "Oh my gosh, talk about whiplash. This is the very reason we are down there."

I can give you countless examples. I think that the one that stands out for me the most was a game, Houston Texans, Gary Kubiak was the head coach, he collapsed at halftime. And this story was no longer about sports. It was about a man's life. Bob Costas was in the studio, Al Michaels and Cris Collinsworth were in the booth, and I was on the field. And this became about: Is this man going to live or die? None of us knew. And we had to cover this.

And so I was the set of eyes — even though we had cameras, you needed that presence on the field to get up close, to look, to observe, and then to chase down everybody in the building that you possibly could to advance the story: find out how he was, what hospital he is going to, who's going to take over the coaching duties, how is this impacting the psyche of the team, what is the GM going to do, how soon will this guy be out? All of these different stories became very important within the context, not only of the game, but within this team's future. So if they decide again, if anyone says, "We really don't need sideline reporters," do it at your peril.

It's an excellent point. Thank you for sharing that because it really puts it into context. It's an extreme situation, but sports are live. This is what happens, life happens, and I think it's also a fair point to make that there really is no going back. If you get used to watching sports now, it would kind of be like going back to standard definition. You just can't do it: You're used to high def. You're used to that intel that you get from a sideline reporter and you don't want to be without it.

Real quick, you guys mentioned Gregg Popovich. I love Gregg — he and I had a great relationship when I was covering the NBA. And one of the ways that I approached it was I didn't talk to these guys on-camera unless it was required in the broadcast. Usually at halftime, I'd walk down into the tunnel and talk to one of the coaches heading into the locker room and then the other coach heading out of the locker room, *off*-camera. And I'd take these copious notes, and then I'd pull it together, and I got some of the best quotes I've gotten in my career from Gregg Popovich.

So it's important to note that it's circumstantial, it's how you approach it, it's the tone of your question, it's how you frame the question, it's all of these things that don't come in your first year of experience. It comes after, again like I said, getting that trust and that relationship with the coach that they know they can trust you with something, like the quote that he gave me at one game where he was really down on his team and it was fantastic. I wish I could remember it word for word, but I can't. But the point is that if you interview these people, maybe eight times out of 10 you get meh, but maybe those other two times you get gold, and it's worth the investment.

One thing we just wanted to mention now is about Charissa's apology because she did issue a statement. We had some thoughts about it because that's what we do. We create and advise our own statements for our own clients, and then we learn from others and pick ones that

we think are good or bad or could have been better. I was wondering what you thought of her public statement and apology after the fact, after things kind of got blown up bigger than she probably expected. What was your take on what she said?

I didn't think it was real cogent, coherent. It suggested she denied saying what she actually said. I don't think she had people like you helping her out with this. I would lay a lot of money on that bet that she didn't have professionals helping her, and I think that was to her detriment and that's unfortunate. She should have. But she went with this statement. I think it hurt more than it helped. And to say, "I never did this, words matter, I think I misrepresented myself" — well, wait a minute [*laughs*], I don't know how we can misinterpret what you said. So there was probably a much better way, and she probably could have used your services in this instance. I think it hurt more than it helped.

I agree, and I think it was a case of her trying to clarify. She used the words "I'm sorry." But I think overall it was very lacking. I had to read it several times before I deciphered what I believed she meant. Which was probably to the effect of "I didn't actually attribute it to a coach, so I was generalizing." Okay, but I think the tone was a little bit off. I think it came out a little bit too defiant.

I certainly don't mind her defending herself to the best she can, but I think it needed a little bit more ownership, a little bit more humility, a little bit more of something that proved that she recognized the extent of it. Like, "You know what? When I saw my words in print, I realized what I didn't at first. Journalistic integrity is of the utmost importance. I took that for granted. I regret saying it." Just something that humanized it a little bit instead of being a little bit too defiant.

There's that balance between you want to be authentically you, but there are people who really can help you [*laughs*]. They're considering your best interests. And they say, "Let us help you shape this, because we're really good at this," and I'm certain that didn't happen in this case. So, yes, I get the sense that there were a lot of people, whether it was Fox, Amazon, her, her friends, whatever, who really felt like, "Oh, this will blow over, this is not that big a deal." I only have my own experiences. I think if this happened at NBC, where I finished my career, she would have been pulled off the air for at least a week or two.

It's funny that you said that Amazon and Fox might think it might blow over, because I don't think we've heard anything from them, which was very surprising. While it hasn't gained more media attention and it seems to have blown over for now, and I emphasize for now. It could come back to bite them. It's a calculated risk for them because I think they knew and came up with this strategy that they weren't going to respond. Were you surprised that they did this as well? I know you said NBC would've taken you off air and maybe also released a statement, but were you surprised that they said nothing?

I was. I was. This is your employee. This is someone you present as the face of your programming every single week. And so, yes, you are in part responsible for all of this. Now you have a little bit of a problem on your hands, a problem of credibility. As someone said to me, "She's now just going to become this string of memes." And it continues — here we are, it's still continuing. You see these memes of Charissa holding a mic and "According to Charissa Thompson ..." [*laughs*]. Whether you think it's unfair or not, it was an unforced error and there were probably much better ways to handle it.

I would also point out, and this was brought to my attention, not that I didn't know it, but it was sort of brought into focus for me by someone who is a very, very experienced writer whom I respect and I won't name, but who said to me, Amazon is owned by Jeff Bezos, who also owns *The Washington Post*, which is supposed to be this bastion of journalistic integrity. So while she may not have done this while an employee of Amazon, what are you saying to your entire organization by not speaking about this, by ignoring it? I think that's a really relevant question.

I think there's several reasons why, and I wanted to get your

thoughts on these as well. Part of it, you could look at it and say, they had their first-ever Black Friday game that they paid a considerable amount of money to get and they had this Garth Brooks concert that they were promoting afterwards. They probably didn't want the distraction. But I also think it might be a sign of the times. Have journalistic standards just gone by the wayside in the social-media era? Is it a case of it matters and people are upset about it, but people just shrug their shoulders about this stuff and just kind of move on because we're in this era of everyone having this immediate platform at their fingertips. What is your take on all that?

You know, there's probably a lot of truth to that [*exhales*]. And I exhale because it is disappointing. Even when I read publications, whether it's online or a hard copy of something, which I rarely read anymore, but anyway, if you're reading a publication, whether it's the *L.A. Times* or the *New York Post* or whatever, and you see a typo. I ask myself, how in the hell does a typo get through in an article in one of these major publications? *Sports Illustrated* is now facing this backlash for maybe potentially using AI-generated stories written by writers whose names no one knows. These things matter. We're getting so far from the truth anymore and that should matter a whole hell of a lot.

So whether it's a typo, whether it's writing something you have to apologize for and retract later because you so wanted to be first on this story, our motto was always we want to be first, but we want to be right. We don't want to have to clean up the mess on aisle nine. So I'm disappointed in all of the things that I see. Listen, when I worked at NBC, if there was a typo, even at CBS, if there was a typo on a graphic, oh, I mean, you were not going to be the same the next day if you committed that typo. You were going to get your ear torn off basically. So these things are just sort of like, oh, honest mistake, that's okay, we'll clean it up later. I don't know, I guess I'm a little more detailed than that. And so that is possible that we're just too, whatever, "We didn't really think she was a journalist anyway." Well, I don't know, our standards in a lot of areas in this country are lowering. And so I guess we should expect that it would impact journalism as well. And it really has in a big way.

It's disappointing. The last thing to cap this off, and I don't know the extent to which you can do this, but if you were talking to Charissa, or someone who had her ear, what would you say, or what advice would you give her from a public-facing standpoint: "Going forward this is what I think you should do to restore your credibility"?

Given the set of circumstances we have right this moment, and I am not a pro at this like you gentleman are, but I think I would say, "You really do have to understand your position here — you're the face of this program." You can say, "Well, I'm not a sideline reporter anymore" — *it doesn't matter.* You still are the conveyor of information, so maybe a step back in humility, maybe let's try one more time at that apology statement, or cleaning this up. But you have to understand your role. I think a lot of these people see themselves now purely as entertainers, and there is some truth to that, but when you are conveying information, just like you wouldn't want to get a *stat* wrong, you want to maintain a sense of credibility top to bottom.

Clearly her career is not over. She's going to withstand this, and she's going to have to have a really thick skin to get through some of the memes that are going to come her way. There have been a lot of people coming to her defense, and I'm sure she's enjoyed that. I think some of the damage has been done, unfortunately, and because her apology, her Instagram post, was sort of hastily thrown together and put out, I don't know how you — I would ask you guys, how would you turn that around? Because it's out there — what do you do with that now?

I think you can always lean on perspective, and the public is forgiving if you *do* have the right message, which is what we're always preaching about. I think it might be the type of thing, maybe it's even after the season, maybe she does a sit-down interview with somebody and just kind of — doesn't have to bare her soul — but just addresses it a little bit differently and is more forthcoming and at least makes an effort to put it behind her. Because, to your point, there are a lot of bright things ahead for her. It's not like her career is done, but in order to — I don't want to say satisfy the masses — but I think in

order to move past it and get that off your shoulder, it's better to put it out there that you kind of lived and learned a little bit.

It's in her best self-interest. Not necessarily interest in how she sees the public looking back at her, but how she sees herself in all of this. And that does require humility, it requires some grace, it requires a shift in understanding what this all means. I think that's a good idea to do the postseason sit-down interview. I'm curious if that happens, where it might happen. Where would you guys put her? Is this an Oprah thing or is this another podcast?

It could be sometimes you go back to the scene of the crime. I wouldn't necessarily do that in this case. Maybe it's an Amazon thing. Maybe it's a Fox thing. Obviously you can go where your connections lie. But it could be something independent, maybe on the same network with somebody else that would give you a fair treatment.

And it doesn't have to be a fluff job, but just somebody who wouldn't be so totally forgiving and, on the other hand, wouldn't also be unrelenting. Somewhere in the middle, where you could be fair. I think it would go a long way.

It's not even that you have to make a bigger deal out of it. It is a big deal, but it doesn't have to be that deep-voice intro of *"Now we have a special edition. . . ."* There wasn't a crime committed in that sense. But it does warrant something where, again, I think the word you and I both used was *humble, humility,* a better understanding with the benefit of perspective. Hopefully that will be in her future. I think it would help.

I hope so, too. She's a nice person.

20

BOB COSTAS:
"ALL YOU HAVE TO SELL IS THE
INTEGRITY OF THE COMPETITION"

Podcast Interview Recorded
May 24, 2024

Few people in broadcasting over the past half century have played as big a role in the way fans consume high-level sports as the incomparable Bob Costas. We were fortunate to be joined by the uber-talented and articulate member of the Sports Broadcasting Hall of Fame for a discussion about all of the new challenges related to sports betting that have arisen for leagues, commissioners, coaches, officials, the athletes themselves, and, of course, fans.

A 2018 Supreme Court ruling has led to such betting being legalized in 38 states and counting. That, coupled with smartphone technology, has made sports betting more convenient for fans than it's ever been. This new normal presents a myriad of potential pitfalls that crisis communicators need to be aware of and prepare for as best they can. Player-prop bets (on player performance or stats) are of special concern.

We also discussed with Costas the high-profile gambling scandals in 2024 around Los Angeles Dodgers superstar Shohei Ohtani, who was a victim of his interpreter, and basketball pro Jontay Porter, who in April of that year received a lifetime ban from the NBA for violating its gambling policies.

In addition to the decades of general sports knowledge Costas has amassed, he's shown himself to be an astute observer of human behavior as it pertains to sports fandom. This, coupled with his experience of having grown up in an environment and era where sports betting played a significant role, made Costas the perfect guest for this discussion.

So, let's start with Shohei Ohtani. Just a little bit of background to refresh everyone's memory: This past March we learned that Ohtani's interpreter, Ippei Mizuhara, had been stealing money from him. The amount turned out to be more than $16 million to cover his gambling debts. Someone in Ohtani's camp had initially set up an interview for Mizuhara, and he claimed that Ohtani knowingly was covering the debts. But that quickly got changed and Ohtani said, "No, I've been the victim of a massive theft." When that happened, I sort of stopped in my tracks. But what was your reaction?

Well, my first reaction was that baseball is collectively praying that this does not directly implicate Ohtani because they're boxed in by their own explicit rules. Rule 21 specifically says that if you bet on baseball at all while you're an active participant — manager, coach, umpire, and, of course, player — if you bet on baseball, apart from a game in which you're participating, that's an automatic one-year suspension. If you're found to have bet on baseball, and you're participating in that game, there's no wiggle room. It's lifetime banishment. Just ask Pete Rose. Just ask Shoeless Joe Jackson — it was actually an ex post facto rule when Judge Landis came in, but he made the rule, and you didn't have a players association then, and so Joe Jackson was banned from baseball, along with seven other members of the Chicago White Sox from 1919.

It seems, and there are always — in a conspiracy-theory world and all kinds of stuff on the internet and whatever attitudes some people have — there are always going to be people who are not satisfied with the, quote, official explanation. And I don't know if the ongoing federal investigations, the FBI and whatnot, if they're closed now, since Ippei has, in effect, pled out and will accept whatever the penalty may be, and he's going to do significant jail time, there's no question about that. But if there is an investigation or a report out of that investigation still forthcoming, we may learn a little bit. [*Editor's note: On June 4, 2024, Mizuhara did officially plead guilty in federal court to bank and tax fraud for stealing nearly $17 million from Ohtani's bank account. In February 2025, Mizuhara was sentenced to 57 months in prison.*]

But based on what we now credibly know, Ohtani is not implicated. He's a victim. Perhaps he should have been more attentive, or those around him who are charged with protecting his interests should have been more attentive, to what was going on. But there is no solid indication that Ohtani himself was gambling and using Ippei to place the bets, or that he had knowledge of the size of the debts, or what Ippei was up to. So based on what we know now, it would appear that Ohtani is in the clear.

I want to piggyback on the most important point, that it doesn't appear that Ohtani was involved at all, but as you said, that's not going to stop the theories about him being connected in some way, shape, or form. There was a recent report that a former teammate was connected to the whole gambling operation as well. So you're still seeing conspiracy theories about whether he was involved or not, but it really hasn't affected his play, which I think is interesting because probably for 98 percent of people, it might. But do you think this could harm his reputation long-term? Because these doubts could follow him for the rest of his career.

But if we find out nothing more than what we presently know — which is not to say that there is more to know, maybe this is the full story and Ohtani was a victim, and he was not a participant — then that's not going to haunt him his entire career. It's not going to be a part of his obituary up at the top, like Pete Rose. No such penalty is going to be forthcoming to him.

And while this part is just speculation because every person reacts to a circumstance differently, but if Ohtani was burdened by a guilty conscience, it's certainly not affecting his play. He appears to have a clear head about it all, and so far his version of the story has not been credibly contradicted. So, in this world where anybody can put anything online or there's a zillion sports talk shows and some are more responsible and careful and credible than others, almost any idea can be floated out there. And then somebody says, "Oh, I heard someplace or I read someplace ... " But that doesn't mean that there's any truth to it necessarily.

I want to transition a little bit into the broader scope of sports betting that we have in this country right now. The landscape changed a lot in 2018, when there was the Supreme Court ruling that ultimately led to now 38 states having legalized sports betting. And now it's just as easy as a few taps of the phone for anyone over 21 to partake.

So I want to speak to you a little bit about the whole legalization argument, which is not unlike the whole recreational-drug argument of "make it legal so we could regulate it." I think most people realize that that's one of the benefits, whether you're on one side of the fence or the other, but it's probably what led to Jontay Porter being caught in the NBA — and we'll get into player props in a little bit. But what's your take on that? Do you feel that it's too far gone at this point, it's better that it's legal, we'll be able to catch more people who are cheating? Or do you feel like the downside is that we're making it *more available* to more people. Which is the lesser of two evils there for you?

Well, I don't want to seem like a scold or that I'm moralizing. Gambling has always been part of society and it's always been connected to sports. I did a commentary about this on HBO a couple of years ago. And my own dad was an inveterate gambler, back when you had to gamble with a bookie, and most of those bookies were connected to the mob. There was a certain Damon Runyonesque kind of glamour to it if you looked at it through a certain prism. It was clandestine. And interesting — in quotes — "interesting characters" populated that gambling universe.

Now, though, you have this [*holds up cell phone*], everybody's got this. And so it's right at your fingertips, and it's addictive. Previously, you had to seek it out. And if you lived in Omaha, there wasn't a casino in Omaha. You had to go to Vegas. And Atlantic City is relatively new when you talk about that kind of legalized gambling. So it was just more difficult to access. Now it's right there on your phone, and we know that it's addictive in a variety of ways. What you watch, what you read — it's addictive.

And so if it's that easily accessible and if a whole generation of young people, including athletes, have some form of attachment to their phones and everything's so easy to access, the law of averages is such, and common sense is such, that some of those people are going to become addicted to it. If they're addicted to their phones, eventually you'll become addicted to some of what the phone gives you access to, including gambling. There's a rush to gambling. There's an adrenaline thing about it. The risk. The possibility of loss and the possibility of gain.

And so it's just crazy to think that you're not going to have some athletes as the years go by — and a generation turns over more quickly than it used to because of the circumstances around us — with the next wave of athletes, and including some that are out there now, like Jontay Porter, they will have essentially grown up with legalized gambling and easily accessible gambling. And if enough of them dabble in it, even if most of them do it just for kicks and there's no real harm, the law of averages says that some will become addicted and some will also get in with the wrong crowd and maybe think that there's something exciting about being able to influence the outcome, not just of a game, but of bets.

And maybe I'm jumping ahead here on what you want to talk about, but with Jontay Porter, it's amazing that they even caught it because it's *so* under the radar. Let's take a guy who isn't a gigantic star, and let's have him influence prop bets that don't necessarily influence the outcome of the game. When the line moves too much, there's too much action on one side or another, that's always been alarm bells in Vegas, for old-school bookmakers, and now for legalized gambling. If the line moves too much, they adjust. But if you're talking about little prop bets, I don't know that there are enough safeguards and enough security forces to pick up on every one of those. [*Editor's note: In July 2024, Jontay Porter, former player for the NBA's Toronto Raptors, admitted he manipulated his stats so his co-conspirators could win bets based on his performance. He did so, he said, "to get out from under large gambling debts." The league had already handed Porter a lifetime ban following an internal investigation.*]

And we know that in the NFL, I don't know the exact number, but I'd say it's probably approaching a dozen players have been sanctioned, not for throwing games, not for betting on games in which they participated, even if they bet on their own team to win, but for betting on NFL games and they've been sanctioned for it. The rule is clear, it's right in front of them, but young people do crazy things, more so than their elders do. It's just part of being a kid, especially a kid with a lot of money in some cases.

The majority of people are betting on the leading scorers, leading rebounders, things like that. When you find players like a Jontay Porter or another low-level guy who might have an over-under of scoring three and a half points, it's a little more difficult to some degree. So due to those circumstances, as you're probably aware of, there have been a lot of discussions about legislation, and with professional sports leagues, about what to do with player props and how to possibly regulate them. Because it's a serious problem when guys that you never heard of can fix or alter their stats to make some type of money on themselves. So do you anticipate any regulatory changes in the future regarding these player props?

I think that all the leagues have to safeguard here. All they have to sell — no matter what else may disillusion us about sports for one reason or another — all you have to sell is the integrity of the competition. Now you're possibly on a slippery slope. You can't ignore the gigantic infusion of revenue that legalized gambling has meant to every league and every sports entity. The very leagues that used to say that legal-ized gambling would be the death of sports as we know it not only now accept it, but they embrace it and encourage it. It's all around you. Every game you watch, every program, every pregame show gives you the odds and various prop bets as well.

So you're in bed with it, but at the same time you know that you're playing with fire, and if it affects the outcome, or the *perception* of the outcome, the *perception* of the integrity of your product, that's going to be a problem for you.

I'm not knowledgeable enough to know what steps could actually be taken. If betting on sports is legal, I don't know that you can tell BetMGM or FanDuel or whatever it might be that you can't put out prop bets, that you can't accept prop bets, which are obviously more problematical than just the over-under or the outcome of the game itself.

I think it's already getting to a point, where for a large portion of the audience, sports is more transactional than emotional. You hope your team wins, but you desperately want your bet to win. Even before gambling was legalized in this form, I remember Peyton Manning telling me, I don't know, maybe 10, 12 years ago, "You know, I run into people and they say, 'I have you on my fantasy team,' and they're upset with me because I handed the ball off at the two-yard line in-stead of throwing for a fifth touchdown, instead of the four I already had, because in their fantasy league that would have helped them more." So the best strategy, the outcome of the game, is incidental to their bet.

Now that betting has exploded and is so much more widespread, that attitude is going to permeate all the more. And then when you're looking at NIL [name, image, and likeness] and the transfer portal [the NCAA's system for student-athletes to transfer schools], not that there's anything that you can argue logically against it, but it changes people's perception of what they're watching, what their loyalties are, what their loyalties should be. It's a brave new world, and I'm not quite sure where it takes us.

With Jontay Porter, one of the interesting things that came out of it,

of course, was that NBA Commissioner Adam Silver banned him for life. That's interesting because it hadn't happened in 70 years. So it begs the question about the challenges that the leagues and the commissioners are facing. I've seen Silver, and Rob Manfred as well from MLB, talking about how they'd like to have more input and more leverage with all these betting apps to talk about what works and what doesn't on the player-prop side specifically. What do you see as the role of Silver, Rob Manfred, NFL Commissioner Roger Goodell, and NHL Commissioner Gary Bettman in the world of sports betting at this point?

Well, if the genie isn't completely out of the bottle, they have a legitimate interest in saying, look, *we* create the product, we — MLB, NBA, whatever it may be — *we* create the product. *You*, a betting site, you glom on to that product with no investment in the product itself. It's already there. It's been there. Now you're attached to it. Yes, we'll collect revenue from this, but we have an interest in this and in truth, in an enlightened fashion, a casino, a bookmaker, they don't want, unless they're an individual that's desperate, they actually want trustworthy competition. That's what their business is based on. So there's a mutual interest here.

And you could see the commissioners — I don't know that they have any legal authority to do it, I'm not an expert on that — but you could see them getting together with the various betting sites and saying, look, let's see if we can pull back on the aspects of this that are most problematic. And it's the prop bets that clearly are the most problematic.

Every time you turn on the TV, you're bombarded by FanDuel, DraftKings, ESPN Bet, all these online sports-betting operators that make it accessible for you to use. And it kind of just changed how we view the sports-betting arena and industry. I think it probably brings more eyeballs to the screen, but with attention spans already shrinking more and more all the time, do you feel that it has fostered more of a highlights-only type of viewing experience? Maybe we call it something like the "NFL RedZone effect," where fans may only want

**to see the big plays, or I only want to see when a team's about to
score.**

Even before 2018, and the Supreme Court decision that legalized gambling pretty much across the board — I think it's now in 38 states, and
eventually we know it's going to be 50 or close to 50 — even before
that, the circumstances you're describing were well underway. Short
attention span, highlight shows, people watching sports events in a
different way than they used to. Various influences — the internet
fosters conspiracy theories.

I mean, look, way before there was legalized betting there were
always concerns in the NBA. Fans felt, wait a minute, Sacramento goes
against the Lakers in — what was it? — 2002 Western Conference
Finals, "the league wants the *Lakers* in the final, not the Sacramento
Kings. So all the calls are going to go the Lakers' way." Now, of course
in basketball, you know there could be a foul or some kind of violation
on almost every play. And is that a block? Is it a charge? You know,
those things are in a vague area, more vague than "safe" or "out."
Here's the replay, let's take a look, as long as we got the right angle,
even if it's by an inch, it's safe or out. Some of these other things are
more judgment calls. Do you call pass interference there or don't you
in an NFL game?

So there were always those suspicions and always those conspiracy theories. Now you throw gambling into the mix and people being
more savvy about media, the rights to purchase entities. You know,
"NBC is going to buy the NBA." "It would be good for NBC and for the
NBA, for the Knicks to play the Lakers in the next NBA final." Well,
that's always been true. But that didn't stop San Antonio from getting
to the finals five or six times or whatever it was.

But people are going to believe what people are going to believe. If
you give them any reason for suspicion — it's just human nature.
There are a percentage of people that are going to feel that way, especially if they are rooting for a team from a smaller market. You know,
"Oh, you want the Dodgers to win. You don't want the Diamondbacks
to win." You know, that's just — it's kind of human nature. And then
when gambling comes into the picture, there's another reason for

people to have suspicions, whether those suspicions are well-founded or not.

Cris [*Crisis Communications in Sports* co-host Cris Bruce] had a little bit of a wry smile on there because he's from Philadelphia, and when the Sixers were playing the Knicks, we kind of went to war over all that, all the calls. So yeah, he was sure that the NBA just wanted the Knicks and wanted New York in there.

Because Philadelphia is Podunk, right, Cris [*laughs*]? Philadelphia might as well be Fayetteville. Right? A tiny little market with no sports history. Poor Philadelphia [*laughs*].

Bob, I have one more question for you because I wonder if there is — and I don't mean to say that it's all negative — but if there is a positive to all this. So, in thinking about the way sports betting has generated interest and the eyeballs that it brings to the screen — and I'm thinking specifically about women's college basketball or just women's basketball in general — you had this amazing season where players like Caitlin Clark and Angel Reese were commanding terrific television ratings. Their games had the highest TV ratings they *ever* had and were also *the most bet on* women's basketball games ever. So whether it's a case of people are watching because they bet, or were betting because they were watching, in your mind, does it matter if it grows the sport and raises the profile?

Well, I think in the case of the women's college basketball and now the WNBA, I think it's they're betting because they're watching. I don't think they're watching because of the bet. This may sound like chicken-and-egg stuff, but I think that Caitlin Clark and others brought honest attention to women's basketball. And then, inevitably, if the number of eyeballs increases, some of that increase is going to include people who say, "What the hell, I'm watching this, I might as well bet on it." So that's almost like a collateral aspect of it.

But no entity is immune. You can actually get a bet down on a Division III college basketball game. You can get a bet down on a volleyball game between, I don't know, Drake and Bowling Green — Drake the university, not the hip-hop guy [*laughs*]. So, it's out there, and those sort of, little kiss it off, "Gambling problem? Call . . . " Yeah, right.

Again, I'm not moralizing about it. My dad bet huge sums of money with bookmakers. And some of it I found interesting. It's part of what drew me to sports because he didn't bet on races or poker games or crap games. He bet on ball games. So I have mixed emotions about it, and I'm not moralizing. It's legal, and a lot of people do it just for fun, and they do it responsibly. But there will be inevitable collateral damage both to individual lives of gamblers, especially young people prone to addiction and easily influenced. There'll be that. And then there will be inevitably, over time, there's going to be a scandal here and there. You know, the Jontay Porter thing did not scandalize the NBA. It ruined *his* career, but it didn't scandalize the NBA. But it is a warning signal that the next time it could be worse. [*Editor's note: In January 2025, a Las Vegas man was arrested and charged in connection with the illegal betting scheme involving Jontay Porter.*]

Absolutely, that's so true. And you reminded me of a quote I read from Rob Manfred. As an example of sports betting perhaps going too far, he said, "Do we really have to bet on what the first pitch of the game is going to be?" And he went on to say that maybe we need to lower the limits that you could bet on things like that. So I suspect that those are the types of things they'll start with and will try to make some ground up there.

And you know what happens with all gamblers, when they get more desperate, then they double down: "I bet on the Yankees to win the game, but the Tigers scored five runs in the top of the first. So it looks like the Yankees aren't going to win the game. But now I've got a whole array of prop bets between the bottom of the first and the ninth inning that maybe I can recoup my investment because I think I'm going to lose the primary thing" [*laughs*].

And by the way, this reminds me of an old joke that my dad loved. And this joke has continued for decades and decades. In fact, Robert

Wuhl used it once on an episode of *Arliss*. The basic premise is, a guy starts gambling as the baseball season begins. Nothing goes right, he's down 10 grand. The football season begins in September. No luck at all. He's down 20 grand. Basketball starts, he's trying to recoup his investment. He's down 25 grand. He confides in his buddy. He says, "I don't know what's going on, it's the worst losing streak ever. The bookies are all over me. If I don't pay up, they're going to break both my legs." And the guy says, "Have you tried hockey?" And the guy says, "Hockey? What the bleep do I know about hockey???"

[*Laughs*] It's a point well taken. It's so true. It is an addiction, but it is something that you could enjoy responsibly. But even when you're not betting a lot, you're still invested. You could have a five-dollar bet, but on the principle, you just want to win it. You want to come out as a winner.

And I'm sure there's a lot of that just to make it interesting. Somebody's 10 bucks, 20 bucks, whatever it is, right? To make it "interesting." There's no harm and it's no different than a Nassau on the golf course. But if it was confined to that, then we wouldn't be having this conversation.

Editor's note: See chapter 5 for blog posts on gambling, including one on Ohtani.

AFTERWORD

Jim Rocco

Perhaps the single most important sentiment I've written that I hope readers take away from this book is "For sports fans, there's sports, and there's everything else."

Now I'm not suggesting that things like health, love, and being in the company of good friends are less important than watching a game (though my wife wonders sometimes), *but* there is an undeniable allure, uniqueness, and universality to sports that I truly feel needs to consistently be top of mind for communications professionals. We live in a time where so much of the content we consume is scripted, recycled, and regurgitated, and because of that, the emotional, unpredictable occurrences and outcomes of sporting events serve as a welcomed and much-needed respite for so many people.

It's through this prism that comms pros should operate when they find themselves entangled in a sports-related crisis. Or better, when they are planning for a sports-related crisis. Simply recognizing that the passion elicited by big-time sports should play a significant role in how you construct your strategies and public-facing statements is vitally important.

So good luck and [fill in your favorite sport adage here]!

Thom Weidlich

I'm not the sports guy — I'm the crisis comms guy. Still, working on this book has been gratifying. For example, I've learned that basketball *isn't* the one with a goalpost at each end of a 100-yard grassy field.

No one interested in crises and how organizations deal with them can ignore sports. It's fascinating how many issues crop up in this area and how varied they are. It's frustrating that sports organizations don't take responding well to them more seriously. Every indicator is that, increasingly, public reputation can make or break an organization, team, league, or player.

The only way to navigate that is to be familiar with the types of crises that arise in sports and best practices in terms of how they've been dealt with.

With this book we tried to take readers on a deep dive into actual crises that sports professionals and organizations face and also give them great commentary from our podcast interviews. We believe that, combined with our introductory chapters, this provides a strong grounding in sports crises — and the fundamentals of crisis communications more generally.

ACKNOWLEDGMENTS

Many people assisted in putting this book together.

Mostly we want to thank our colleagues at PRCG | Haggerty and PRCG | *Sports*: Sandra Prendergast, Lucy O'Brien, Cris Bruce, and Joe Grigas. Sandra, who is also a big part of the Hart + Harvest publishing imprint, helped hugely with production and design. Cris and Joe checked facts. All helped with proofreading. Cris and Joe were instrumental in doing many of the original podcasts. Lucy proofread many of the original blog posts.

In addition, we have former colleagues to thank. Isaac Benjamin worked on the earlier podcasts and wrote one of the blog posts here. Rachel Gamson edited early blog posts and wrote two of them. Michael Trancucci helped with the blog "Postgame" updates.

Our colleague and partner Eric Rose of EKA PR in Los Angeles co-wrote one of the blog posts. David Aretha helped with his excellent proofreading.

We, of course, owe a special thanks to our podcast interview subjects whose transcripts are included here: Mary Carillo, Kery Davis, Jay Horwitz, Andrew Brandt, Michele Tafoya, and Bob Costas.

Thanks to all of you!

INDEX OF CRISES

INDEX OF CRISIS CONCEPTS AND SCENARIOS

www.ingramcontent.com/pod-product-compliance
Lightning Source LLC
Chambersburg PA
CBHW071714120626
46550CB00001B/225